ON OUR WAY

ON OUR WAY

Christian Practices for Living a Whole Life

edited by Dorothy C. Bass & Susan R. Briehl

UPPER
ROOM BOOKS®
NASHVILLE

The Upper Room® Web site: www.upperroom.org

UPPER ROOM®, UPPER ROOM BOOKS® and design logos are trademarks owned by The Upper Room®, a ministry of GBOD®, Nashville, TN. All rights reserved.

Unless otherwise indicated, scripture quotations are from the New Revised Standard Version Bible, copyright 1989, Division of Christian Education of the National Council of the Churches of Christ in the United States of America. Used by permission. All rights reserved.
Scripture noted NIV is taken from the Holy Bible, NEW INTERNATIONAL VER-SION®. Copyright © 1973, 1978, 1984 International Bible Society. All rights reserved throughout the world. Used by permission of International Bible Society. Scripture note AT is the author's translation; AP indicates author's paraphrase. Scrip-ture noted KJV is from the King James Version of the Bible.
         Pages 238–239 constitute a continuation of this copyright page.

At the time of publication all Web sites referenced in this book were valid. How-ever, due to the fluid nature of the Internet some addresses may have changed or the content may no longer be relevant.

Cover and interior design: Jason Gabbert / www.thedesignworksgroup.com
Cover image: shutterstock.com
Typesetting: PerfecType, Nashville, TN
First printing: 2010

            LIBRARY OF CONGRESS CATALOGING-IN-PUBLICATION DATA
On our way : Christian practices for living a whole life / edited by Dorothy C. Bass and Susan R. Briehl.
         p. cm.
   Includes bibliographical references
   ISBN: 978-0-8358-1016-6
1. Christian life. 2. Spiritual life—Christianity. I. Bass, Dorothy C.
II. Briehl, Susan
   BV4501.3.0475   2010
   248—dc22   2009041855

            Printed in the United States of America

ON OUR WAY

Contents

*in the real world . . .

*for the good of all . . .

*in response to God

*Living a whole life

attentively . . .

together . . . in the

real world . . . for

the good of all . . .

in response to God

1 * An Invitation

Dorothy C. Bass

I see in the rising generation a passionate yearning to live in a way that is good for our endangered planet, life-giving to others, and attentive to the presence of God. *On Our Way* is a response to this yearning. It is offered by a group of authors who belong to the diverse, imperfect, amazing community that has gathered around Jesus Christ across the centuries. Humbly, hopefully, and drawing on the deep wisdom of scripture and Christian tradition, these writers wrestle with questions of how to live alert to the needs of the contemporary world. Together, their chapters guide readers into the heart of discipleship: love of God and neighbor embodied in an ongoing way of life.

Wrestling with questions about how to live your life is part of being human. Where are you heading, and why, and with whom? Such questions are not reserved for people in a certain historical period or stage of life, but they are especially urgent—and especially difficult to answer—for those coming of age in the twenty-first century. In today's world we all find ourselves overwhelmed with information but often moving too fast to seek wisdom. We are aware of massive problems but often disheartened about our ability to address them. As members of a growing, mobile, and religiously diverse global population, we are denied easy certainty. Amid widespread

> **"** Wrestling with questions about how to live your life is part of being human. **"**

social and cultural change, we are given both the freedom and the burden of choice in many areas of life.

The years following high school, college, or graduate school provide crucial opportunities for considering your life as a whole. In modern industrial and postindustrial societies, those coming into adulthood generally are expected to develop vocational and personal commitments more or less on their own. So at a certain point in life, off you go, down one road or another, making more and more decisions on your own about money, relationships, what to study, what work to do, and how to respond to war, racism, poverty, violence, sickness, and need. Questions about how to spend your one, God-given life become more insistent—and also more important, because how you live will have consequences not just for yourself but also for the world.

On Our Way invites you to explore a way of life that takes shape in response to the active presence of God in and for the world. We sometimes call this a way of life abundant, remembering the proclamation that Jesus came into the world to bring not just life but life that is abundant (John 10:10). All who embrace this way are joined to Jesus and to the community of Jesus' disciples across the ages. Rooted in ancient wisdom while also moving toward the future, this way of life overflows with God's justice, mercy, and love—not only for the sake of those who believe but for the good of all.

*Exploring a Way of Life Abundant

Rather than considering this whole way of life at once, our focus will be on a number of practices that give it substance and shape. Attention to practices is helpful because it makes a way of life, which is a very big thing, more visible and more open to engagement, criticism, and transformation. Noticing, understanding, and living specific practices require us to see and do things that are of immense importance to the way of life in and for the world to which people of faith are called.

In the pages ahead, authors who have found themselves called to this way of life delve deeply into twelve practices that have been and continue to be important aspects of Christian life. Other practices could also be included, to be sure, but this set covers a wide enough swath of experience to show how practices can serve and strengthen a whole way of life. Each of these practices addresses fundamental needs that appear in every life and every society—the need to learn, for example, or to gain material sustenance, know another person intimately, care for the earth, or encounter strangers without harm. These are things that all people—not just those who are Christian—do, so basic are they to who we are as human beings. What has been important to Christians over time—and what we now long for in our own day—is to do these things in ways that embody God's justice and compassion for all.

Practices come to fruition in the lives of real people in the real world. Therefore Susan Briehl and I selected authors who bring personal passion and unique life experience to each of the practices under consideration. These authors, who come from a variety of backgrounds and Christian denominations, are people of inspiring commitment and deep insight, and it is a privilege to bring what they have written to print. These authors also bring profound awareness of how challenging these practices and the way of life to which they belong can be. The life to which Christ has called them is abundant, but it is not easy. Even while sharing vivid examples of how these practices have helped life to flourish through the centuries and in the present day, they never overlook their difficulty. These practices have been neglected, thwarted, and abused in the past, and those who join in them continue to struggle, stumble, and fail today. Those who desire to live these practices in our own time will need to do so not with optimistic idealism but with hopeful realism.

All the practices in this book bring us to places of risky engagement where the pain of the world and awareness of our own shortcomings will pierce our hearts. Though they are for our whole lives, when we join in these practices it becomes impossible to ignore just how not-whole we and our world actually are. Practicing peacemaking, for instance, we come face to face with the hatreds and grievances that foster violence, enmity, and war—including ugly passions we might not have recognized within ourselves. In the midst of this practice and the others, our preconceptions, our sense of righteousness, and even our bodies may shatter to pieces. Suffering—that of others, our own, and even the pain of a wounded creation—will be unavoidable. Again and again, this way of life passes through the valley of the shadow of death. Yet these same places can become sites of communion with God, other people, and creation, sites where God's shalom erupts into the world.

Because of our special concern for those who are coming of age today, Susan and I also selected authors who care deeply for men and women in their twenties, and we urged them to give special attention to the shape of Christian practices during this stage of life. At the same time, the entire team that created *On Our Way* insists that practices such as these are for our whole lives. We need to embrace them, as we are able, whether we are five, twenty-five, or ninety years old—as the authors, aged from twenty-four well into our fifties, try to do ourselves. These practices are also for our whole lives in that they touch every aspect of personal and social experience, from sexual intimacy to global economic justice.

*Finding Your Way Through This Book

> To embrace a way of life abundant requires us to be **attentive**. No one can live this way in isolation from others; life abundant depends upon and arises within life **together**. It does not lead into a fantasy future or purely spiritual realm but **into the real world**. There, Christians practice these practices not for our own sake but **for the good of all**, and not by our own power or vision but **in response to God**, whose own grace and call provide this way of life.

This summary provides a map through the territory ahead. *On Our Way* is divided into sections that highlight these five characteristics of the way of life we aim to portray. In a sense, any division into sections is somewhat artificial, since *every* practice requires attention and is lived together in the real world, for the good of all and in response to God. Indeed, the practices are inextricably interwoven at every turn: walk down the path of one practice, and you'll soon discover that it intersects with all the others.

Practice doing justice; see how this impacts the practice of making a good living, and be summoned to know and love your neighbors of other faiths. Discern God's call regarding what you will do with your life, and find yourself immersed in studying Christ and the world. Share your life with friends, and get together to sing your life to God with all the breath in your God-given body. No practice can exist alone, even though each practice does emphasize a specific dimension of the whole.

*ATTENTIVE   To live attentively in the midst of countless distractions is an immensely challenging and highly countercultural stance. The two practices in the first section—study and discerning God's call—demand our attentiveness, and at the same time they foster within us a greater capacity to be attentive. Focusing on things that really matter requires us to resist powerful pressures and unexamined assumptions—a potentially dangerous act that can unearth insights and questions that lead us beyond the boundaries of certainty. The Christian practice of study, Matthew Myer Boulton shows, includes unlearning as well as learning, and doubt as well as belief. His chapter invites disciples (students) of Jesus (the rabbi, or teacher)—many of whom are also students in higher education—into the work and the wonder of honest learning, especially the learning that comes from ongoing attention to the Bible and to the "book" of nature. In the subsequent chapter, Jennifer Grant Haworth explores the practice of discerning God's call, especially in times of uncertainty about one's direction in life. By telling the stories of those who have struggled to find a vocation, offering disciplines of prayer and conversation that foster attentiveness, and urging attention to the needs of the world, she invites readers to listen for God's call to them.

“ The practices are inextricably interwoven at every turn: walk down the path of one practice, and you'll soon discover that it intersects with all the others. ”

*TOGETHER   When we are called by God, we are also called into community with one another. To be with others in a truthful and life-giving way—sharing time and place, worry and support, trust and meaning—is a fundamental need of every human being, from the dependency of early childhood through every stage of life. The three chapters in this section explore various dimensions of life together. In his chapter on living as community, Jonathan Wilson-Hartgrove describes the surprising, exasperating, and joyful reality of the Christian community in which he lives, placing it in the context of God's own communal being as Trinity and the church's enduring call to become one body, the body of Christ in and for the world. In no other way than through community can the loneliness each of us has experienced be addressed, and only in community with others can risky and compassionate practices for the sake of justice,

" When we are called by God, we are also called into community with one another. "

compassion, and peace be sustained. In the following chapter, Stephanie Paulsell probes friendship and intimacy. Here risk and vulnerability are powerful forces—but so is trust when it emerges within relationships that are honest, attentive, and reverent. Both Jonathan and Stephanie discover wisdom about community and friendship in the writings of friends and lovers from the ancient and medieval world; our practices, they help us to see, are enriched by continuity with the practices of our ancestors in faith.

The third practice in this section, singing our lives to God, explores music as a form of communal abundance on both Saturday night and Sunday morning. Here Tony Alonso, a musician and composer who serves a university's worshiping community, shows how our singing is connected to the music of all creation and to the testimony of the people of God across the ages.

*IN THE REAL WORLD   Christian practices are not ethereal and ideal but fleshy and imperfect. For good and for ill, they come to life in concrete historical situations shaped by distinctive social, economic, and cultural forces. The practices in the third section of *On Our Way* highlight the concrete character of Christian practices. Dan Spencer, an ethicist and environmentalist in Montana who sometimes calls himself a "geologian," helps us to recognize the practice of creation care as one that is grounded in scripture and crucial to faithful living. Through this practice, we honor and respond to God's sacramental presence in the material world, and we grow in love for all our neighbors, both humankind and otherkind. In the subsequent chapter, an ethicist takes a realistic view of need, desire, and money in the rapidly changing global economy. By considering personal, community, and global economics as interrelated dimensions of a single Christian practice, Douglas Hicks challenges us to renewed and responsible living that serves the good of all.

Finally, Evelyn Parker explores a practice that touches each of us intimately and that also empowers us to touch one another with care and respect: honoring the body, the Christian practice that reflects God's affirmation of our amazing, fragile, finite embodiment. Evelyn begins by telling of her tender care of her dying father and concludes with reflections on exercise and rest; between these bookends, she also ponders the brokenness of this practice in some churches as she reflects on HIV/AIDS and racism. This practice, like all the others, takes place in the real world, with all its brokenness and sin.

*FOR THE GOOD OF ALL   The three practices in the fourth section directly address the reality of brokenness and sin in today's violent, divided world. Christian practices, far from being the isolated and isolating activities of an exclusive community, are given to Christian people so that we

"Christian practices are given to Christian people so that we might become light and yeast—beacons and agents of God's justice, mercy, and love for all."

might become light and yeast—beacons and agents of God's justice, mercy, and love for all. Scott Alexander, a Catholic whose life's work is to raise up Catholic leaders with a deep respect for Islam and a profound love of Muslim peoples, provides a compelling account of a practice that should be of urgent concern to all contemporary Christians: knowing and loving our neighbors of other faiths. In the following chapter, Mary Emily Briehl Duba explores peacemaking and nonviolence, another practice that is desperately needed in our war-torn world. Through inspiring accounts of peacemakers in scripture and history, and through thoroughly realistic accounts of the tough decisions that face contemporary peacemakers, including herself, she challenges readers to reflect far more deeply than most of us have done on Jesus' affirmation of those who make peace.

Doing justice, the practice explored in the final chapter in this section, is set forth by Joyce Hollyday, who calls our attention to the prophets of ancient Israel and to the struggles of those who work for justice in South Africa, the United States, and elsewhere. All three of these authors have strong personal commitments to the practices of which they write; these chapters are passionate, authentic, and well informed. Their accounts of the practices that enable them to live for the good of those they may never know personally—those who are oppressed or marginalized, those from whom their own communities are estranged, those whom many of their peers see as enemies—challenge us all.

*IN RESPONSE TO GOD   Finally, Susan Briehl writes of living in the presence of God. Her chapter probes the profound mystery of this way of abundant life: its reliance on God. As Susan explores this practice, every other practice also appears, for as channels of God's love to us and to all, all Christian practices are rooted here. In poetry and prose, she depicts a God-given way of life that is attentive both to natural wonders and to

" ... the profound mystery of this way of abundant life: its reliance on God. "

humankind's suffering and sin; that gathers us together with ancient singers and contemporary street people; that leads into a world so real that doubt and death are not denied; and that turns us outward, from self-concern toward all the world. This way of life is nourished by scripture, prayer, and the communal worship of God.

I am grateful to all the authors for the riches they have spread before us. As you read the chapters in this book, I hope that you will also explore at first hand the practices and the way of life they comprise. Find others who also yearn for abundant life with God and others; and share your questions, and your life, with them. You can do this by becoming part of the ongoing community that has been pondering such questions for millennia and living out its answers through a way of life abundant—the church, which exists near you as a Christian congregation. It will not be perfect, and neither will you. But you will be on your way, by the grace of God.

Living a whole life

*attentively . . .

together . . . in the

real world . . . for

the good of all . . .

in response to God

2* Study

Matthew Myer Boulton

S ay the word *study* and most people will take you to mean something like what you are doing now: reading a book, your body arranged in a posture of concentration, probably silent and solitary. Say the word *Christian* and most will take you to mean something about "faith in Jesus Christ" or "believing what Christians believe about God and the world." But a closer look at *study* as a *Christian* practice puts both terms in a new light and suggests that even Christianity itself is something quite different from what many people suppose it to be.

By all accounts, Jesus of Nazareth wasn't much of a reader. The New Testament writers do portray him as an educated, literate man (in Luke 4, for example, he reads from the scroll of Isaiah, and in John 8, he "writes with his finger on the ground"), but if we search the Gospels for the verse, "And then Jesus retired for an afternoon of reading," or, "Then Jesus reminded the disciples to bring their Bibles with them to Bible study"— our search will be in vain. There were no "Bibles" in those days, for starters. Rather, there were only rare collections of sacred scrolls, kept safe in synagogue libraries and pored over by a small, elite class of intellectuals. Jesus knew these scriptures exceedingly well, it's true, but if the Gospels are any guide, he came by this knowledge not only or even primarily through reading but through listening and conversation. Even at twelve years old, Luke reports, Jesus found his way to the temple in Jerusalem, "sitting among the teachers, listening to them and asking them questions" (Luke 2:46). His teaching too was most often conversational. Jesus was a member of a predominantly oral culture, and though he often would quote sacred texts, his ministry was expressed mostly in spoken words rather than written ones. "Beware the scholars," he was fond of saying (Luke 20:46).

But if Jesus was no scholar, he was a consummate student: of conversations, of communities, of religious practices, of God's activity in the world, and of human struggles, failings, blessings, and hopes. Accordingly, he called other students to "follow him," which meant to walk alongside him, observe him, listen to him, argue with him, argue about him, and thereby be shaped and formed in relation to him along the way. The word *disciple* means "student" or "learner"; the word *rabbi* means "teacher"; and perhaps the earliest name for the movement of students following the rabbi Jesus was "the Way" (Acts 9:2). These basic, original terms suggest that early Christianity was an unfolding program of study. Like every such program, this one included growth, setbacks, misunderstandings, new insights—and so, for each disciple, an ever-stretching, ever-developing imagination. "You have heard it said," Jesus preached to devotees and bystanders alike, "but I say to you. . . ."

*Banana Men and Fireworks

The afternoon our two-year-old son, Jonah, knocked out one of his two front teeth, I was the parent on duty. We were playing together in the living room—me sitting on the couch, Jonah standing beside the coffee table—repeating again and again what had become a common routine: Jonah handing me a crayon, telling me what to draw, and then coloring in (and around!) my outline. Mind you, there were two things, and two things only, that Jonah demanded I draw in those days: first, a "banana man" (a banana outfitted with an oversized pair of glasses), and second, "fireworks" (the Fourth of July had only recently passed, and Jonah was still fascinated with those "big booms" in the sky).

On that particular afternoon, I was bold enough to propose a third alternative. Why not combine these two images into *a banana firework?*

Jonah's eyes slowly widened, the possibilities flickering across his mind like roman candles—and then, before I knew it, the dawning prospect of a "banana firework" proved too exciting for his two-year-old body to bear. He broke into a kind of celebratory jig, dancing his way along the side of the coffee table—and then promptly took a tumble, catching his front teeth on the table's edge as he went down. I can still see and hear that tiny white tooth skittle across the hardwood floor, like a miniature hockey puck headed for the hearth. I scooped Jonah up in my arms and dashed to the kitchen, the better to deal with the blood and the tears.

There was not much of either, as it turned out. When I sat Jonah up on the kitchen counter to get a good look at his mouth, the face that met me was more stunned than frantic. "Big boom," he said repeatedly, in varying tones of voice. "*Big* boom. Banana fireworks!" As the conversation continued, it became clear that Jonah was making sense of the accident—and his missing tooth—by attributing it to the "banana fireworks" themselves, and the "big boom" they had obviously just produced. He was using the terms available to him to interpret his experience, and in the context of his two-year-old logic and imagination, it made good sense to conclude that the boom that dislodged his tooth and the boom made by a banana firework were in this case the same boom.

Someday more terms will become available to Jonah, and he will learn that there are no such things as banana fireworks, that crayon drawings don't cause explosions, and that when he was two years old, he lost his front tooth because he lost his balance. Someday he will learn about baby teeth and adult teeth, about dentists, about how to use a toothbrush properly. Someday when even more of the world becomes available to him, he will talk to his mother about her year in Haiti as a local liaison for dentist delegations from the United States. That may be the day Jonah learns that there is a place, just over six hundred miles from Miami, where millions of people don't have toothbrushes at all.

At each one of these stages in Jonah's learning, he will unlearn things too. Just as one day he will leave the idea of "banana fireworks" behind, he will likewise unlearn that there is a tooth fairy, that dentists mean him harm, and that everyone in the world has a toothbrush. And somewhere along the way, it pains me to write, he will also have to unlearn the idea that human beings always or even typically take care of one another the

> **"** Following him, we learn—and unlearn.
> Following him, we grasp—and relinquish. **"**

way we should. Jonah will both learn and unlearn, grasping and relinquishing, as broader and deeper ideas replace relatively narrow and shallow ones.

To be human is to be enrolled in this great course of study. Like a snake continually shedding its skin or a gymnast moving to higher levels of difficulty, the student, the disciple, the pilgrim, moves along a path—older ideas giving way to newer ones. Or more typically, the new ideas are added like mosaic tiles, such that the old ones are not discarded but rearranged into altogether different designs.

Almost instinctively, any of us embarking on an itinerary like this one will want a guide—or better yet, a fleet of guides, mentors sensitive enough to let us make use of our relatively immature ideas as long as we need them, and then, when the time comes, to challenge us to let those ideas go. Such guides often go by names like "Teacher," "Master," or, among Jews in first-century Palestine, "Rabbi." Christian life is a life of study, and Christian disciples are students following a rabbi from Nazareth, who sets the course and the pace. Following him, we learn—and unlearn. Following him, we grasp—and relinquish. Following him, we understand—and discover things we have misunderstood.

And so as a Christian practice, study is not synonymous with reading books or with academic reflection, though it may well include these. Instead, Christian study means a particular kind of attending to Christ and the world, a particular stance of curiosity, vigilance, and openness to learning—an openness that extends even to unlearning what we have previously learned to take for granted. According to the New Testament, Jesus never says, "Study this or that book," but he does effectively say, again and again, "Study the world." Read it with care. Be curious, watchful, adventurous, and open. Are you consumed by worry? "Consider the lilies, how they grow." Want to be truly generous? "Consider that poor widow, how she gives." Want to learn how to love? "Consider that Samaritan, that foreigner, how he lives with compassion." Want to learn how ι "Consider that tax collector, that traitor, how he calls on God." Wa enter the kingdom of heaven? "Consider this child, this little one, a. learn to be like her."

Imagine living this way. Imagine each day—with its various scenarios, encounters, projects, and wildflowers—as part of a grand divine curriculum laid out before you, a lifelong education meant to form and shape you into the person God calls you to be.

Also note, in the brief list just mentioned, the role models recommended by Jesus are usually overlooked, outcast, or dismissed; and yet the good rabbi directs our attention precisely to them and away from those we might expect: successful people, religious leaders, honorable patriots, experienced adults. Thus Jesus seems to say: as you study the world, consider especially those places and people you might not ordinarily notice or admire. Wherever you go, and whomever you meet, be ready to learn; to help compensate for your blind spots and biases, cultivate the habit of giving attention to those you would otherwise be most likely to neglect. That way, you may miss less of the divine curriculum. That way, you may continually practice a stance of humility, receptivity, and discipleship. That way, you may most beautifully and properly "study"—an English word that comes down from the Latin studere, "to be diligent" or "to be ready."

Imagine living this way, diligent and ready, as alert in the woods as in the library, and as attentive to our enemies—our own "Samaritans" and "tax collectors"—as we are to our friends. Christian study invites us to follow Jesus as far into the world as we can go, attending to him and to the beautiful, broken creation we see, hear, and touch through him. Most fundamentally, Christian study means attending to life: learning about it and at the same time learning how to become more deeply engaged in it.

*Attending to Life

The chair was orange and brown and impossibly plaid, worn out but still more comfortable than any other spot in the apartment. I was in graduate school, and this was my chair. It slouched in the corner, ugly and amiable, a floor lamp on one side and the door to the porch on the other.

Mostly I sat there at night, reading by lamplight, my legs thrown over one of the chair's arms. I must have been bored or indifferent for plenty of long hours in that chair, but I don't remember any of those now. What I remember are the times I was amazed. Amazed to be reading words written, say, some sixteen hundred years ago, and then amazed to catch a glimpse of a brand new idea by way of those words, to have my mind stretched and shaped, as if a fourth-century African, for instance, was reaching across the sea and the centuries all the way to me, sitting sideways in my favorite chair.

My roommate in those days, an astronomy major, kept an excellent telescope up on the roof under a big blue tarp. The light from those twinkling stars you see tonight, he used to tell me, originated ages ago—one, forty years; another, four thousand—and yet at just this instant, all those lights arrive here on Earth. Seeing stars, he explained, is a kind of looking back in time. Put differently, seeing stars is the past making contact with the present, right here and right now, lighting our way in the middle of the night.

So it is with books, and with oral traditions of knowledge and insight. Each text or tale or piece of wisdom is a radiant point in the cultural sky, more or less brilliant, its light originally shed in the past and received here and now. The collections many traditions call "scriptures" (literally, "writings") are in fact treasuries of this kind of illumination. The world's sacred traditions are among the very oldest lights in the firmament of human civilization, stars that have guided lost travelers over the longest lengths of time. As nowhere else, in scripture the past makes contact with the present. Arguably this contact goes both ways. This is the wonder of traditions that cascade down generations: facing one direction are readers and listeners looking up and back into the heavens of history gone by, and facing the other are writers and speakers looking out and ahead into the heavens of history yet to come. Who's to say that Saint Augustine wasn't dimly aware of readers like me as he wrote? That my apartment's little pool of lamplight wasn't a tiny, numberless star in some fourth-century African sky?

For many people today, and in particular for students currently enrolled in programs of formal education, "attending to life" means regularly connecting past, present, and future in just this way. For these, it means attending to texts, traditions, and libraries, as well as to classes, projects, papers, and deadlines. Even though Christian study is broader than books, the academy can be fruitful ground for Christian discipleship. There are challenges, of course: formal education can be a death-dealing business. Too often school can be an experience of constantly being measured and only rarely measuring up, constantly trying to understand and only rarely feeling understood. "Beware the scholars," Jesus still warns.

At the same time, formal education can be a breathtaking feast of ideas, colleagues, and opportunities to grow—a bountiful, life-giving turn along a pilgrim's path. For Christian pilgrims, the difference between these two experiences of formal education—as death-dealing and as life-giving—may hinge on properly setting such schooling within the wider context of Christian discipleship. In other words, the key to healthy academic study may be "attending to life" in more ways than one.

First, healthy study attends to life in the sense of showing up, of being there, of putting yourself in life's way. There is a difference between dissecting a dog in a laboratory and playing with a dog in a yard; both may serve as ways to learn about dogs, but stay too long at the dissection table, and more than just your clothes will reek of formaldehyde. Your mind will too. In your educational training, it's best to spend plenty of time out in the proverbial field, where living things play and thrive: "consider the lilies of the field, how they grow" (Matt. 6:28). Besides learning to take things apart, analyze, dismantle, debunk, and expose, good education incorporates learning to put things together, enjoying things whole, and making lots of room for delight in discovery. Keep company with colleagues and teachers who take palpable pleasure in their work and who refuse to take it too seriously. Keep a close watch for where "life" is breaking out and do whatever it takes to show up when it does. Attend to life. Jesus sums up his mission in this nutshell: "I came that they may have life, and have it abundantly" (John 10:10).

Second, healthy study attends to life in the sense of mindfulness, of paying attention both to the subject matter of our studies and to the broader contexts in which our learning takes place. This requires intentionally clearing space for concentrated attention when we read, write, think, and discuss, and cultivating habits of mind that are as poised and alert as circumstances allow. The Gospel writers report that Jesus regularly retreated from the crowds to pray, often heading up into the hills. This withdrawal was by no means mere piousness but a practice of lucidity and grace, of staying awake and aware of what his work was actually all about.

> **"** Jesus characteristically points our attention in surprising directions, . . . toward the poorly lit margins where the outcasts and the overlooked dwell. **"**

Mindfulness also implies developing a certain kind of peripheral vision. As we have noticed, Jesus characteristically points our attention in surprising directions, away from the bright lights of worldly prestige and toward the poorly lit margins where the outcasts and the overlooked dwell. In an academic context, this suggests intentionally balancing conventional classroom learning with studies in other places and from other teachers; even within the classroom, there are plenty of margins and outcasts worth noticing. Consider, for example, fellow students who don't speak up much in class discussions or who may feel like outsiders for any number of reasons; then seek them out—not in acts of self-satisfied charity but humbly and respectfully, as one colleague hoping and expecting to learn from another.

And third, healthy study attends to life in the sense of caring for it, waiting on it, protecting it, and helping it to flourish. For Christians, the "greatest commandment," the organizing task under which all other tasks find their proper place, is the single command to a double love: "You shall love the Lord your God with all your heart, and with all your soul, and with all your strength, and with all your mind; and your neighbor as yourself" (Luke 10:27).

Clarifying this instruction with a story, Jesus points to a Samaritan— again, someone his disciples would consider an enemy, as Scott Alexander notes in the chapter on knowing and loving our neighbors of other faiths. In the story, this enemy becomes the featured role model for neighborliness, as Jesus commends the Samaritan's tender attention and care for a suffering stranger (Luke 9:51-56; 10:25-37). Here "attending to life" manifests as the meticulous work of bandaging the man's wounds, pouring oil and wine on them, carrying him to an inn, paying all costs, and promising to return—in short, the Samaritan "took care of him" (Luke 10:34). If this commentary on what Christians often call "the greatest commandment"— loving God and neighbor—is taken seriously, then a Christian's whole life, including her life of study, must take shape as just this sort of "taking care"—of serving, guarding, and restoring the world by building up from ruins, as the prophet Isaiah puts it (Isa. 61:4). In part, this is rigorous intellectual work: after all, the command specifically includes a call to love God "with all your mind." And in part, this is practical, local work, as tangible as oil, bandages, and blood. Thus "the greatest commandment" is also a compact manifesto on the true unity of a learning mind and a caring hand. In essence, Christian study should always and everywhere be neighborly work. In a word, it should always and everywhere be love.

*It Is Also Written

One of the oldest ideas in Christian thought, going back at least as far as the early third century, is that God's authorship includes not just one "book" but two: the "Book of Scripture" and the "Book of Nature," which is to say, the Bible on one hand, and the created world on the other, from mountains to Mozart. According to this view, scripture provides crucial interpretive keys (the stories about Jesus, for example) for reading the rest of creation; with these keys in hand, reading the world is a Christian practice as indispensable as reading the Bible. Both "books" deserve our attention; and, properly read, each leads the student more deeply into the other.

Studying scripture is one of the most fascinating, adventurous, and controversial practices of Christian life, since scripture itself is nothing if not a fascinating, adventurous, and controversial conversation. Think of the Bible's opening pages, for example, where two quite different creation stories sit side-by-side. In one poetic, intricately structured, majestic vision, humanity is created *last* of all creatures. In the other poetic, dramatic tale, a human being is created *first* of all creatures. Evidently whoever juxtaposed these stories made no attempt to combine them or hide their disagreements. It is as if the Bible itself makes an announcement at the very entrance to its library: "What you will find here is no single line of thought but many, an assorted treasury of stories and songs and poems and letters; and sometimes these treasures disagree. If you listen, then, what you will find here is a choral symphony, complete with grand recurring themes, counterpoint, and dissonance. And most fundamentally, dear readers, what you will find here is a diverse repertoire of resources for your worship and life as community, your interpretation and spiritual exercise, your reflection and discovery, your conversation with other Christians and your dialogue with those who treasure other texts."

Thus the Christian Bible, contrary to what many people think, is by no means a singular, consistent presentation; no amount of interpretive ingenuity can make it so. In fact, the Bible seems designed to resist such oversimplification, not least because both "testaments" begin with multiple, partially incompatible accounts (two creation stories and four Gospels). For attentive readers today, this plurality presses the questions of proper interpretation and use; in effect, it forces us to ask one another, "How do we make sense of this diversity, and relate it fruitfully to our life together?"

In other words, scripture's sometimes harmonious, sometimes cacophonous complexity precludes our ever simply identifying "what the Bible says." As we read and interpret scripture, we must ask not only "What does the Bible say?" but also inquire "How do we best coordinate the various things it says?" and "Which of these things should be emphasized and used to interpret other passages?" We find exactly these sorts of questions whenever "scripture" shows up inside biblical narratives themselves.

For example, early in Matthew's Gospel, the devil confronts Jesus in order to tempt him, first taking him to the temple's pinnacle, and then twice quoting Psalm 91: "Throw yourself down," the tempter purrs, "for it is written, 'He will command his angels concerning you,' and 'On their hands they will bear you up'" (Matt. 4:6; Ps. 91:11, 12). But Jesus, having none of this, counters scripture with scripture: Psalm 91 with Deuteronomy 6, saying, "It is also written: 'Do not put the Lord your God to the test'"(Matt. 4:7, NIV; see Deut. 6:16).

That little phrase "it is also written" is the indispensable basis and refrain of Christian biblical interpretation. Though Deuteronomy 22 states that a new bride found by her husband not to be a virgin shall be stoned to death by the men of her town (Deut. 22:20-21), *it is also written* that above all, God requires us to "do justice, and to love kindness, and to walk humbly with God" (Mic. 6:8). Joseph, faced with Mary's surprising pregnancy, interprets the law as a guide toward mercy, not violence (Matt. 1:19). Thus Joseph attends to life, and for Matthew, this merciful act of scriptural study sets the gospel story in motion. Matthew describes this act of interpretive daring as an indication of Joseph's righteousness, a commendable example of the "It Is Also Written" school of scriptural interpretation. Thus even on scripture's own terms, discovering "what the Bible says" in the sense of the various ideas and stories and instructions it contains is one thing; discovering "what the Bible says" in the sense of how these various ideas, stories, and instructions are best coordinated and applied to life is quite another. For this latter task, we need be good students not only of scripture but also of creation.

*Knowing the Neighborhood

A story told during a seminar discussion:

> Yesterday my roommates and I made a feast for dinner. We'd invited nearly a dozen friends, and so we spent all day shopping and cooking from scratch: two big pots of soup, two loaves of homemade bread, a giant salad full of vegetables, and two pecan pies for dessert. But then, at about three o'clock, just as we were putting the pies into the oven, the phone calls started coming in.
>
> One by one, our friends called to cancel: one couple had car trouble, another was sick, another was overwhelmed with work. It was uncanny. By five o'clock, all but one person had backed out—and then the phone rang one more time. And so there we were, three people surrounded by enough food for fifteen.
>
> And then it hit me, probably because of the reading we've been doing in this class. I remembered the parable Jesus tells about the great banquet [Matt. 22:1-10; Luke 14:16-24] and how when the invited guests refuse to come, the hosts go out into the streets and invite the poor and the blind and the lame. And I thought: this is our chance to enact the parable. This is what we are supposed to do with all this food we've made.
>
> But I didn't say anything. And so we just ended up doing exactly what you'd expect us to do: we called around to a couple of other friends, had a smaller dinner party, and put the leftovers in the freezer for later. And now today, I'm wondering what happened, why I didn't speak up, why we let that opportunity slip by.

The student who told this story thinks of scripture not as something to be read and interpreted at arm's length but as something to enact. And if I understand her rightly, this enactment is itself an immediate, embodied form of reading and interpretation. In this sense, reading scripture is a performing art, akin to music or drama. Think of how a violinist interprets a well-known violin concerto. She reads it by playing it. She interprets it by making its music in her own particular style, according to her own particular sense of the concerto and of the musicians with whom she performs. The texts of the Bible are like so many musical scores awaiting performers to interpret them by playing them, enacting them, giving them form and life here and now. "Scripture" is made up of "scripts," and all the world's a stage on which these scripts are properly played out. The Bible may be written in ink, but in genuine Christian life, *it is also written* in what we think and say and do.

Jesus would agree. According to Luke, for example, Jesus gives one of his first sermons in his hometown synagogue. In keeping with custom, the attendant hands him a scroll from which to read—on this particular day, the scroll of the prophet Isaiah. Jesus unrolls the scroll until he finds the passage he has in mind, clears his throat, and reads: "The Spirit of the Lord is upon me, because he has anointed me to bring good news to the poor. He has sent me to proclaim release to the captives and recovery of sight to the blind, to let the oppressed go free, to proclaim the year of the Lord's favor" (Luke 4:18-19; see Isa. 61:1-2). Looking up from the scroll and into the faces of those gathered, Jesus adds: "Today this scripture has been fulfilled in your hearing" (Luke 4:21).

Today, in other words, this script is enacted. Today this music is played and heard in all its fullness, beauty, and consequence. Today these ancient lights arrive here and now: "the year of the Lord's favor," prophesied long ago, has begun.

Likewise, the parable of the great banquet in Matthew and Luke is a variation on Isaiah's theme. For just as the prophet put it, "the Lord's favor"—here pictured as an invitation to a sumptuous feast—is extended in a special way to the poor and disinherited. My seminar student sensed a concrete opportunity to participate in this great divine sermon, to "enact" God's good news at her own dining room table—which is exactly the sort of place, presumably, that God intends such graceful music to be played and enjoyed. "*De te loquitur*," Martin Luther is said to have remarked of the Bible: "it's talking about you." This script has your name on it. You have a part to play. This is what "fulfillment" means: fully filled out, right here and right now, as tangible as bread, soup, and pecan pie.

> **" '*De te loquitur,*' Martin Luther is said to have remarked of the Bible: 'it's talking about you.' "**

"Well," someone might respond to my student's story, "I don't know why she didn't speak up, but I know why I wouldn't have. I wouldn't know whom to invite. I don't know anyone personally who was hungry last night or who's particularly poor, for that matter. And even if I do have some acquaintances who might be, it would feel strange and hollow to invite them over for dinner suddenly, like extras in my little morality play." This person may discover the banquet parable functions as a revealing challenge precisely because he cannot easily or gracefully enact it. It can encourage self-reflection: *If my whole circle of friends is privileged, able-bodied, and comfortable, how can I take part in the gospel drama? How can I bring good news to the poor and the hungry and the captive if I have no genuine, reciprocal relationships with people who are poor, hungry, or captive?* The parable prompts this person to think again about his relationships, about who he knows, and who he doesn't know. It raises the question *What in my life needs changing?*

In this way scripture's scripts will at times lead not to immediate performance but to further study and preparation for enactments yet to come. Here Christian "practice" means rehearsal, training, exercise—and when it's done well, it typically involves developing new relationships, new bodies of knowledge, and ultimately, new capacities that lead us into other Christian practices—in this case, into living as community and seeking justice. As in the theater, Christian study frequently involves being an understudy, not only to the good rabbi himself but also to other pilgrims who have walked this way, performed these roles, and played this music before. These mentors can help us discern which scripts we are called to enact down the road, which scripts we are ready to enact today, and which scripts properly interpret, reframe, or rebuke other scripts. For as we have seen, the Bible does not speak with a single voice, and sometimes the intra-scriptural conversation includes critique.

In Mark 5, for example, when a hemorrhaging woman supposedly defiles Jesus by touching his clothes, the rabbi reacts in a way clearly critical of Leviticus 15; or again, confronting a murderous mob in John 8, Jesus effectively critiques Deuteronomy 22 (a passage his legal father, Joseph, critiqued before him). But insofar as these are both cases of Jesus enacting the "greatest commandment" to love God and neighbor, he therefore carries out his criticisms of Deuteronomy and Leviticus by way of other verses in those very books: "You shall love the LORD your God with all your heart, and with all your soul, and with all your might" (Deut. 6:5), and "you shall love your neighbor as yourself" (Lev. 19:18). It is as if Jesus says, "It may be written that this woman has defiled me, or that whoever commits adultery shall be killed—but *it is also written*, on those very same scrolls, that you shall love God with abandon, and your neighbor without separation. And taken together, *these* two verses are the reading glasses through which we best interpret all the others."

Christian study, then, involves the study of scripture, but there is no study of the Bible without the simultaneous study of creation, the "Book of Nature" that encompasses the whole neighborhood and everybody in it. After all, the stages on which scripture's scripts are enacted are set nowhere but *in* the world, from the dinner table to the public square; and at their best, those enactments are performed *for* the world—that is, for the repair, restoration, and life of the world. Therefore, we must "get to know the neighbors" in preparation for good scriptural interpretation and enactment. Where are the places and people most in need of restoration around the world and also around the block? Where is God's Spirit already bringing the dead back to life, and how can we take part? What are the hidden wounds that might be overlooked (the hunger of the poor, the loneliness of the rich, the struggles of the disinherited, the sorrows of the privileged)? And what are the hidden joys that might go unnoticed, the sweet signs of hope we ought to celebrate with vigor and imagination?

When he was a young man, the Puritan preacher and theologian Jonathan Edwards used to wander the eighteenth-century New England woods, notebook tucked under one arm, scouring the landscape for what he called "types and images of Christ." As he understood it, a "type" was a kind of shadow, impression, or figure of divine speech that God the Creator, in a kind of playful cosmic poetry, has strewn across the world for our benefit: the shape of a leaf, the industry of a spider, the beauty of a flower. In each of these, Edwards saw reflections of Christ and the "good news" of the Christian gospel. And though few people today explore the woods quite the way Edwards did, can we imagine a modern analogy? Can you walk through your life, notebook tucked under one arm, scouring the landscape for reflections of Christ, beauty, joy, good news? And when you find one, in a face or a lily or a breathtaking vista, can you dare to imagine of this shining little passage in the "Book of Nature," *de te loquitur*, "it's talking about you"? Not *only* about you, of course (and so you'll also want to listen with others and join in spreading the word as widely as you can), but still "about you" all the same?

> **❝** Can you walk through your life, notebook tucked under one arm, scouring the landscape for reflections of Christ, beauty, joy, good news? **❞**

*Learning along the Way

On a clear night, the human eye can see two thousand stars, more or less, which is far too many to count. Indeed, along with the grains of sand on the seashore, the stars are the poets' favorite figure for "the innumerable," "the incalculable," and in that sense "the wondrous." These days Jonah and I are reading the Winnie-the-Pooh books at bedtime, and we are both smitten with the enchanted forest at the end of the series. The trees there can't be counted.

But suppose you set out to study the stars? With even a simple telescope, you can see two hundred thousand of them, and with a model like the one my roommate kept up on the roof, you can see not only stars but galaxies. Today that former roommate is a professional astronomer, and he tells me there are more than a hundred billion galaxies in the universe, each with something like a hundred billion stars—more or less. So much for counting. We live in Pooh's forest, each and every one of us, wonders amid wonders.

We can pursue Christian study properly only as a practice of humility, never mastery. The more we learn, the more we come to appreciate how much we have yet to learn about the world and about ourselves. As Socrates famously put it, the wise man is the one who knows he knows nothing—or, in Paul's terms, "Knowledge puffs up, but love builds up" (1 Cor. 8:1). Rather than accumulating knowledge for the sake of our own power, a true course of Christian study develops a stronger and stronger sense of our own ignorance, and a wider and wider openness to the natural wonders all around.

We are children, every one. Like Jonah sitting on the kitchen counter, each of us uses whatever terms are available to us to interpret our experience. In this way, with our childlike logic and imagination, we make as much good sense as we can of the world, "banana fireworks" and all. As we learn and grow along our pilgrim's path, what now seems like good sense may well come to seem like nonsense, and a new world will open up ahead of us. Two thousand stars will give way to two hundred thousand, which in turn will give way to incalculably more. And so on. These two books, scripture and nature, are inexhaustible—which is what we'd expect, after all, of God's own works of art.

And so from this point of view, *study* is by no means limited to what you are doing now: reading a book, your body arranged in a posture of concentration, probably silent and solitary. Rather, your studies will continue the moment you look up from this page—your eyes coming to rest on yet another folio in the great book of nature all around us. And your studies continue as you live out each day in the company of other learners, immersed in this unfolding divine curriculum with its various scenarios, encounters, projects, wildflowers—and books, including (and for Christians, especially) the "Book of Scripture," that great library, repertoire, and ongoing conversation.

Finally, *Christian* is by no means strictly synonymous with "faith in Jesus Christ" or "belief in what Christians believe about God and the

> **"** We watch Jesus, listen to him, argue with him, argue about him, and so are shaped and formed in relation to him as we go. **"**

world." As every student knows, over the course of an education, beliefs grow and change, weaken and strengthen, arrive and depart, develop and evolve into entirely new forms. We learn—and unlearn. Like the disciples in the Gospels (reliable examples, after all, not of faith but of the lack of it), Christians are best characterized not as those who "believe" but as those who endeavor to follow Jesus: we are his hapless, stumbling students. We walk with him, notebook tucked under one arm, scouring the landscape for teachers: the widow, the traitor, the child, the fields. We watch Jesus, listen to him, argue with him, argue about him, and so are shaped and formed in relation to him as we go. From moment to moment, we may or may not "believe" in him or in this or that article of Christian orthodoxy. In fact, if we find ourselves lacking in these respects, we merely confirm our place in the company of disciples, those poor students whose "little faith," as Jesus puts it, is dwarfed by the smallest speck: "If you have faith the size of a mustard seed . . ." (Matt. 14:31; 17:20).

At its heart, a Christian church is not a community of faith but a community seeking it—following Jesus, learning to believe along the Way. On any given day, we may or may not "have faith." We may or may not believe or love or build up from ruins. We may or may not doubt or dispute or lose heart or complain. But we do follow. We do study. We do explore and engage, attend and interpret, rehearse and enact. And as often as we can, we do turn off the lamp, climb out onto the roof, and behold the inexhaustible sky.

3* Discerning God's Call

Jennifer Grant Haworth

F ew things cause more anxiety, incite more fear, or generate as much daydreaming as the question *What do I want to do with my life?* This is especially true when major life decisions demand attention, as they often do during our twenties. From picking a major to selecting a career, staying single or getting married, following our dreams or playing it safe, decisions are the stuff of early adulthood.

Just ask Kate, who came face-to-face with these questions soon after graduating from college. Although Kate believed she had already thought things through, she was thrown into an existential tailspin when she found herself working long hours at a job she thought she'd love but, instead, hated. "I've been told I have a future here," Kate, a former student of mine, told me. "But I don't even care. My work doesn't make a difference beyond pleasing my boss. And I'm always working, so I never see my fiancé or my family. I'm so frustrated I limp home every night and cry."

"Why not quit?" I asked, rather matter-of-factly.

"I can't!" she lamented. "I have bills to pay and a wedding to help finance. I feel trapped. I can't tell you how many times I've wondered, *Is there more to life than this?*"

Fortunately, for Kate and for all of us, the answer is yes! As people of faith, we believe that when God knit us together in our mother's womb (Ps. 139:13), God had more than work in mind for us. Calling us each by name (Isa. 43:1), God longs for us to live fully into our vocations.

What is vocation? At its core, vocation is a call from God to love and to grow in love—with self, others, and God. We respond to this invitation by listening carefully to our own experience in the light of God's loving presence. In doing so, we discern what the writer and theologian Frederick Buechner says is "the place where your deep gladness and the world's deep hunger meet." Each person's unique calling gathers together those talents and passions that bring joy; and it discloses where, how, and with whom sharing those talents and passions will bring more love and life into the world. Father Michael Himes has described our calling as our "particular way of self-gift" that, once discovered, leads us to make loving decisions to "give oneself away."

We begin to learn about our vocation through a centuries-old Christian practice known as *discernment*. Through individual reflection and conversation with others, the practice of discernment challenges us to pay attention to and understand our experience, encouraging us to become more familiar with and sensitive to God's action in our lives. When discernment becomes a habit of our heart, mind, and soul, it leads us more honestly into our deepest self and also prepares us to go out to live God's love in our world.

While discerning our vocations, or callings, is a lifelong practice, in this chapter I am exploring vocational discernment in early adulthood.

" Practicing discernment means attending to what is truly important—and really real—in ourselves and in our world. "

Grounded in both individual attentiveness and communal reflection, vocational discernment as a Christian practice invites us to notice where and how we are experiencing God in our daily lives. Practicing discernment means attending to what is truly important—and really real—in ourselves and in our world. As Ray's story illustrates, this is often easier said than done.

*Whose Life Am I Living?

Tall and tan, Ray is a surfer who grew up on the beaches of suburban Los Angeles. Not an "academic type," Ray excelled as an athlete and played water polo during college. "I loved the competition, and I loved being part of a team. All I wanted to do was hang out at the pool with guys who weren't thinking past winning our next game." Reflecting on that time, Ray, now thirty-one, said, "I had no idea what I wanted to do. I had no clue who I was. I avoided dealing with those questions by living in a bubble for five years."

Ray admitted that as graduation neared, he was scared, because he knew what was around the corner. Ray's dad owned a business. When Ray was growing up, his dad dreamed about his son someday working with him, learning the ropes, and then taking over the company. Ray majored in management—not because he wanted to but because it would prepare him for this future. "I was okay with it during college," Ray said. "The script was set; I'd get my degree and, voilà, I'd have a good job. Meanwhile, my friends were worried about finding employment and paying off their school loans. Given what they faced, it seemed selfish to want more for myself."

Ray did go to work for his dad. Five mornings a week he got up at 5:00 AM, put on a shirt and tie, and commuted two hours in heavy LA traffic. Five evenings a week he drove back. On weekends Ray and his girlfriend spent time alternately looking at condos and escaping to the mountains, where he "found his breath again" while cycling on physically demanding trails.

Ray made his father proud. "Apparently, I was a natural," he told me. "Dad promoted me, gave me an impressive title, and raised my salary. I looked like a success, but I felt like a total failure. I didn't like the work. I hated the commute. Every time I put on that tie, I felt like I was choking off my voice. I lived for the weekends. Biking brought me home to my soul and gave me the space to quiet the noise and hear God's voice."

Although it took him another few years of long commutes (which he learned to value as quiet time for reflection), Ray eventually found the courage to tell his dad that running the family business was his dad's dream but not his. "It was one of the most difficult moments of my life," Ray confessed. "I didn't want to disappoint him. Here I was, the family business talent, making a lot of money and on the verge of buying a great condo, and I was choosing to leave all of it without any clear idea of what I would do next. I had discovered that none of that was as real to me as the voices I heard biking on the backwoods trails of the Santa Monica Mountains. It sounds crazy, but I heard God telling me, *Ray, there's more to life than this. It's time to leap and trust that the net will appear.*

Ray took the leap and spent a year talking with people he admired about how they learned to live their dreams. He racked up a load of debt, but he felt it was what he had to do to discover where he was being called. Today Ray helps to run a production company that tells the stories of people who have overcome fears, doubts, and the expectations of others by listening to and acting on the voice of the genuine in themselves. By listening to his experience and longings, Ray discerned a way of making a good living by using his gifts as an entrepreneur to inspire the thousands of viewers who see the company's films each year.

*Are You Stuck in the Crosscurrents?

You've heard it. Your sister says, "I know you want to move, but I hope you'll stay close to home." A friend remarks, "You love to argue. You'd be an awesome lawyer." A professor scribbles on one of your papers, "You write well. The academic life may be calling you." A tiny voice inside you whispers, *I'd love to write and work from home*, but a loud voice then booms, *It took you how long to earn your degree? How much do you owe in student loans? I don't care if you're not thrilled with your life. Get used to it.*

None of us is immune. Voices from within and without compete for our attention, often pushing and pulling us in every direction so noisily that we can't hear the one that asks, *Is this the real me? Is this who God is calling me to be?* As Ray experienced, certain voices can choke the life out of us. My friend Bill Creed, SJ, offers a helpful image for such voices: they are like the surface crosscurrents on a river—easily visible and pulling in various directions. But beneath the river's surface, Bill says, a far mightier current flows, moving the river gently but steadily toward its mouth, its true end.

In my work with twenty-somethings, I've heard about the many voices that act like crosscurrents, overwhelming the deeper current of vocation and calling. Ray's crosscurrent was listening too closely to his father's hopes for his life rather than his own. Efforts to please our parents, distinguish ourselves from siblings, and compete with peers often generate powerful surface-level tensions. Ray also struggled with the voice of professional success, which too often translates in our culture as good pay and lots of possessions. The voice of doubt can also be loud, especially for the many who are still trying to identify their talents, strengths, and limits. *Am I good (or courageous or committed or even crazy) enough to do this?* the voice of doubt asks. *If I choose this, will I have to say no to that? What if this doesn't work out the way I planned?*

Closely linked to the voice of doubt is that of fear. This voice causes some to retreat into compulsive busyness at work, at home, in relationships, in social life, even in free time, as a way to avoid listening to the deeper voice within. Fear can also lead to stalling and lethargy; people move numbly through daily life, frightened even to ask, *Is there more to life than this?*

One of my favorite spiritual writers, Henri Nouwen, recognized the seductive power of these voices. In his bestselling book *Life of the Beloved*, Nouwen wrote that all of us live in a "world filled with voices that shout: 'You are no good, you are ugly; you are worthless; you are despicable; you are nobody—unless you can demonstrate the opposite.'" Trying to respond to these voices by proving our worth can lead to endless efforts to please others—parents, mentors, bosses, peers—and to unsatisfying careers and lifestyles that fit the culture's definition of success, not our own. When this happens, Nouwen saw, we often stop listening to the deep river of our lives, letting the surface currents determine our direction. We begin to avoid risk. We grow anxious or restless, depressed or angry, because we just can't seem to wrap our hands around anything that brings forth the response, "Ah, yes, that's it! That's the truth I've been seeking, the bedrock that makes me know that I matter, that helps me to see that there is a meaningful way to live."

People of faith need not despair, Nouwen insisted in his writings. If we will just stop, interrupt the surface noise, and listen, we will hear a voice speaking life to us. "I have called you by name, from the very beginning," this voice will say, according to Nouwen. "You are mine and I am yours. You are my Beloved, on you my favor rests. I have molded you in the depths of the earth and knitted you together in your mother's womb. I have carved you in the palms of my hands and hidden you in the shadow of my embrace. I look at you with infinite tenderness and care for you with a care more intimate than that of a mother for her child. I have counted every hair on your head and guided you at every step. Wherever you go, I go with you, and wherever you rest, I keep watch."

The voice that calls us Beloved is the voice of God. Once we claim the truth that we are God's beloved, we recognize surface crosscurrents for what they are: forces that have no real hold on who we most deeply are.

*What Life Wants to Live in Me?

Through individual reflection and conversation with others, the Christian practice of discernment invites us (1) to pay attention to our daily experience and what it stirs in us; (2) to reflect on what we notice there, sorting and sifting in order to understand what is leading to greater life and love and what is not; and (3) to take loving action on what we have learned. When done faithfully, discernment draws us closer to God, opening our heart in ways that lead us to make more loving choices for ourselves and our world.

Before exploring this three-part process, I need to say a word about the role of desires in Christian discernment. As Jesuit priest James Martin reminds us, human desire (the word comes from the Latin *desiderare*, "to long for") plays an important but often overlooked role in the spiritual life because it inclines or motivates us to act in certain ways. Our desires can be shallow or deep, fleeting or enduring, from God or from something other than God. One task of discernment is to grow in awareness of which desires lead us closer to life, love, and God, and which ones lead us away.

Spiritual writers from a variety of Christian traditions agree that our most authentic desires are God-given. The Protestant theologian and psychologist James W. Fowler makes this point simply: "What God wants for us and from us has something central to do with what we most deeply and truly want for

> **"** Our desires can be shallow or deep, fleeting or enduring, from God or from something other than God. . . . Which desires lead us closer to life, love, and God, and which ones lead us away? **"**

ourselves." Similarly, the contemporary spiritual writer Margaret Silf, who was trained in Ignatian discernment, observes that "for those whose hearts are, deep down, directed towards God . . . the deepest desire will be in tune with God's dream for them, and for all of creation." Bringing God's dream for us to birth, writes Silf, is "the amazing vocation of every believer."

But how can we discern what our deepest, God-given desires are? The insights of a sixteenth-century soldier-turned-priest have been helpful to me and to millions of others. For Ignatius of Loyola, the first step was to slow down, open his eyes a little, and pay attention to the love and life that had a hold on his heart. Ignatius was born into a wealthy Spanish family in 1491. His parents hoped he would make them proud by serving as a courtier and knight who would marry a wealthy royal. His friends urged him to go out drinking, gambling, and fighting. And all around him, Ignatius felt the pressures of a society that rewarded ambition, valued the acquisition of wealth, and required conformity to social expectations.

Ignatius did not buck these pressures. He served ably as a courtier and soldier in the service of King Ferdinand of Spain. He was admired by friends as a fun-loving sport who didn't hesitate to engage in swordplay to win the attention of a beautiful woman. His emerging success as an aristocrat, however, came to an abrupt halt at age thirty, when a cannonball shattered his leg while he was defending a royal fortress in Pamplona. Ignatius went home to his parents' castle to recuperate and to figure out what he was going to do with the rest of his life.

For the next eight months, Ignatius lay in bed as his leg healed, though it would never be the same again. He passed the time by reading. Although he had requested stories of knightly valor, the castle had only two books: one on the life of Christ and another on the lives of the saints. For months, Ignatius alternated between these two, reading, reflecting, and paying attention to the daydreams they generated in his imagination.

Ignatius slowly noticed that two daydreams vied for his attention. One was the heroic dream of knightly ambition and military glory; the other was a newly emerging dream of serving a different King. While his heroic dreams brought fleeting delight, over time they left him "dry and discontented." In contrast, his dreams of serving God and imitating the saints left him feeling full of life. He later wrote, "I paid no attention" to these feelings at first, but "one day my eyes were opened a little and I began to wonder at the difference and to reflect on it. I learned from experience that one kind of thought left me sad and the other cheerful. Thus, step-by-step I came to recognize the difference between these two . . . the one being from my own sinfulness and vanity and the other from God."

Ignatius's daydreams provided a window into what gave him life. His deep desire, he came to understand, was not to win the admiration of his friends or to meet the expectations of his parents; rather, as Nouwen might have put it, it was to "become the Beloved." Motivated by the love he experienced in his daydreams, Ignatius discerned that what *really, truly, authentically* had a hold on his heart was God. Despite many setbacks, Ignatius would spend the next several years walking the path to "I know not where" in search of an elusive "I know not what." Eventually, while studying at the University of Paris, he met others with whom he could explore his deep desire to serve God. In 1534, Ignatius and a small group of his friends formed a community known as the Society of Jesus, or the Jesuits, which would later grow into one of the largest religious orders in the history of the Catholic Church.

When we open our eyes a little, we will, as Jesus says to Nathanael, "see greater things" for ourselves and our world (John 1:50). Practicing this kind of seeing will require us, as it did Ignatius, to become aware of God's action in our lives; to reflect on our experiences in order to understand which lead us to greater life and love and which do not; and to act lovingly on what we've learned, even if it means that we must walk a path to "I know not where."

*Becoming Aware

Three large lithographs by the American painter Georgia O'Keeffe hang in my office. O'Keeffe, who like many artists managed to see the extraordinary in the ordinary, created paintings in which ordinary things—flowers, buildings, desert landscapes—are transformed into powerful abstract images. Once, when asked why she painted so many flowers, O'Keeffe responded, "Nobody sees a flower—really—it is so small—we haven't time—and to see takes time, like to have a friend takes time."

Yes, to see or to have a friend does take time. Discerning God's call takes time too.

Discernment begins with choosing to slow down and open our eyes a little. The first step in developing a discerning heart is to pay attention to where God is active in our lives, and to do this alone and with others. There, in the stuff of our everyday experience—our hopes, our fears, our dreams, our routines—God is at work, inviting us to notice what brings us joy, what we're good at, and what others need us to do. We can foster

> " . . . to act lovingly on what we've learned, even if it means that we must walk a path to 'I know not where.' "

such noticing through prayer and meditation, service to others, and active listening to the stories of others.

Prayer and meditation allow us to press the pause button and be still, opening a space where we can to listen to God, talk to God, and listen some more. When we read and pray over the daily scriptures chosen for a church lectionary or devotional source, for instance, we connect with God's wisdom and are invited to notice how it connects to our day-to-day lives. Other forms of prayer—such as centering prayer or meditative yoga—can quiet and open us, allowing us to hear more clearly God's voice of love and where, to what, and to whom it is calling us.

The examen, a particular form of prayer used by Christians across the centuries, invites us to stop each day to notice what is leading us toward greater life and love and what is blocking our way. This simple, three-part prayer, often done near the end of the day (examen is short for "examination of conscience") may last only a few minutes. After asking the Spirit for illumination, you ask, *For what moment today am I most grateful?* and *When did I feel most alive today?* You then offer a prayer of gratitude for these blessings, noting that God is always present in any encounter that deepens love and enriches life. After this, you review the day again, asking, *For what moment today am I least grateful?* and *When did I most feel life draining out of me?* You pay attention to these experiences, take note of how you reacted in these moments, and pray for forgiveness in those situations where your response was less than loving or life giving. Finally, you reflect on what you noticed while praying. What feelings arose? How are these connected to specific experiences of the day? What patterns are emerging over time in your reflections? Which experiences make you feel more alive, and which exhaust and deaden your spirit?

While prayer quiets us in order to hear God's voice, serving others often carries us to places where we encounter God in the gritty realities of the world. Here we are invited to become aware of our "deep gladness"— for example, when we experience joy or energy in using a particular talent for the benefit of others—and of the "deep hungers" of the human community for care, for food and shelter, for peace, for companionship, and for so much more.

Recently I met with a twenty-six-year-old graduate student, Shalene, for a spiritual companioning session. After graduation, Shalene had spent two life-changing years in Africa, and now she was excitedly preparing for an upcoming service trip to Kenya.

"What happened while you were in Africa the first time that produced such a change in you?" I asked. "What did it help you become more aware of?"

"In the journal I kept during that time," she answered, "I wrote a lot about how my eyes were being opened in ways I never could have imagined while living in the States. I saw how the everyday decisions I make at home adversely affect the poor in Africa. Everything here is about finding the cheapest price, but in Africa I saw firsthand how the best deal for me is not always good for others.

"I lived with a family that came from a long line of tea farmers. Unfortunately, the Kenyan government had recently moved to a farming policy that placed a priority on cash-crop farming. In this family, the husband was forced to leave their small tea farm—tea was not considered a cash crop—to plant and harvest roses in a government-sponsored operation. He barely made any money. Eventually they lost their farm, which is now producing cash crops for the government. Centuries of love went into that farm, but greed eventually overtook it. Because of this family's heartache, I'll never look at a rose in the same way again."

"That experience helped you to see injustice as more than a concept," I offered.

"Oh yes. And it showed me what I wanted my life to be about. I went to Africa as a social worker who wanted to help people. I came back from Kenya as a more compassionate, humble person who realized that the best help I could offer was to stand beside others working for justice. I know that if I listen enough to my experience, I will hear where God is inviting me to go next."

Shalene's service experience made her more aware of the world's deep hunger, and it also led her to notice the deep currents of justice, kindness, and humility that moved within her. Serving others—especially those who live on the margins—can shed light both on our unique talents and abilities and on the gifts all Christians are called to share: friendship, compassion, hope, love.

Listening to others' stories offers a third way to become aware of God's call. Whether we hear these stories firsthand, read them in a book, or experience them through film, it's important to pay attention when certain stories speak to us. That may happen even as you read the stories in this chapter and throughout this book. As you ponder these stories, perhaps one or more of these practices will call out to you as a vocation, a way of participating in God's life and love in this world.

*Developing Understanding

Through prayer, service, and story, God invites us to wake up and become aware of the many ways in which we can share our talents and gifts with others. That said, awareness without understanding goes nowhere. Understanding develops through reflection, taking the time to see the patterns in our experience and grasp their significance. While we can begin to notice and interpret God's action in our lives individually, if we want to hear deeply, see clearly, and choose wisely, we need trusted companions on the journey.

"The path [to our callings] is too deeply hidden to be traveled without company," writes the Quaker educator Parker Palmer. "Finding our way involves clues that are subtle and sometimes misleading, requiring the kind of discernment that can happen only in dialogue." We need other people to help us discern our callings, Palmer continues, because "the destination is too daunting to be achieved alone: we need community to find the courage to venture into the alien lands to which the inner teacher [God] may call us."

For at least three centuries, spiritual directors and Quaker clearness committees have accompanied seekers on the journey of discernment. Both can provide the companionship we need to sort and sift through our experiences, clarifying which are leading to greater life and love and which are not.

Spiritual direction usually occurs within the context of a one-on-one relationship. Its focus is on encouraging people to become more aware of God's movement in their lives, inviting them to grow in intimacy with God and to respond lovingly to God. Directors prompt directees to reflect on their experiences and to pay attention to the feelings they evoke. They help directees to notice patterns in their lives, including those that consistently deepen their relationship with God, give them energy and life, grow their hearts in love and joy, and inspire them to share their talents and gifts with others. And because all this is done in a context of trust and support, directors also encourage directees to identify tendencies that might be deceptive or destructive to their discernment. When done faithfully, spiritual direction often guides people to live more fully into their Belovedness, their authentic callings.

Quaker clearness committees, in contrast, offer a group approach to discernment. Since the seventeenth century, members of the Society of Friends (Quakers) have gathered in face-to-face groups to help one another better hear and understand God's voice in their lives. These committees assemble most frequently when a member (or a couple, family, or other group of members) is standing at the crossroads of an important decision. A Quaker approach to discernment is grounded in the assumption that every person has an "inner teacher" who longs to guide us more deeply into our deepest truth. Quaker clearness committees focus on listening attentively and walking compassionately with a member as he or she explores varying choices. Rather than offering opinions or advice, committee members ask questions that emerge from deep listening to the member and to the promptings of the Spirit in the accompanying silence—questions meant to assist the member in sorting through thoughts, feelings, choices. As the member reflects and responds, Quakers trust that the inner teacher will be heard more clearly, leading the member to choose the more loving and life-giving choice.

Whether we walk with one companion or several, we need the guidance, support, and insights of others as we travel the pathways of discernment. Each individual, shaped by a particular history and point of view, can see only partially. Reflecting on our experiences with trusted others can prevent us from being blinded by our own arrogance or deceived by our own insecurities. Discerning in community can encourage us to continue our search. And sharing our thoughts with others who listen in love can enrich our understanding of the God-given desires that lead us to live more fully into our callings.

*Acting Lovingly

Discernment does not end with becoming aware of how our experiences are drawing us closer to or further away from God. As Timothy Gallagher, a Roman Catholic priest, has pointed out, "the life of discernment calls for a person willing to act." When God has shown us greater things for our lives and our world, we eventually must decide what we want to do with this knowledge. How will we act on what we've learned, if we act at all?

Christian wisdom teaches that a sound decision is one that will grow our heart in love, bring us and others life, and reflect the "fruit of the Spirit." Looking back on his own long process of discernment, Father Pedro Arrupe, a twentieth-century leader in the Society of Jesus, wrote that "finding God, that is, falling in love in a quite absolute, final way" is what leads a person to a vocation. "What you are in love with, what seizes your imagination, will affect everything," he continued. "It will decide what will get you out of bed in the morning, what you will do with your evenings, how you will spend your weekends, what you read, who you know, what breaks your heart, and what amazes you with joy and gratitude. Fall in love, stay in love, and it will decide everything."

If growing in love is an important guideline to follow in making a decision, then growing in life is not far behind it. Any choice that leads to greater energy, creativity, or healing is a life-giving option, since it is always the "Spirit [that] gives life" (John 6:63, NIV). "Jesus, 'God-with-us,' poured his life energy into touching all creation with compassion and healing love," writes Margaret Silf. "He lived out the bias of God towards all that is life-giving, and he teaches and commissions us to do the same. . . . It is in the nature of God always to be weaving the most life-giving outcome from whatever we present." A wise choice fills us with the energy of life and inspires us to share our life with others. To use Michael Himes's terms, a good decision—a real calling—will energize us to give ourselves away.

> **" Fall in love, stay in love, and it will decide everything.—Father Pedro Arrupe "**

Last, we'll know we're choosing wisely if, as we live with our decision and act out of it over time, we (and those we touch) experience the fruit of the Spirit: "love, joy, peace, patience, kindness, generosity, faithfulness, gentleness, and self-control" (Gal. 5:22-23). A wise decision fosters these dispositions, suggesting that the Spirit is at work in us. As Jesus told his disciples, "A good tree cannot bear bad fruit, nor can a bad tree bear good fruit. . . . Thus you will know them by their fruits" (Matt. 7:18, 20).

Eventually, all of our individual and communal efforts to become aware and develop understanding lead to a place of decision. Ray had to decide whether he was going to live his father's life or his own. Ignatius had to choose between serving God or a Spanish king. And Kate had to determine whether to stay in a job she hated or discern a more life-giving course (which she did, eventually gathering the courage to leave her job, enroll full-time in a graduate program, and follow a calling to give herself away as an educator).

We cannot grow into our deepest desires or distinctive callings if we are not willing to become aware of God's movement in our lives, to reflect on this movement prayerfully alone and with others, and to take loving action on what we have learned. This is, in a nutshell, the work of discernment. Practicing it faithfully will help us to discover, over time, the unique gifts God has given to each of us—gifts we are called to share lovingly in healing the world. It will help us to notice the deep hungers of the world. And time and again it will reveal how much God loves each of us individually, and how much God loves this suffering world, inspiring us to make decisions that, in gratitude, "pay forward" more love and life to ourselves, our neighbors, and our God.

*How, Then, Shall We Live?

In these pages I have shared words of wisdom concerning discernment and what this practice promises to reveal about the ways God calls us to live—together, as members of the body of Christ, and uniquely, as individuals called by name to share our unique gifts with others. Now there is one more word I want to share, one that is as important as any of the others: *patience.*

Although we live in a culture that believes our questions will be answered if we just work hard enough, study long enough, or throw enough money at them, the Christian practice of vocational discernment reminds us that quick answers and fixes are illusions. Life is a mystery: not a single one of us knows for certain when a new life will begin or a current life end. A life well-lived keeps us focused on God, continually moving us into the depths of the mysterious river that sustains us. Trusting that we are held by God in the midst of these waters, we are set free to love the questions, not be terrified by them. And we come to love the mouth from which all questions are ultimately answered. We are set free to live in patience and hope, even while our discernment continues. "Be patient towards all that is unsolved in your heart and . . . try to love *the questions themselves,*" the writer Rainer Maria Rilke once advised a young poet. "Do not now seek the answers, that cannot be given you because you would not be able to live them. And the point is, to live everything. Live the questions now. Perhaps you will then gradually, without noticing it, live along some distant day into the answer."

It is the vocation of all Christians to keep living life's questions throughout our lives, turning our ears daily toward God as we seek to respond to God's call to us and to our world. If we do this, we will no doubt be invited to travel the path of "I know not what." When I respond to that invitation in my own life, I still often wonder where I am being led. But I am sustained by a felt knowledge that I am lovingly led by God.

" For surely I know the plans I have for you, says the Lord, plans for your welfare and not for harm, to give you a future with hope. Then when you call upon me and come and pray to me, I will hear you. When you search for me, you will find me; • if you seek me with all your heart, I will let you find me.—Jeremiah 29:11-14a "

Living a whole life attentively . . .

*together . . . in the real world . . . for the good of all . . . in response to God

4* Living as Community

Jonathan Wilson-Hartgrove

I t's the Sunday after Thanksgiving, four in the afternoon, and I'm busy making sweet potatoes and stuffing for twenty-five. Sarah's at the other house setting the table. I run over to get some butter, and we banter about whether it's better to set two separate tables in the kitchen (for more seats) or to keep them both together (so we can all face each other). We have this same argument every year. I finish the potatoes—fifteen minutes late—and Leah helps me carry them to the other house. I walk past the garden to the back door, which enters to the kitchen. Rodney and Marcus are at the sink doing dishes. I notice that the tables are still together.

The Sunday after Thanksgiving is an annual feast day for the extended family of the Rutba House community. We are a community of Christians who try to pray together and support one another in the kind of practices this book is about. I live here with my wife, Leah, our son, JaiMichael, and nine other folks (this week). We're a group of married and single people who share two houses, food, money, and a common life of prayer and discipleship. Sometimes we call ourselves a "new monastic community" because we've learned so much from the monastic movements that have carved out space to live as countercultural communities throughout the history of the church. But our annual Thanksgiving feast is a good reminder that we're really just a big family, extended beyond the ties of biology because we've become brothers and sisters of Jesus.

Before dinner we gather in the living room with sparkling grape juice in Mason jars to remember the past year and toast the good gifts God has given us. I look around at the faces and wonder how we ever got together. A carpenter who used to teach English. An ex-con who works the door at a blues club. A single mother who cleans up at a nursing home. A mother of three who shares kid duty with her husband while they're both in graduate school. A college student who lived at Rutba in high school, home for the holiday with two new friends. A computer analyst. A retiree. A six-month-old baby.

This is the community God has given us. We're black and white (and shades between), rich and poor (according to the IRS), formally educated and streetwise. We're an odd bunch—a "peculiar people," you might say. Maybe an act of God is the only thing that could have brought us together. We raise our Mason jars to give thanks and sing a classic from our neighborhood church: "Thank you, Lord. . . . You been so good. . . . I just want to thank you, Lord."

*Longing for Life Together

Sociologists call places like Rutba House "intentional communities," and I'll admit that it takes a good bit of intentionality to make life together happen. But I don't know that good intentions are what brought us together. Sometimes people who stop in to observe our communal life will say something like, "Oh, this is so beautiful . . . you must be saints." But we're always quick to clear up their misperception (if they stayed another day or two, I suspect it would clear itself up). "No, we're not saints," I usually say. "We're broken people who live together because we know we can't make it on our own."

Living as community is the practice of sharing our lives through mutual care and hospitality with all of God's people so we can be reconciled to the God who made us (Eph. 2:15-16). Truth is, when Jesus calls people to follow him, he calls all of us into community. "I ask . . . on behalf of those who will believe in me through their word," Jesus prayed, "that they may all be one. As you, Father, are in me and I am in you, may they also be in us" (John17:20-21). The great gift of God's incarnation in Jesus is that we are all invited into the beloved community of God's family.

This beloved community takes many different forms. In the early church, community emerged in the homes of wealthy Christians who invited poor neighbors to eat and worship with them. For much of church history, the local parish has been a place where Christian brothers and sisters connected as members of an extended family in their village or town. During the liberation struggle in Latin America, "base communities" of people who read scripture together and worked to put its liberating message into action developed among poor campesinos.

There is no ideal form of Christian community. In the places where we are, the practice of living as community calls us to ask, "How is God leading me deeper into life with other people?" I should confess at the outset of this chapter that I'm no expert on community. But I've felt the need to share life with others, and I've received the great gift of people who are willing to share their life with me. I feel like I know what Dorothy Day, founder of the Catholic Worker Movement, was talking about when she remembered her life as "the long loneliness" (also the title of her autobiography). "We have all known the long loneliness," Day wrote, "and we have learned that the only solution is love and that love comes with community." I don't know a better summary of what life is about.

That deep desire for connection—for the embrace of others who love me and help me know who I am—has been like a song in the background of my life since I was a child. I grew up in a tobacco farming community that was disintegrating as the sons of farmers took jobs in the city and migrant workers did more and more of the fieldwork. Like many sons of Stokes County, North Carolina, I left in search of something better. A few years later, on the campus of Eastern University in the suburbs of Philadelphia, I fell in love with the poetry of Wendell Berry. His descriptions of a place in Kentucky reminded me of the hills in Western North Carolina and the voices of men who sat on Coca-Cola crates at John Brown's Country Store and told stories. And I grew nostalgic for a community I'd never really known—a community that had, perhaps, never fully existed. Yet, somehow I knew community was what I was made for. The long loneliness inside of me whispered that I could not rest until I'd found a life to share with others.

Community is "in" these days. Real estate agents offer homes to up-and-coming young Americans in planned communities. College students and young professionals stay connected through virtual communities of social networks and second-life alter egos. Community gardens, community art collectives, and community coffee shops have become the hallmarks of hip urban life. Madison Avenue knows this, of course. Not long ago, an automobile manufacturer was promoting sales through ads that urged car buyers to join "the Saturn community." Marketing firms create ads that touch a deep human need. What is more, they touch it at a time in history when the social fabric that holds communities together has been stretched thin by the pressures of a highly mobile economy. The more fragmented life becomes, the more we feel our need for community.

Take, for example, the promising college graduate who decides to go to law school. Let's call her Christa. She was born in New York City, when her parents were in grad school there. Christa's family moved to Atlanta when she was three, but she really considers Buffalo home because that's where she moved with her mom to be close to family after her parents divorced. She went to college in Chicago, graduated at the top of her class, and has applied to law schools in three different states. Whichever school Christa chooses, she knows she probably will have to spend her summers somewhere else if she wants to get the best internships. And she hopes to clerk for a Supreme Court justice in DC after graduating.

If you had a chance to read Christa's blog, you'd know that Christa longs for community and commitment. Throughout college she volunteered as a tutor at an inner-city elementary school. She fell in love with the kids there and found meaning in her time with them. She really wants

❝ We have all known the long loneliness,
and we have learned that the
only solution is love and that love comes
with community.—Dorothy Day **❞**

to get married and have a family herself but feels like she needs to settle down first.

Christa dated a few guys in college but didn't want to get too serious. She's afraid of reliving her parents' failed relationship. She was in a Bible study in college with some girls who really helped her to grow and took care of her, but Christa never found a church where she felt at home.

Now Christa is back in Buffalo for the summer. She'll be moving soon, so she takes Sunday mornings to catch up on sleep. With a little more time to reflect, though, she admits that she's not satisfied. Her life feels scattered. She wants more of the stuff that matters and knows law school won't provide it. How is she going to find what she really longs for?

Christa's deepest hunger is for community. In her quest to find who she is as an adult, she has felt the long loneliness and her need for the mutual care of a life shared with other people. She feels alone—but in fact she is far from the only one who experiences this hunger. This is a desire that she shares with all human beings.

Of course, Christa's socioeconomic situation has shaped the options available to her in this quest for belonging. Because she went to college and has access to the Internet, Christa connects with friends on Facebook. If she had grown up in East L.A., she might be exploring her identity with the group of guys who gather after work to play soccer four nights a week. If she had been born in inner-city Detroit, she might have joined a gang. If she'd been a poor girl in West Virginia, she might have signed on with the army.

To say that the desire for partnership is a basic human desire is not to say that any of us necessarily knows what to do with it. A seemingly endless quest for connection sends some people reeling from one unhealthy relationship to another. The long loneliness has been the driving force behind the Ku Klux Klan, the Bloods and the Crips, the Khmer Rouge, and the Interahamwe of Rwanda (just to name a few not-so healthy communities). The more deeply we feel the need for community in a fragmented world, the more likely we are to create exclusive communities where we feel safe. Wanting desperately to keep the little community we have, we are tempted to cast out anyone we think is not like us.

You don't have to be living on the edge to succumb to this temptation. While the poor may band together in gangs or hate groups, middle-class Americans also form exclusive and unhealthy communities along lines of

> **"** We long for community—all of us—but our longings can be turned toward good or evil in a world broken by sin. **"**

race, class, and nationalism. It's no accident that one of the most unifying causes for middle-class Americans in the twenty-first century has been the "war on terror." Without a deeper vision for community, we easily identify ourselves by saying who we're against.

We long for community—all of us—but our longings can be turned toward good or evil in a world broken by sin. The question is not really whether we'll live in community. We are always a part of many communities because the fabric of our lives is interwoven with neighbors near and far—even with the earth itself. But how do we know what good community looks like? How can we keep from following a natural desire to an unnatural and destructive end? We need a story we can trust that tells us who we are.

*What People Were Made For

I grew up on the Bible, memorizing verses to back up the doctrine that my church thought important. Most of those verses were about how Jesus died to save me from my sin. Eventually I decided to study the biblical languages. When I did, I discovered that almost all the "yous" in scripture are plural. This startled me because I had learned to read Scripture as if it were written to *me*. I had to sit down and reread the whole Bible. What difference does it make if this whole book is written for a people called to walk with God in the world? I started at the beginning and read about how God created everything in the beginning, carving out a space in the midst of chaos to make a home with people. Genesis 1:27 really jumped out at me:

> So God created humankind in his image,
>> in the image of God he created them;
>> male and female he created them.

I'd been told all my life that I was special because I was created in the image of God. But I'd never listened to what Genesis said that image looked like—namely, a "them." When God went to create humanity, he created a community. Or, maybe I should say *they* created a community. "Let *us* make humankind in *our* image, according to *our* likeness," Genesis says (1:26, emphasis added). Could this mean, I wondered, that God is not a *he* but a community who in turn was *creating* a community, "according to our likeness"?

When I went to seminary later and read some good theology, I learned that my question had actually been pondered by others for centuries. Christians have long read this verse as an early indication of the Trinity, in which God is three persons forever giving themselves to one another so fully that they are also one being. God is the beloved community of Father, Son, and Holy Spirit. To be created in God's image is to be made for life together.

When you read the New Testament with this in mind, you notice how Jesus is always inviting people into a new community (often through actions that echo God's work of forming community among the twelve tribes of Israel). Jesus calls twelve disciples, interprets Israel's law for them in the Sermon on the Mount, insists that outsiders are welcome in God's family, heals people who are broken by oppression, expands the boundaries of what it means to be family, denounces corrupt religious leaders, reteaches God's manna economy by feeding the five thousand, and proclaims the year of Jubilee. After doing all of this, Jesus explains to his disciples that the way of God's community is so counter to the selfish ways of the broken human community that it is going to get him killed.

At Jesus' lowest point, his little community of disciples runs off and leaves him. Peter refuses to admit that he ever knew Jesus. It's hard to imagine a more broken community than this one. But Jesus gets up from the dead to prove that God is able to overcome the very worst brokenness. The resurrected Jesus tells his disciples that if he ascends to heaven, he will send the Holy Spirit to enliven their communal life with the very same power that was in him.

In the book of Acts we read about how God's Spirit came on the disciples at Jerusalem and inspired a life together unlike anything they had known before. "Now the whole group of those who believed were of one heart and soul, and no one claimed private ownership of any possessions, but everything they owned was held in common. With great power the apostles gave their testimony to the resurrection of the Lord Jesus, and great grace was upon them all" (Acts 4:32-33). Suddenly there was a community of people who lived together peaceably, sharing what they had so that no one was needy.

People who heard about this community were fascinated by it. The good news about Jesus wasn't just a set of propositions about how God could fix their sin problem. It was a concrete community that promised to fulfill their deepest longing. It's little wonder that Acts says, "And day by day the Lord added to their number those who were being saved" (Acts 2:47).

I'm a follower of Jesus today because I stumbled into a little Christian community just as I was beginning to ask critical questions about the church in society. I wanted to know why Jesus said "blessed are you who are poor" (Luke 6:20) while most of the church was eager to achieve middle-class comfort. I wanted to know why Jesus blessed the peacemakers (Matt. 5:9), but many Christians waved the flag in a time of war. I wanted to know how in the world you could give to whoever asks (see Luke 6:30) if the beggars are always begging and the hucksters are always hawking their wares.

As I was asking those questions, God led me to a community of imperfect people who opened their door to strangers, visited with homeless friends on the street, shared their incomes in mutual care, and talked about Jesus with an authenticity I hadn't witnessed before. As I got to know those folks, I learned of other communities like theirs all over the country. Beneath the radar of American Christianity, many of them had been living the way of Jesus quietly for decades. As I visited and talked with these communities, I realized that they didn't think they were doing anything very new. They'd simply joined the long tradition of communities who have tried to live in the way of Jesus since the book of Acts.

*The Witness of the Saints

In almost every era community movements have arisen to ask, *How can we live the way of Jesus faithfully in a new time?* One consistent stream of these communities is the movement known as monasticism. When the Roman Emperor Constantine offered his favors to the church and transformed it from a persecuted minority into the established imperial religion, men and women now remembered as the desert fathers and mothers went out into the Egyptian wilderness to discern a new way of life. Monasticism was born in the way of life these desert Christians developed.

One leader of early monasticism, Pachomius, was born in Upper Egypt at the end of the third century, the son of a Roman soldier. He grew up knowing next to nothing about Christianity. When he was a teenager, he ended up in prison, not for causing trouble but because of political changes. A prisoner of war, he sat in a barren cell, uncertain what fate awaited him.

While Pachomius was in prison, some people came by every day to slip food into his cell. These weren't his guards but people coming to help him of their own will. Pachomius asked one of them who they were and learned that they were followers of a man named Jesus who had told them to visit prisoners and feed the hungry. Impressed by the generosity of those Christians, he joined them when he was released from prison. He learned from a desert father named Palemon how to live as a hermit and followed that way of prayer and simplicity for a number of years. But in a recurring dream, Pachomius saw Christians living together in community that filled the earth with "sweetness"; this life was like "honey covering the earth." Deciding the dream came from God, he set out to found a

12 Marks of a New Monasticism

1 Relocation to the abandoned places of Empire.

2 Sharing economic resources with fellow community members and the needy among us.

3 Humble submission to Christ's body, the church.

4 Geographical proximity to community members who share a common rule of life.

5 Hospitality to the stranger.

6 Nurturing common life among members of intentional community.

7 Peacemaking in the midst of violence and conflict resolution within communities along the lines of Matthew 18.

8 Lament for racial divisions within the church and our communities combined with the active pursuit of a just reconciliation.

9 Care for the plot of God's earth given to us along with support of our local economies.

10 Support for celibate singles alongside monogamous married couples and their children.

11 Intentional formation in the way of Christ and the rule of the community along the lines of the old novitiate.

12 Commitment to a disciplined contemplative life.

community for monks at Tabenna. Today Pachomius is considered the father of communal monasticism, also called cenobitic monasticism.

Such movements have emerged over and over again in church history. Monastics inspired by the communal way of life developed by Saint Benedict in fifth-century Italy still pray and work in communities of vowed women or men all over the world. Other Christians have created communities of Christian brothers or sisters who went out into the world to serve God among the poor. When the advent of a cash economy transformed social life in Europe, for example, two wealthy Italians from Assisi, Francis and Clare, renounced their own privileges to start orders (that is, ordered communities) of this kind, in celebration of God's great sabbath economy. The point of monasticism is not that everyone should live as monks do. The point is that, with God's help, we can make it possible for people in different times and places to develop life-giving ways of being in community.

There is a new monastic movement today. The grassroots emergence of communities of intentional discipleship, which has been happening in Western Christianity for about seventy-five years, gives me great hope that we can indeed follow Jesus in a post-Christian era. This is one of the main places where community is flourishing in the church today. But these communities do not exist for their own sake. The proliferation of new monastic communities is a sign for the whole church that the world is hungry for the way of life Jesus taught and practiced. The practices that mark new monastic communities may have to be modified in different contexts, but they offer hope that people can receive the gift of God's way in the world.

*Demonstration Plots of the Kingdom

A Ugandan friend tells me that when he was growing up in the village, farmers used to travel to towns to see the demonstration plots planted by agricultural schools. In these plots they could observe new irrigation techniques and the effects of various planting methods. They could taste the cabbage that had been grown in a new way and compare it with cabbage from their own fields. The demonstration plots existed for the good of all the farmers in the region.

Because Christian community always exists for the sake of the world, the reconciliation and mutual care that we practice within the church is

> **" Like leaven in the bread dough, we live the beloved community . . . so that the world can see something of the life that's really life. "**

meant to be like a demonstration plot for the whole human community. Christians don't practice community for our own sake. Like leaven in the bread dough, we live the beloved community all people were made for so that the world can see something of the life that's really life.

I'm greatly encouraged by the Christian Community Development Association, a network of six hundred churches and ministries that have sprung up over the past twenty years in America's blighted urban neighborhoods. Focusing on church-based indigenous leadership development, these ministries offer a holistic vision of God's kingdom through job programs, worship services, prison reentry programs, schools, health clinics, summer camps, and housing programs.

For CCDA churches and ministries, "thy kingdom come on earth as it is in heaven" is more than a prayer to God. It is an invitation to get to work, ensuring that each person in their neighborhoods has what he or she needs to flourish as a child of God. The community God has made them part of inspires them to work for the betterment of the neighborhoods and the creation of a different kind of community for all people. CCDA emphasizes the importance of commitment to a neighborhood and its people. "If you're not going to stay fourteen years," I heard one CCDA leader say, "don't come." His point, of course, was that community takes time. You can't create it overnight. In places where trust has been broken and people have been abused, it may take a whole generation to build genuine community.

Community takes time wherever we are. In a highly mobile culture, we have to be intentional if we are going to get our roots in deep enough to find the waters of belonging in the communities where we live.

A Christian family living on a suburban cul-de-sac one day realized that they didn't know the names of anyone in the neighborhood except the couple who had just moved in next door. So they invited the new folks next door over for dinner. They shared with them their desire to know their neighbors, and both families said they'd try to meet someone else on the street. A few years later, this little cul-de-sac in the suburbs has a dinner together at one family's house each week. They share garden tools and babysit each other's kids. The ones who are interested sometimes pray together. It's a nice reminder that, wherever we are, Jesus is right there. And that if you love your neighbor as yourself, you are far more likely to end up sharing life with your neighbors.

Many people go to church looking for something like this kind of neighborliness. However, just showing up once a week for worship with a large group of strangers is rarely enough. One of my friends has described the difference she experienced between just going to church and becoming an "intentional churchgoer." At a Thursday-night Bible study in a local parish she attended as a young, single woman she found a space to know others and get involved in their lives. "Supported and challenged by one another, transformed into an intentional family of prayer and sharing, we were a small community within a larger one," she writes.

Small groups are a wonderful way to carve out space for community within local churches. People who make the effort to know one another, pray with one another, read scripture together, and talk honestly about discipleship almost inevitably end up eating together. In the breaking of bread, we begin to realize what it means that because we eat one loaf, we are members of one body. And church is no longer the place you go (or don't) on Sundays. It becomes the people who help you remember who you are.

A church that forms community around food isn't only a better community for its own members. It can also foster community with neighbors and friends who are not part of the church. My friend Fred Bahnson manages the Anathoth Community Garden, which was started by a United Methodist church in North Carolina. After a brutal murder left everyone in their rural area afraid, this congregation had a vision that connection to the land could be an important part of the healing process for all. And so this church decided to start a garden where anyone could come, put in a few hours a week, and take home fresh produce in season.

Fred tells me that the garden has become a place where old farmers talk with college students from the nearby universities. Kids doing community service work beside grandmothers who grew up gardening. A Zen Buddhist has become one of the most active members of the garden. He brings his famous stir-fry to garden potlucks and enjoys the fellowship. Without much fanfare, a little Methodist church has created a space where friendship can happen. And a neighborhood that was traumatized by murder isn't as afraid anymore. This neighborhood is becoming a community.

*Finding a Place to Practice Our Faith

A few years ago I was asked what I liked most and what I liked least about life at Rutba House. The best thing about community, I replied immediately, is knowing that there are people who love you, even though they really know you. And then I added this: the worst part is trying to love all those other people, even though you know them.

I don't want to give anyone the false impression that community is easy. I'll never forget the time I was speaking in class about God's gift of community and a Korean student in the back row raised his hand to say, "You know, I grew up in a tight-knit ethnic community. I felt suffocated, and people were always in my business. I've had enough of community."

I had to admit that he had a point. Community can be pretty messy. Any group of people can devolve into an insular, self-serving club for the self-righteous. Or it can spin apart when well-meaning people focus so much on reaching out that they forget to take care of their own brothers and sisters. It's hard to strike a balance between caring for one another and remaining open to outsiders.

All communities also have to deal with money, sex, and power (the traditional monastic vows of poverty, chastity, and obedience are an attempt to address these issues head-on). Most communities mess up sometime with all three of these issues. Community doesn't make people perfect. As a matter of fact, it usually helps us see better how imperfect we are.

The Rutba House offers hospitality to people who are homeless for one reason or another. Most of the long-term members of our community are white and fairly well-educated folks who grew up in stable families. Most of the guests we host, however, are poor and black. They've spent much of their lives scrambling to survive.

Now, I would like to think of myself as a good and generous person who shares with people in need out of the goodness of my heart. But after living with needy people, I know that's not true. I'm easily annoyed when I feel like someone is lazy. I don't like to feel like I'm being used, and I'm not very good at talking to people about it. There's a part of me that wants to kick difficult people out of my life (I call this "the other 'F-you'"—the curse that says, "Forget you").

But even though community has exposed my selfishness, it is also the context where Christian practices have begun to make sense for me. My self-defensiveness has led me to say things I wish I hadn't said. In order to go on sharing life with people I've hurt, I've had to ask for forgiveness. I see now that forgiveness is tied up with conversion—that to be forgiven is to be changed. Some of our hardest guests have held my hand and helped me on the way to holiness.

The sort of radical practices that Mary Emily Briehl Duba writes about in her chapter on "Peacemaking and Nonviolence" are much easier to imagine in the context of community. One church in Chicago decided to harbor AWOL soldiers during the Vietnam War. Members made the decision in a discernment meeting where one of the members said to another, "If the police come and find the soldiers in your house, I'll take care of your family until you get out of jail." Followers of Jesus can never forget that this way of life got our Lord killed. But neither should we forget Jesus' words from the cross to his mother: "Woman, here is your son" (John 19:26). In community we are not left alone, even by death.

Making a good living is another practice that is facilitated by the practice of living as community. After all, individuals and single-family units don't often have much wiggle room when expenses are subtracted from income at the end of the month. Sharing resources in community creates new possibilities through an economy of scale. By sharing space, for example, individuals can significantly reduce their monthly expenses. But you don't have to share a house to live in community. At a church in Iowa a member who works for a large software company came to his fellow church members saying he was going to have to move his family to another state in order to keep his job. The church prayed together and decided it was best for the family not to move. They pitched in and paid the guy's monthly salary until he found a new job in their town. Stories like that make me think Jesus was telling the truth when he said, "The Spirit of the Lord is upon me, because he has anointed me . . . to proclaim release to the captives" (Luke 4:18).

This church was helping the family to make a good living, but it was also helping them engage faithfully in discerning God's call at a point of vocational crisis. As noted in the chapter on discernment, reflection on vocation needs to happen at least partly in community. If vocation is about knowing who we are and how we fit into God's story, other people who love us and know us well often see our vocation more clearly than we can ever do alone. Wherever that genuinely happens, community is formed.

L'Arche (which means "the ark" in French) is an international network of small communities where people who are mentally disabled are the "core members." Living with them are people who are "temporarily abled." These residents recognize the essential dignity of their disabled friends by sharing life together, not as helpers but as people who genuinely need each other.

L'Arche was started by Jean Vanier, a promising young PhD in philosophy who asked his priest what he should do with his life after grad school. Vanier recalls that the priest said, "There are two disabled men living in a house down the street. Go live with them." Vanier was so transformed by

> **The cry of people with disabilities was just a very simple cry. Do you love me?—Jean Vanier**

the experience of living with those two men that he has spent the rest of his life living in community with people who are mentally disabled. "The cry of people with disabilities was just a very simple cry," Vanier says. "Do you love me? That's what they were asking. And that awoke something deep within me because that was also my fundamental cry. . . . I knew the need to be both accepted and admired." Vanier has gradually learned a wisdom that his academic pursuit of philosophy had not provided: the wisdom of love. Finding a place where we know that people love us is crucial to all of us as we discern our vocations.

But if everyone needs community, that doesn't mean that we all have to find it in the same place. Sometimes when I talk about new monasticism, someone will ask, "Are you saying that everyone needs to live in intentional community?" I always say, "Oh no! That would take a very large house."

Life in community is not for everybody. At their best, communities like L'Arche and Rutba House are laboratories where Christian practice can be explored for the sake of the whole church. You don't have to live with the mentally disabled to learn that you need people who love you. But wherever you are, what Vanier has learned is true. Christian community is about finding those relationships that make a life of faithfulness possible where you are.

I know a group of women who gather to pray together once each week. Over the decades, they have prayed one another through marriage difficulties and child-rearing challenges, church conflict and financial crises. On more than one occasion, they have acted to become the answer to one another's prayers. When Mary knew that Sylvia was struggling to care for a sick child, she would regularly drop by with dinner in a casserole dish. Ann, who is a teacher, has intervened for more than one of the other women's children when they were having a hard time at school. Some women have come and gone from the group. They've all suffered loss. But each of them knows that they are loved by God and by God's family.

This kind of community is more and more difficult to sustain in a highly mobile and extremely fast-paced culture. Who has time to sit and listen to the same people every week for years? After all, the people you commit to may just move next year . . . or next month. Indeed, some of them almost certainly will.

But community is not an ideal. It doesn't happen when perfect people get together under just the right conditions. Community is the discipline of giving ourselves to others because we know we need them. Doing so, we open ourselves to all the heartache that life with others will inevitably involve. But we also open ourselves to God's gifts, including community itself. For in the end, community is always a gift.

On a small college campus in Tennessee, I ran into some students who were trying to take seriously the call to community. Living together in dorms, these guys had experienced how proximity allowed them to know one another's lives well. But they also knew that their lives were very much the same. So they started asking how they could share life with people who are not like them.

Not far from their campus, they discovered, there was a house where men who had been in prison were living together to share expenses and hold one another accountable. The students started going over to eat with these men once a week. After a while, the guys in the halfway house asked if some of the college students wanted to live with them while they were in school. Now a couple of rooms in the house are set aside for college students to live with the ex-cons every semester. Students who have lived there say they learned more from the experience than they did in most of their classes.

Like the ex-cons who are transitioning back into society, those students don't live together forever. Some stay for a semester, some for a year. They graduate, get married, join churches, have kids. They may go on to be lawyers, doctors, teachers, or entrepreneurs. But they are different. They know deep down in their bones that the people who end up incarcerated are not unlike them. They've learned how prison exposes the weakness of our social networks. They know, as Dorothy Day said, that "the only solution is love." Wherever they go, they are people who will work to build up community not only because they need it, but because we all need it to survive.

*Coming to the Table

It's Monday, the day after our Thanksgiving feast at Rutba. After fasting from breakfast and lunch (which we especially needed after eating like we did yesterday), we break our fast on Mondays with our weekly thanksgiving—what the church calls Eucharist (*eucharistō* is Greek for "I give thanks").

We gather in the same living room where we sat together yesterday offering toasts. In silence we remember the past week. One member confesses a lack of trust that has been making him anxious. Another confesses anger. We try to tell the truth about our brokenness—how we have failed to trust Jesus and have hurt one another. We admit that community is hard. We can't do this by our own strength.

But then we also remember, in the words of our simple liturgy, that "in the name of Jesus Christ, we are forgiven." In God's great story our fragmented lives have been re-membered—put back together again—by the love of Jesus. And now here we are at Jesus' own table. "To eat the Body of

> **In God's great story our fragmented lives have been re-membered—put back together again—by the love of Jesus.**

Christ and to drink the blood of Christ," declared the fifth-century bishop Augustine of Hippo, is to be "incorporated in the unity of His Body." Jesus gives himself to us as bread and wine. So we share the gift with one another.

I turn to Dan, tear off a piece of the loaf, and say, "this is the body of Christ." I watch as he chews, and I trust that he is becoming what he eats. In what can only be described as a mystery, Dan is becoming Christ's body for me.

Our weekly thanksgiving is a simple act, often filled with the sounds of children crying, the kitchen timer beeping, a guest knocking at the door. But I think it's where we remember that community is coming to the Table by faith. The Orthodox theologian Alexander Schmemann wrote that "we [offer] the bread in remembrance of Christ because we know that Christ is Life, and all food, therefore, must lead us to Him."

All of our eating points to this mystery: that, somehow, we are the body of Christ. So we eat together with one another, with our neighbors, and with the strangers who show up at our door. Sometimes we get the feeling that we might have "entertained angels without knowing it" (Heb. 13:2). And sometimes we say with the psalmist "you prepare a table before me in the presence of my enemies" (Ps. 23:5). But we keep coming back because we believe this practice of living as community opens us to life with God. We keep coming because we've seen enough to know that this way leads to life.

5* Friendship and Intimacy

Stephanie Paulsell

Ralph Waldo Emerson once asked, in an essay on love, "What [is] so delicious as a just and firm encounter of two, in a thought, in a feeling?" And truly, is there anything more pleasurable in life than the first steps into intimacy with another person? Is there anything more wonderful than meeting someone and finding, unexpectedly, that you are in deep agreement about what matters most and have more to say to each other than could be said in a lifetime? Is there anything more delicious than a first confidence given, a first secret tenderly received, a first kiss?

Friendship is such a deep and genuine joy that human beings have always celebrated it in our art and literature. The ancient *Epic of Gilgamesh*, sometimes called the world's oldest story, has also been described as a "hymn to friendship." The story of the relationship between Gilgamesh and Enkidu explores the ways in which friendship makes us both strong and vulnerable, and how an intimate relationship with another can alter us, shape our character, change our lives. Ancient philosophical movements often viewed friendship as a spiritual practice, indispensable to a life lived well. Epicurus, Cicero tells us, "says that of all the things which

> **"** Is there anything more delicious than a first confidence given, a first secret tenderly received, a first kiss? **"**

wisdom provides in order for us to live happily, there is nothing better, more fruitful, or more pleasant than friendship." Aristotle, in his powerful analysis of friendship in his *Nicomachean Ethics*, writes that "without friends no one would choose to live, though he had all other goods."

If you've ever shared a secret with a new friend only to discover your secret was not safe, however, you know that cultivating the shared intimacy of friendship holds risks as well as pleasures. If you've ever befriended someone, not because you were drawn to her but because you calculated that her friendship would be advantageous to you in some way, you know that the practice of friendship can be manipulated and misused. If you've ever experienced any kind of intimate relationship so controlling or so driven by one person's bottomless needs that it cut you off from other relationships, you know that intimacy can turn inward in harmful ways, shrinking the boundaries of our lives rather than enlarging them.

Friendship requires trust, and trust requires faith in one's friend. Friendship is a relationship of reciprocity, in which one friend does not wield power over the other. Even the most intimate friendships require a degree of distance that allows friends to develop, each independently, while still responding to the claims friendship makes on them. And friendship requires deliberate cultivation. It's natural to be drawn to another person, but cultivating a friendship over time, as friends move and change and grow, does not always come naturally.

> Easy at first, the language of friendship
> Is, as we soon discover,
> Very difficult to speak well, a tongue
> With no cognates, no resemblance
> To the galimatias of nursery and bedroom,
> Court rhyme or shepherd's prose,
>
> And, unless often spoken, soon goes rusty.

The poet W. H. Auden is right: while the early days of a n
ship are full of words, eagerly shared, sustaining that exchange
in a context where trust, reciprocity, and enough distance to be
selves are prized takes constant practice. Other intimacies—th
nursery or the bedroom, as Auden says—can be buoyed along for a time
by galimatias—nonsense. Not friendship. The warm repetitive murmur-
ing between lovers, or between parents and their small children, cannot
keep a friendship afloat. It is conversation, Emerson wrote, "which is the
practice and consummation of friendship." But the language of friendship
must be deliberately sought and cultivated across the boundaries of lives
lived more separately than family members or lovers, lives shaped by other
intimacies, other commitments, yet still bound together by love.

At the heart of Christian faith is the conviction that our life with God
and our life with others are one life. *When you clothe your naked brother or
feed your hungry sister*, Jesus teaches in Matthew 25, *you care for me*. Loving God with all one's heart, soul, strength, and mind and one's neighbor
as oneself was the bedrock of the Jewish tradition inherited by Jesus and
passed along by him to his followers.

Friendship—a particularly wonderful manifestation of our life with
others—appears in the history of Christianity both as a vital Christian
practice and as a way of describing intimacy between Christ and humanity. In his teaching, Jesus, especially the Jesus of John's Gospel, speaks of
the claims friendship makes on us—and on him—in the strongest possible
words: "No one has greater love than this, to lay down one's life for one's
friends," Jesus says to his disciples. "I do not call you servants any longer,
because the servant does not know what the master is doing; but I have
called you friends, because I have made known to you everything that I
have heard from my Father" (John 15:13, 15). The letters of Paul often
describe Christian life itself as rooted in the practices of friendship: "Bear
one another's burdens," Paul writes in the letter to the Galatians, "and in
this way you will fulfill the law of Christ" (6:2). The Wisdom Literature
of the Bible is full of practical advice on cultivating and nurturing friendships, with an emphasis on whose friendship to seek (the wise) and whose
to avoid (scoffers), lifting up practices that build up friendship (forgiveness) and warning against those that tear it down (dwelling on disputes).
Biblical Wisdom Literature also cherishes the idea that intimate friendship

with God is possible. "In every generation," the author of the Wisdom of Solomon sings, "she [Wisdom] passes into holy souls and makes them friends of God, and prophets; for God loves nothing so much as the person who lives with wisdom" (7:27-28).

But isn't Christianity about loving strangers and our enemies more than it is about loving our friends? Didn't Jesus say that even tax collectors love their friends? Doesn't Jesus ask us to practice solidarity with all people rather than focusing on our relationships with particular people, whose company we enjoy?

Yes, Jesus did teach solidarity with others, even those whose company we do not eagerly seek. Yes, he answered the lawyer's question—"Who is my neighbor?"—with the story of the good Samaritan, for whom the well-being of a helpless stranger was as important as his own or that of his friends. Yes, Jesus calls us each and every day to radical practices of relationship anchored more in our common humanity than in the common interests that provide the wellspring of our friendships.

But does Jesus' call to make our own the concerns of others, including strangers and enemies, mean that we ought not seek out friendships with those to whom we are drawn and in whose company we feel most alive? On the contrary, our capacity for the radical practices of relationship to which Jesus calls us depends upon our ability to initiate friendships and to welcome offers of friendship from others. In a way of life made up of Christian practices, friendship and intimacy are crucial to the practices of nonviolence and peacemaking, honoring the body, and living as community. Friendship teaches us to care about another's pain, another's joy.

How can Christianity give us any guidance for our friendships and intimate relationships today? Valuing work and vocation as we do in modern societies, we are often starting over again when we move for education or a new job, seeking out friends in new places. Our attention is pulled in a thousand different directions, and our capacity for being fully present to one another slowly and quietly erodes as our capacity for multitasking grows. Our "social network" may expand when we accumulate online friends whom we have never met, but we go for long stretches of time without being in the same physical space as those we love the most. We even have a name for the struggle to remain intimate with another person from whom we live far apart: long-distance relationships.

Does Christian faith have anything to do with the way we seek and make and cultivate intimate relationships? Is there anything we can learn from Christian practice about how to find a good friend, or how to be one? Would thinking about friendship as a Christian practice, necessary to the Christian life, make any difference in how we practiced our friendships? Would understanding our life with others and our life with God as one life enable us make choices about friendship, intimacy, and love that cause love to flourish and grow? Can Christian practice help us learn how to nurture relationships that will last?

*Friendship

"Friendship demands a religious treatment," Emerson believed, because reverence is such a necessary part of friendship. We should revere our friends, Emerson insisted. "Treat your friend," he advised, "as a spectacle." Stare in open admiration.

And for what do we revere our friends? For Emerson, we admire the merits our friend possesses that are not ours. "Stand aside; give those merits room; let them mount and expand," Emerson advises. Friends do this for one another: they make room for each other's gifts to expand and grow. If we cannot delight in the gifts of our friends, if we begrudge them our admiration and the admiration of others, or if we experience their successes as somehow a diminution of our own, the friendship will stall and wither. Friendship is a school for developing the generosity of spirit that every intimate relationship requires. Indeed, friendship "is acquired by competition in generosity, not by a haggling over its prices," as Saint Ambrose put it long ago.

Novelist Virginia Woolf compared her friends to lamps mounted on a carriage: "There[']s another field I see: by your light. Over there's a hill. I widen my landscape." For Woolf, friends enlarge one's world. Even if we see eye-to-eye about many things, our friends are not us, and their perspectives, their vantage points differ from ours. They allow us see farther than we can on our own. They widen our landscape. As Christian ethicist Paul Wadell puts it, "One reason we like our friends and want to be with them is precisely because they are *not like us*." If a friendship cannot sustain two different perspectives, if one friend resents or fears the other when she disagrees with him or views a situation differently than he does, then the friendship will not grow. If one friend relies on the other to be and think and act a certain way and cannot tolerate any change, the friendship will not develop. It is a very great pleasure to see eye-to-eye with a friend. But if we find we are looking to our friendships only to confirm our own perspective and never to challenge it, then we need to think again about what it means to be a friend. And if we find that our friend requires one way of thinking and acting from which we can never deviate, then we may be stuck in a relationship that limits our growth rather than making room for us to become our best selves.

Our friends also call forth our reverence because they remind us of the profound friendship that animates the life of God. God exists in relationship: Father, Son, and Holy Spirit. In our friendships, Simone Weil observes, we see "an image of the original and perfect friendship that belongs to the Trinity and is the very essence of God." The ordinary practices of cultivating a friendship have the potential to draw us more deeply into God's own life. Aelred of Rievaulx, a twelfth-century Christian writer, even proposed that what is true of love in the passage "God is love, and those who abide in love abide in God, and God abides in them" (1 John 4:16b), can be said of friendship. "God is friendship," Aelred says. Those who abide in friendship abide in God, and God abides in them.

Friendships are often born from the discovery of some common interest or even some common complaint. And, God knows, finding someone who agrees with our complaints and critiques can be bliss! However, that bliss can be so pleasurable that we get stuck there, sharing complaints with each other repeatedly, going over and over what quickly becomes well-worn ground. This is especially true with friendships that take root, as many do, at work. The boss is a jerk, let us count the ways! What is fun at first can easily become repetitive. Such friends will need to develop other points of intersection in order for their friendship to grow.

> **"** 'God is friendship,' Aelred says. Those who abide in friendship abide in God, and God abides in them. **"**

One of the great pleasures of friendship is the feeling of being truly known by another. In the early days of any friendship, we try as best we can to make ourselves knowable. We talk about what kind of music we like, what books we love, what films we've watched over and over again. As we share these bits of information, each person builds a portrait of the other.

The truest friend holds that portrait loosely, though, rather than insisting that her friend stick to the script (even a script of the friend's own devising). If you've seen the film *Juno*, you'll remember that when Juno MacGuff, a pregnant teenager, meets the family she hopes will adopt her baby, she is immediately drawn to the husband. Both Juno and the husband love music, although their tastes are different; they take pleasure in educating each other in their likes and dislikes. The wife seems bourgeois and staid, more interested in her Pilates machine and her bathroom renovations than in the debates over popular culture that Juno and the husband enjoy.

But the husband cannot see beyond the inspiration he draws from Juno's young, smart perspective into her real needs, desires, and vulnerabilities. Overidentified with the portrait of Juno he has pieced together in his imagination, he wrongly believes she'll applaud his announcement that he is leaving his wife to pursue a career in music. Instead, Juno is appalled, and their friendship ends abruptly. The seemingly boring wife turns out to be the one capable of courage, generosity, and friendship. She offers Juno what Juno most wants and needs—a loving and stable home for her baby. And Juno turns out to have the deep insight of a true friend, recognizing who the wife truly is. When the husband is out of the picture, Juno tells her: "If you're still in, I'm still in."

Our friends help us to be ourselves, but they also help us to be more than we knew ourselves to be. In his *Confessions*, the early Christian writer Augustine tells the story of the death of a beloved friend with whom he shared "a friendship that was sweeter to me than all sweetnesses that in this life I had ever known." Augustine tells us that he had turned his friend away from Christian faith and led him toward Manicheanism, another religious movement of the time. When his friend became deathly ill, however, his family had him baptized as a Christian. When the friend's health subsequently improved, Augustine joked with him about this baptism, expecting his friend to follow his lead. Instead, "with a sudden confident authority which took me aback," the friend told Augustine that if he wanted their friendship to continue, he must not speak so cynically to him. A few days later, his friend did die, leaving Augustine wild with grief. His friend's unexpected admonishment remained lodged in his heart, where it did its transforming work on him over time, contributing to Augustine's own conversion. The friend's refusal to play the role Augustine expected helped open a space in which Augustine could risk seeking his own truest self.

Because of all the ways in which friends can deceive one another—and themselves—as they try to cultivate friendships, some Christians have tried to avoid being seduced by pleasures that feel like friendship but might really be an infatuation or an attraction that would lead away from the freedom to become ourselves fostered in genuine friendship. Aelred of Rievaulx, in his essay "Spiritual Friendship," developed what he called "a formula for friendship whereby I might check the vacillations of my loves and affections." His formula goes like this: don't rush into intimacy. Choose your friends carefully, and let your friendship develop slowly. Observe a probationary period, in which you discover whether or not your friend can be trusted. Once you are satisfied that you have a found a good friend, cultivate your friendship, and, above all, be loyal.

Emerson agrees with Aelred on the importance of moving slowly, not out of fear that the person may not be worthy of our friendship but out of reverence for the other. Our friendships fail, Emerson says, when we rush at "a swift and petty benefit," locking our friend into an identity as someone who meets our needs, agrees with our opinions, benefits us in some way. Knowing a friend—really knowing—takes time, and presence, and patience. It's not possible to speed up the process of coming to know someone; it's the work of a lifetime. Friendship cannot be rushed, even over the Internet. We lack reverence for our friend when we behave as if it can.

Churches are good places to encounter potential friends and good places to practice revering them. Where else in our culture can we go to encounter people of all ages and backgrounds, to get to know others across the many boundaries that divide us and impede our friendships? Where else are we invited to cultivate friendships with those who may be much older or much younger, wealthier or poorer, less educated or better educated, than we are, people whose work is unlike ours, whose origins are unlike ours? Where else are we invited to regard one another in the light of God? And where else can we pray for our absent friends in a community that cares about our friends because they are ours? Praying for our friends is an indispensable practice of friendship for Christians. Prayer is a way to dwell with our friends—even those at a distance—in the presence of God. Through prayer, we come to know our friends—to reverence our friends—in new ways. And through our love for our friends, which leads us to prayer, we come to taste and see the goodness of God—the "spiritual fruit," Aelred says, of friendship.

*Intimacy

For Aelred, friendship is a supremely humanizing practice. As friends, we learn to cherish and to be cherished, to delight in each other's good fortune and to bear each other's burdens. The intimacies of friendship give us pleasure and enlarge our lives.

But Aelred also knew that friendship draws its humanizing power from a paradox: the intimacies that bring us joy also make us vulnerable. Once we have opened ourselves to a friend, we have to rely on our friend to shelter our vulnerability. And, of course, sometimes friends do not take care with each other's hopes and secrets. Friendship can survive absence, anger, and frustrations of various kinds. But, Aelred says, it can't survive the disclosure of secrets or the infliction of a "treacherous wound." Betrayal and treachery will kill a friendship every time.

Intimacy is always a risk, whether enacted in the sharing of one's most private thoughts or through the physical intimacy of touching and being touched. When intimacy involves bodies, though, both the pleasures and risks of intimacy increase. Naked and undefended, we must rely on the one with whom we are intimate not to exploit our vulnerability but to reverence it.

"Did I even know I had a body/before that kiss broke its boundaries?" the poet Karin Gottshall asks. A first kiss can feel that way, can't it? One minute we are there, alone with our thoughts, self-contained; and the next, we are made vividly aware of our body in relation to another's body. We feel just how embodied we are and how very much that matters. "Touch . . . makes the body real to us," Mark Doty writes.

> **"** Naked and undefended, we must rely on the one with whom we are intimate not to exploit our vulnerability but to reverence it. **"**

The reality of the body undergirds every Christian practice, and attention to the body's pleasures and pains is necessary to practicing them well. Without a sense of ourselves as embodied creatures, we can't begin to honor our bodies or the bodies of others. Nor can we care for the body of the earth without a sense of our bodies as a part of God's good creation. Seeking justice, making a living, peacemaking, living as community—all these practices require a clear view of our bodies in relation to other bodies. Cultivating intimacy with another can teach us how interdependent our desires are with the desires of others. We can begin to seek ways of living to honor that interdependence.

If we are lucky, our first kisses and caresses, and all those that follow, will be marked by the same reverence Emerson talks about in relation to friendship. There is nothing more cruel than violently crossing a body's boundaries. It is no wonder that rape often becomes a weapon of war and genocide, the devastation of a people one body at a time. Even a thoughtless, careless crossing of the body's boundaries can cause pain. When we approach another's body without reverence, the potential for doing harm is great; just as when we pursue a friendship for its advantage to us, we potentially can inflict what Aelred calls a "treacherous wound" on our friend.

When intimacy of any sort is entered into with reverence, though, we find our own deepest pleasure in seeking to give pleasure to another. When we seek after intimacy with reverence for our beloved, desire leads not to exploitation but to what poet Mark Doty describes, in his meditation on the death of his lover, Wally Roberts, as "participation, the will to involve oneself in the body of the world." Doty says, "We are implicated in another being, which is always the beginning of wisdom, isn't it—that involvement which enlarges us, which engages the heart, which takes us out of the routine limitations of self?"

Desire as the beginning of wisdom—certainly the Song of S
jewel of biblical Wisdom Literature, supports this idea. A tes
mutuality in love, to the beauty of the human body, to the g
sexual desire and the power of love, the Song of Songs speaks the language
of desire. A woman, "black and beautiful," and a man, "radiant and ruddy,"
catalog every inch of each other's body, every smell and taste. "Your navel is
a rounded bowl that never lacks mixed wine," he says to her. "His cheeks
are like beds of spices, yielding fragrance. His lips are lilies, distilling liquid
myrrh," she tells her friends. "Your two breasts," he sings, "are like two
fawns, twins of a gazelle." "I am my beloved's," she exults, "and his desire
is for me."

Because the Song of Songs describes desire, it inevitably expresses the
pain of separation, of missed meetings, of absence. Running through the
streets looking for her lover, the woman says to the daughters of Jerusalem:

if you find my beloved,
tell him this:
I am faint with love. (5:8)

The man in the Song is at least as vulnerable as the woman. He speaks
of her as a mare let loose among Pharaoh's chariots by the enemies of
Egypt; he feels as undone and out of control as Pharaoh's stallions in the
presence of a female horse. He is "held captive" in the tresses of her hair.
This sort of shared vulnerability is not what we expect to find when we
open our Bibles, but there it is: a Song of mutuality, the lovers evenly
matched in the force of their desire, equally vulnerable in their desire to
be desired by the other, as determined to give pleasure as to receive it. The
Song tells of lovers well matched, luxuriating in their intimacy, an intimacy grounded, perhaps, in friendship. "This is my beloved and this is my
friend," the woman sings at the end of a long description of the beauties of
her lover. This is my beloved, and this is my friend.

Of course, many of the ideas about sexuality we inherit from Christian faith are not about sexual pleasure but, instead, about refusing sexual
relationships. The Song of Songs celebrates the exquisite flame of sexual
desire, while Paul says it is better to marry than burn with passion. Augustine famously refrained from becoming a Christian until he was sure he

could live without sex. We seem to be in a world of extremes: extreme pleasure in intimacy at one end, extreme anxiety about intimacy at the other. What does any of this have to do with us, and our own sexual lives?

Christians' anxieties about sexual intimacy have often been translated into a suspicion of human sexuality itself. It's a difficult legacy that seems to leave us with nothing but a list of dos and don'ts, instructions on boundary lines. That can make it easy to dismiss what Christians like Paul and Augustine have to say about sexual intimacy.

But perhaps it is possible to hear in their worries not just a fear of women or a denigration of the body (although these forces are certainly present) but also an honest acknowledgment of the power of sexual desire, a struggle to understand their vulnerability to it, and a real desire for freedom. It is possible, as Augustine knew, to be imprisoned by desires and to become locked in patterns of satisfying them that use others as a means of one's satisfaction only. It is possible to be led by desire away from one's most profound aspirations, away from the life one hopes to lead. And it is possible to fall into an intimacy that barricades one from the world rather than leading to a deeper engagement with it.

Does this mean that we should be afraid of our desire for intimacy? Should we repress it, rein it in somehow, to avoid being swept away in a direction we did not choose? Oh, God, no. Our desire for intimacy makes us vulnerable, to be sure, but it also forms us to receive the world with reverence and awe. "Ah, you are beautiful, my love; ah, you are beautiful," the lovers repeat to one another in the Song of Songs. And as they breathe in each other's beauties and breathe out their praise, they discover that the whole world is beautiful and worthy of reverence: the fields, the orchards, the fruit on the trees. Becoming intimate with each other, their intimacy with all of creation increases.

Even as we open ourselves to receiving another and the world as lovers, though, there is good reason to apply Aelred and Emerson's advice for friendship to a physically intimate relationship: Don't rush. Develop trust. Seek the good of the other. Let the fruit of intimacy ripen, as Emerson might say. Treat a growing intimacy as something precious to be sheltered and nourished rather than rushed, and shelter your beloved's vulnerability with care. Cultivate fidelity. And don't lock the object of your desire into a script of your own making. Prepare to be surprised.

Physical intimacy requires the cultivation of generosity every bit as much as friendship does, perhaps more. And the cultivation of imagination. To be intimate with another person, we must always be imagining the other's feelings, hopes, desires. We have to imagine those desires as best we can, knowing all the while that we cannot ever know even our closest friends and beloveds completely.

For no matter how intimate we are with another, no matter how well acquainted we are with every inch of our beloved's skin, we remain mysteries to one another. The lovers in the Song of Songs are beautiful, to be sure, but they are more than their beauty, more than the sum of their glorious body parts. And that *more*—so much more difficult to describe than lovely hair or firm breasts—is also what we reverence when we love. The day we believe we know everything there is to know about our intimate beloved is the day our love will cease to grow. We can always go more deeply into the mystery of each other. There is always more to know.

" No matter how well acquainted we are with every inch of our beloved's skin, we remain mysteries to one another. "

*Covenant

Entering into a covenant with another person is a way of turning toward the mystery of each other with deepest reverence. Marriage is an act of faith because we can never know each other completely, or know what the future holds. That is why, as the poet Wendell Berry puts it, marriage "must be an unconditional giving, for in joining ourselves to one another we join ourselves to the unknown."

All Christian covenants take their shape from the covenants God made with Noah, with Abraham, with Israel. I am yours, God promises, and you are mine. We belong to each other, come what may. So like a marriage is God's covenant with Israel that Jews and Christians alike have often found the pleasures and pain of marriage reflected in scripture. The prophet Hosea, mourning his wife's adultery, has been read as the story of Israel's unfaithfulness to God. The erotic poetry of the Song of Songs has been understood to reflect God's passionate love for Israel. "Who is that coming up from the wilderness, leaning upon her beloved?" (8:5) One answer Jews and Christians have given is: Israel, leaning on her lover's arm. And indeed, the Song of Songs is sung every Passover as a reminder that God delivered Israel from slavery in Egypt not only because God was contractually obligated to do so according to the covenant. God delivered Israel from slavery because God loved her, passionately.

Just as God's covenants structured the people of Israel's life with God according to promises of presence and fidelity, marriage offers human beings a way to live according to such promises. But marriage does not "make two people one," as we sometimes say in weddings. No matter how profound the intimacy between the two making the covenant, each person's inner life, each person's history, will always be unique, separate from the inner life and history of the other. We remain mysteries to one another, full of secrets, always. Thank God that this is so. The joy of living in covenant with another person comes not only from comfort and familiarity but also from discovery.

But without practices of attention, fidelity, and presence that keep us reverently attentive to each other's mystery and committed to a lifetime of trying to know each other more deeply, the fact that we are mysteries to one another can bring more pain than joy. The husband in Jane Smiley's novella *The Age of Grief*, having welcomed home his wife who has just ended an affair with another man, reflects, "It seems to me that marriage is a small container, after all, barely large enough to hold some children. Two inner lives, two lifelong meditations of whatever complexity, burst out of it and out of it, cracking it, deforming it." Even held by promises, marriages can lose their elasticity. In the midst of building a career or raising children, it is all too easy to take a marriage for granted, to become distracted from the work of being present to each other, and to find one day that we have become not mysteries to each other, but strangers.

In the covenant of marriage, our bodies keep us separate, but they also have the potential to draw us near to one another. Through the ordinary gestures of our bodies, we enact our covenant in preparing food, sharing meals, making love, taking walks, maintaining our household, reaching out for an embrace. It's through our bodies that we live out the promises made at weddings. And it's through our bodies that we fail in our promises and through our bodies that we ask for forgiveness and begin again. An old form of the marriage ceremony uses these words for the exchange of rings: "With this ring I thee wed, *with my body I thee worship*, and with all my worldly goods I thee endow." *Worship* is not too strong a word for the reverence from the body to the whole person that marriage requires.

What else do we need to keep our marriages elastic enough for "two inner lives, two lifelong meditations of whatever complexity" to expand and grow? We need courage to imagine each other's pleasure and each other's pain. We need a willingness to find words to try to say what we mean. We need a willingness to fall silent, knowing that language cannot do all the work of love. We need confidence that love is the only way of being that will never fail, never cease, never vanish away. We need to practice fidelity—sexual fidelity, to be sure, but also fidelity to each other's hopes and aspirations. We need to live as though the bonds of love that join us, that cause us to take responsibility for each other, are somehow eternally true.

"Sexual love is natural," Wendell Berry writes, "but marriage is not," just as the impulse to express ourselves is natural, while the forms of poetry are not. Marriage is a form with certain limits, certain requirements: fidelity, presence in sickness and in health, living together until death parts us. Every married person knows what it feels like to come up against those limits. That is when marriage truly begins, when we learn to live and love and seek each other's good within the promises we have made. A lot of the time we will do this without thinking. But at other times, living within the limits of our vows will not come naturally. At those moments we have the opportunity to learn not only the pleasure of reverence but also the work of it. And those are the moments when we might learn that we and our beloved are more than we imagined ourselves to be. "The impeded stream," says Berry, "is the one that sings."

Even if marriage is not "natural," it is certainly a natural aspect of creation to desire intimacy. When love is met by love strong enough to motivate two people to join themselves to the unknown, it surely is a sign of the most mysterious possibilities creation holds. Marriage means the deepening of intimacy and partnership. It means the creation of new relationships between families and friends. It means a turning inward toward each other, and a turning outward, together, toward the world. And it means so many things that two people making lifelong promises to each other in the presence of their friends and of God cannot begin to imagine. Two individuals join in marriage not because they know exactly what it is going to mean but in order to find out what it means.

The covenant of marriage is a new vocation, even for those who have lived intimately for years. Marriage is not simply a private agreement between two individuals but something that comes to life within a community. When we witness the exchange of promises at a wedding, we become that community for the two people joining each other's lives. We enter into a new relationship with them and with one another. By our pres-

" Marriage means a turning inward toward each other, and a turning outward, together, toward the world. "

ence, we pledge ourselves to honor their vows and to support them in the deep pleasure and the difficult work that living out those vows will bring. Celebrating a marriage is a way of saying that we believe it is still worth hoping in this world, still worth making a home in it, still worth our most radical promises. Witnessing wedding vows is holy work.

One of the most famous wedding stories from the Christian tradition is the story of the wedding at Cana, the story in which Jesus changes jars of water into wine to help the celebration along. The Gospel of John presents the wedding at Cana as a story about Jesus, and the church celebrates it as Jesus' first miracle. The story tells us nothing about the bride and groom, not even their names. But surely it is the ordinary miracle of two people pledging themselves to each other until death parts them that opens a space for all the other miracles of the day. For it is precisely when people make radical commitments to one another and to an unknown future that the boundaries between water and wine, between earth and heaven, even between the flesh of two separate people seem so permeable.

*One Life

"My friends have come to me unsought," Emerson writes. "The great God gave them to me."

Friendship and intimacy are gifts from God. In creating us as embodied, vulnerable creatures, God has placed us in one another's care and given us responsibility for one another's good. Certain relationships develop in ways that give us deep and abiding pleasure while enlarging our imaginations and extending the boundaries of our lives. That experience teaches us a great deal about God's hopes for human life. Christian discussions of friendship and intimacy use the strongest possible words: there is no greater love, Jesus taught, than laying down one's life for one's friends. Although we may never be called upon to die for our friends, we are daily called upon to offer ourselves to them, which does involve, as the Christian tradition has long recognized, a little death. We are called upon to live as if another's good and another's pleasure are as important as our own.

In cultivating friendships and intimate relationships, we have the opportunity to discover our best selves, to find new possibilities within ourselves that we could never have imagined if we had not risked ourselves in relationship with another. Friendships and intimate relationships are treasures—gifts from God—to be tenderly held and carefully cultivated, never to be rushed or taken for granted or used for any other purpose than honoring the mystery of the other. For when our relationships take root in reverence, our life with others and our life with God is truly one life.

6* Singing Our Lives to God

Tony Alonso

T he hills are alive with the sound of music, with songs they have sung for a thousand years," Maria sings from the hilltops in the opening scenes of *The Sound of Music*. "The mountains and the hills before you shall burst into song, and all the trees of the field shall clap their hands," cries the prophet Isaiah in the Hebrew scriptures (Isa. 55:12).

What does a nun in a big-screen musical have in common with an ancient prophet? Both of them know that the whole world is filled to the brim with song—the howling cry of the wind, the boisterous boom of thunder, the soothing tap of rain, the crashing of ocean waves: the world is alive with song. The cosmos itself vibrates with sound as the earth turns around the sun and the moon and the planets spin through space. The creatures are singing too. Birds chirp and whales moan. Dogs bark and lions roar. God sang creation into being, and creation has been singing ever since.

We who are human also have a song to sing. Mothers sing lullabies to their children. Grieving families sing *alleluia* through their tears. Mexican immigrants cry out "*¡Resucitó!*"—"He is risen!"—celebrating Jesus'

> **"** The howling cry of the wind, the boisterous boom of thunder, the soothing tap of rain, the crashing of ocean waves: the world is alive with song. **"**

deliverance from death because they too need deliverance. Protesters sing "We Shall Overcome," trusting that right will prevail over economic and political injustice. Hawaiian storytellers chant tales of their ancestors, ensuring that they will be remembered in the next generation. Choral ensembles and street musicians sing songs that have shaped their own lives and the lives of others. These are the voices of young and old, rich and poor, people of every color in every corner of creation singing their lives to one another and to God.

*Music and Faith: An Intimate Bond

My cousin is a musician whose music could not be more different than my own. I write communal music for worship, and he writes a fusion of reggae, hip-hop, and rap. When I lead people in song, it's usually in our university chapel with a group of students who have chosen to spend their Sunday nights in church. He performs in the late hours of the evening and the early hours of the morning for patrons of clubs and bars. But in the music he writes and plays with his band, I hear an expression of desire for unity, peace, and reconciliation—the same unity, peace, and reconciliation we are singing about at Sunday evening Mass. He connects deeply with his fellow musicians and his audience—just as I do with the worshiping assembly and my fellow music ministers. These are very different but equally authentic expressions of faith.

For centuries distinctions have been made between sacred and secular music—as if we could divide music that is connected to God from music that is not. But God is always speaking, God is always listening: in the concert hall and on the street corner, at the protest march and at the child's bedside, at our Saturday night parties and in our Sunday morning worship. I think it is more helpful to ask *Does this music lead us to God?*

The kind of music that reverences the presence of God in and around us doesn't depend on which instruments are used or when the music was written, where the music is being played or what the musicians look like, or even whether the lyrics mention God. When the Spirit is at work, there is no limit to the ways music can deepen us in faith. Many musical expressions have the potential to bind us more closely to one another, to give voice to the longing of our hearts, and to lead us to God, the composer of all song.

What does your heart yearn to sing to your beloved, to the world, to God? Have you ever made a mix CD for a friend or a family member? That

For centuries distinctions have been made between sacred and secular music—as if we could divide music that is connected to God from music that is not.

unique collection of songs is precious because it reveals your soul's yearning. Have you ever sung in a show choir or a chamber choir? Have you played in a garage band, a marching band, or an orchestra? Were you in a school musical? These experiences too reflect the soul's desire to connect, to be made whole, to find union with others and with our Creator.

Not all music leads to faith and wholeness. In the 1930s and 1940s, Hitler used music filled with messages of division and hatred to form the infamous Hitler youth. To a lesser but still troubling degree, some music today demeans women, glorifies violence, and justifies injustice. Buddhist monk Thich Nhat Hanh, who has spent his life working for peace, warns that some of what we consume can nourish anger instead of compassion. "What we read in magazines, what we view on television, can . . . be toxic," he says. "[A film] . . . can contain anger. If you consume it, you are eating anger, you are eating frustration. Newspaper articles, and even conversations, can contain a lot of anger." Does the music we listen to build up or tear down? Light the way to compassion or perpetuate intolerance? Lead us to God or lead us astray? By asking these questions, we can make musical choices that nourish our souls and lead us profoundly into life.

*Singing a Common Song

I recently attended a Billy Joel concert in a cavernous arena in Los Angeles. Cell phones rang, conversations droned on, people came and went, up and down the aisles, heading for the bathroom or the concession stand. A guy spilled his beer on my lap. It's not easy to feel connected to twenty thousand people in a venue like this. Yet toward the end of the night, Billy Joel came to his signature song, "Piano Man," and everything changed. Whenever the chorus came around, the entire crowd started swaying and singing along. When the band dropped out on the final chorus, the fans took over, and the sound soared through the arena. We didn't need the piano man to sing us a song. We were singing with and for one another. In that moment, in that vast arena, came an unexpected and unsought sense of unity: music bound the crowd together in a way nothing else could have done.

As people of faith have known for centuries, when we join our voices in song, our hearts and minds are also united in a profound though mysterious way. The Spirit dwelling in us sings through us and binds us together. In a world full of dissonance and disunity, a common song can be a step toward and a sign of the unity God desires for us.

Song also connects the present with the past. Several weeks ago I attended the wedding of a college roommate. The reception was a buzz of activity—the clinking of glasses trying to get the bride and groom to kiss again and again, children chasing each other around in circles, people dancing the *Macarena*, and servers preparing to bring out the wedding cake. I was in deep conversation with an old friend when the band began to play Celine Dion's "My Heart Will Go On." Truly, this is one of my least favorite songs, but it was on the radio almost every day of my senior year of high school. The moment that song began, I was back in the transformed school gym, on the angst-laden dance floor with my prom date in her red dress. That was a nice memory. But a song also can evoke a past heartbreak more palpably than an old photograph.

Music can connect us to places we have never been and to ancestors we have never met. I was born in Miami to a father from Cuba and a mother from a small town in Minnesota. We moved to Minnesota when I was five. Life in the rural Midwest in the eighties wasn't particularly conducive to speaking Spanish regularly or finding the ingredients to make Cuban roast pork, black beans, yuca, and coconut flan (we had to carry those back from our Christmas trips to Miami). To keep our Cuban roots alive, my grandfather sent us cassettes of Celia Cruz, Cachao, and Orquesta Aragon—music he loved from his days in Cuba. Whenever a tape arrived, I would run to the cassette player, put it in, and press play. My reaction was visceral. The congas and guiro, trumpets and flutes, the rhythms of the salsa or the *son*—something about all of these resonated in my body and spirit in a way nothing else did, not even other kinds of music.

Hearing, singing, and dancing this music magically connected this seemingly 100 percent gringo boy in small-town Minnesota to an exotic island ninety miles south of Florida. Each of us has a musical DNA. Pay attention to the music that resonates in you—perhaps it is calling you back to your roots. And pay attention to the musical roots of your faith—the melodies, rhythms, and words written on your heart.

What does it mean to sing *amen* over the course of a lifetime, and even in times of doubt? How do the *alleluias* we sang on Easter morning as second graders, when the world seemed so simple, resonate in the *alleluias* we sing as adults at the funeral of a friend, a mother, a father? A word like this, sung over time, can be an anchor in our faith journey, even if we have passed through storms and experienced much complexity and struggle along the way. Words like *Kyrie eleison*—"Lord, have mercy"—can be meaningful even if we haven't sung them for years, when all of a sudden we find ourselves in church again for the first time in a long time, hear a melody, and remember.

These songs connect us to more than our individual faith journeys; they connect us with the generations of Christians who have sung these sacred words, and the psalms, and other hymns and spiritual songs, all to reorient their lives toward God. When we sing these words and melodies, we are one with a motley crew of saints and sinners who came before us.

The next time you are invited to sing *Kyrie eleison* or *alleluia* or *amen*, even if you're not sure what their place is in your life at the moment, consider how those words, those songs, connect you with your own faith journey and with the journeys of those who came before you. Many of them were just as full of questions and struggles as we are.

*The Last Best Place

We are "surrounded by music" but "robbed of song," my friend and mentor Gabe Huck likes to say. Soft rock music plays while we sit in the dentist's chair. Synthesized strings and a drum set fill the elevator with cheesy arrangements of pop hits. A pianist plays show tunes at the mall. Ironically, even as our culture fills itself with more and more music, we desire less and less to sing. Music, like so much in our culture, has become noise—filler constantly present in the background of our lives but never demanding or even inviting our investment or participation.

The last best place we might find a group of untrained musicians sing-

> " We are 'surrounded by music' but 'robbed of song.'—Gabe Huck "

ing together in Western society, apart from the occasional birthday party, is in church. Here music is not relegated to the background but lies at the heart of how we pray. Singing with our faith community is a counter-cultural act in which we become part of a way of life that is deeply life-giving but often at odds with the larger culture. We witness to God's new creation by singing songs of faith and hope at worship and allowing those songs to spill over into the rest of our lives, into the rest of the world.

Most of us are not meant to sing at the Metropolitan Opera House or even to have the lead in a community musical. However, God has given each of us a unique voice so that we can sing our lives to God and to one another, so we can cry out from the depths of our being in good times and bad. Telling a person he or she can't sing is akin to calling a person ugly. We are created in the image and likeness of God—and that likeness includes our voices.

Yet even in church, some people are tempted to mimic the entertainment culture by hiring professional performers or using music that no one can sing or treating the community like an audience. In some churches the music can seem lifeless or disconnected from our human experience. How can it be, we wonder, that music, which was so life-giving and filled with spirit on Saturday night, can be so distant from our hearts on Sunday morning?

Churches become houses of song that engage the complex realities of human life when we sing hymns, old and new, that speak of a God who knows our struggle, our grief, and unbelief. Lyrics like "Take, O take me as I am; summon out what I shall be; set your seal upon my heart and live in me," express our yearning to discern God's call and bring us face-to-face with a God who calls us in spite of our flaws. Words like "Let the banker and the president beware the trumpet's call, And beat swords of greed and commerce into equal shares for all" bring new energy to our discussions about the gospel's implications for public policy and the political process. We are part of the world God loves, both when we are in the church and when we are not. When we sing at worship, we can give voice to all of the longings and truths we have experienced during the week—to all our needs, and all the needs of the world.

*Beyond Words, with Words

Music takes us places words alone cannot. Anyone who has been moved when listening to a symphony or who has sung his sorrow through a cello concerto or her joy through a piano prelude knows this. Even one word sung can express more than a thousand spoken. Think of the famous chorus from Handel's *Messiah*. How could the joy that comes from singing *hallelujah* dozens of times, by high voices and low voices and all voices together, quickly, slowly, softly, and loudly, ever be captured by only speaking the word?

While music transcends language alone, it also anchors language in our hearts. We often tell our story and stay in conversation with God by sharing words set to music. Scripture gives us a profound vocabulary for speaking with God in every season of life. Paul encouraged the earliest

Christians to persevere in faith by persevering in song: "Let the word of Christ dwell in you richly; teach and admonish one another in all wisdom; and with gratitude in your hearts sing psalms, hymns, and spiritual songs to God" (Col. 3:16). To let the Word dwell in us richly is to sing the Word in all its richness. Music imprints the Word on our hearts so that we may make the Word visible in the world. "What we sing, over time, we come to remember," writes composer Marty Haugen, "What we remember, over time, we come to believe. What we believe, over time, we come to live."

When slaves sang, "Go down, Moses, way down in Egypt's land; tell old Pharaoh to let my people go," they weren't merely recounting biblical history; they were fastening their hearts on words to carry them through their struggle. After September 11, 2001, the people of the United States wanted to sing, but we didn't know what to sing. We didn't seem to have words anchored to our hearts that could give authentic voice to our pain and fear. On the steps of the Capitol on September 12, members of Congress defaulted to nationalistic anthems like "God Bless America," when we really needed to be singing with them, "Where are you, O God?" Later, many Christians remained silent during our nation's march to war with Iraq. I believed that if all the Christian communities in the United States, led by their faith in the God of Peace, would speak and sing out against the war, we could prevent it. But what would we sing? I sat down and wrote this hymn:

> Will the circle be unbroken?
> Will the pow'r of death prevail?
> Will the voices seeking justice
> be rejected and grow frail?
> Will revenge replace forgiveness?
> Will our pride replace God's peace?
> Will the innocents be victims
> and the violence increase?
>
> Will the words our God has spoken
> be revised or be ignored?
> Will the love that made and formed us
> be rejected for the sword?

Will the God who cries, "Forgiveness
is the only way to peace,"
be blocked out by cries of anger?
Will the fighting ever cease?

Here the body, blessed and broken,
and the blood of Christ outpoured
is the only food of freedom
for the servants of the Lord.
Here the stories shared at table
call us all to peaceful ways:
show us Christ in all creation,
show us love's the only way.

*Singing with the World

The other day I walked into a Starbucks and was a bit appalled to find myself asking the barista with ease for a "grande, nonfat, two-pump, extra hot, no-foam vanilla latté." It is embarrassing for me to tell you this. Like so many of the authors in this book, my journey of faith leads me to strive for a life that goes against the grain of our sometimes dysfunctional, individualistic culture. But my very particular latté order reminds me that trying to avoid my culture altogether is like a fish trying to avoid water. In the culture in which I swim, getting things exactly the way I want them is a top priority. Companies encourage us in this pursuit, of course, making money by making it easy for us to customize our car, our house, our meal.

This tendency toward individualism extends to music as well. With headphones wrapped around our ears, connected to an iPod containing an extensive selection of our favorite songs, each one of us can choose our own preferred style or song at the touch of a screen. Although music has the power to unite, today music is beginning to build walls as well, perhaps for the first time in human history. New technologies allow us to ignore one another in the car, on the bus, even at home!

The musical isolationism that shapes how many of us experience music today might mistakenly lead us to believe that God is only speaking through that which fits our personal musical tastes or reflects our own culture or native tongue. Several years ago, I was working at a church in a suburb of Chicago where an associate pastor from Nigeria was assigned. A kind, reserved man, he would often go about his work without interacting much with me or the other members of the staff. A few months into his time with us, we sang a song from Zimbabwe, "If You Believe and I Believe." After the liturgy he quickly came to me, beaming with joy. He knew the tune from his homeland, he said, and as a child he had learned different words to it. He began to share other melodies and stories of his homeland. Singing that simple song from Zimbabwe in our suburban parish opened a door between us and bound us together.

Expressing our faith through the music of other cultures can deepen our compassion and understanding. As of this writing, our country remains embroiled in two wars in the Middle East. How many Iraqi or Afghan hymns or lullabies do you know? If you are like me, you know next to none. I can't help but wonder: if we knew well the songs that an Iraqi mother sings to lull her baby to sleep, the songs Afghan children sing on the playground, the songs their families sing at a birthday party, could we so easily distance ourselves from their deep suffering? Could we so easily go to war with those whose songs have been imprinted on our hearts?

Imagine for a moment that you are watching the nightly news. A child sits in a nearby room playing, but her ears perk up when she hears "Iraq" mentioned by the broadcaster. Instead of conjuring images of terrorism or war or fear, it calls to mind an Iraqi song she learned last Sunday at church. She begins to sing the song and asks you to sing along. After the song she asks why the country is on the news. She is inviting you to become with her part of the disarmed and disarming body of Christ in the world.

*Singing to Change the World

Music has the power to change the world. Song can bring down walls. Slaves sang down the walls of slavery. South Africans sang down the walls of apartheid. What shall we sing down? Where in our world do we need to join our hands, our hearts, and our voices right now? Imagine if all who claim the name of Christ put down their weapons and instead armed themselves with song.

If we sing God's song and are not led into the world to be God's compassionate presence, then why sing at all? When music is a true practice of faith, it will lead us into the other practices shared in this book,

> **" South Africans sang down the walls of apartheid. What shall we sing down? "**

and they will lead us to song. I think of a friend who led a tour of the Holy Land that he hoped would enable his group (with members ranging in age from eighteen to eighty) to form bonds of peace and unity with those they would meet. In preparation, he taught them a song in Arabic from West Africa, "*Salaam Aleikum*"—"Peace be with you." At every stop along the way, they sang this song of blessing to express gratitude to their hosts. As it turned out, complete strangers in lands from Israel to Pakistan also knew this song and joined in the singing. As the group departed each place, they felt a lingering connection to the people they left behind. They were learning to know and love people of another faith in a way that no one would ever forget.

Every week thousands of young people travel to France to visit Taizé, an ecumenical community dedicated to reconciliation, understanding, and simplicity. These young people gather from all over the world for simple, meditative prayer. They sing repetitive chants in multiple languages, chants that ultimately lead to silence and contemplation. At the end of their stay, they return home more fully aware that they are living in the presence of God and that they are called to be living signs of reconciliation and peace. The songs of Taizé, now sung in worship all over the world, are crucial to this awareness and will remind the pilgrims of it in coming years.

Each November people from around the country travel to the School of the Americas (SOA) in Fort Benning, Georgia (renamed the Western Hemisphere Institute for Security and Cooperation—WHINSEC—in 2001), a U.S.-sponsored military training school where over sixty thousand Latin American military officers have been trained for violence and torture. People gather there to protest the very existence of this school and to remember those who have been killed in Central and South America by its graduates. Outside the school, leaders of all ages take turns singing out each name from a long list of those who have died. After each name is chanted, the entire group sings "*¡presente!*"—present! Death cannot separate those who have been murdered from the love of God in Christ Jesus. This singing inscribes their names on the hearts of those who have gathered and inscribes Easter hope on their lives. People will return every year to sing that litany, until this school of torture is closed forever.

*Singing to the Lord

I can't imagine protests or rallies without chants and songs. Or Christmas Eve without "Joy to the World." I can't imagine falling in love without a song to express my feelings. Or a breakup without Bonnie Raitt singing "I Can't Make You Love Me." Or my grandfather's funeral without the assembly spontaneously breaking into the Cuban national anthem just as the priest began the closing prayer. Most of all, I can't imagine how I would be in conversation with God without songs to sing.

"Sing to the Lord!" the scriptures say. What I have slowly come to realize is that "Sing to the Lord!" is not just an invitation. It is a command. It is a mandate that comes with no caveats. It is not *sing to the Lord if you have a beautiful voice.* Not *sing to the Lord if you can stay on pitch.* Not *sing to the Lord if you feel up to it.* Not even *sing to the Lord only at church* or *only on Sunday.* Our communal conversation with the world around us, with one another, and with God requires of us a song.

God invites our song. God demands our song. And not because God needs it. Instead, in God's infinite wisdom, God knows that we do.

Living a whole life

attentively . . .

together . . . *in the

real world . . . for

the good of all . . .

in response to God

7* Care for Creation

Daniel Spencer

S tep. Step. Breathe. Step. Step. Breathe. As my climbing partner Dan and I neared the summit of Kintla Peak in Glacier National Park, we paused to catch our breath in the thin air and to take in the stunning beauty of the mountains. Under our feet, bright red and green mudstones were laced with ripple marks and raindrop splatters from waters that covered these lands over a billion years ago, an earlier surface of the earth now raised ten thousand feet above the sea. Fragile but hardy alpine flowers—purple phacelia, yellow glacier lilies, blue lupine—clung to rock and ice.

And in every direction, water. Wispy clouds of vapor above us and glaciers, waterfalls, streams, and lakes below us, gathered from winter storms on the peaks and now making their way down to water the earth. Six thousand feet below, wind rippled across Kintla Lake, reminding us of the wind from God that swept over the face of the waters at the beginning of creation (Gen. 1:2).

All around us blew a gentle breeze, reminding us of God's breathed word separating the earth from the waters, preparing a new world for birds, fish, and beasts—an explosion of life that God saw and said, "This is good. This is very good." At the end of those marvelous first days, in stepped humans—into a world already filled and complete, into an earth story stretching back billions of years, lacking only a creature who could marvel at its beauty and harmony, wonder at its Creator, and breathe out the prayer, "It is good. It is very good."

"In the beginning." Jewish and Christian scriptures begin by celebrating the beauty of the God-created earth and our place in it. Everything that follows in the biblical story is set in the context of the goodness of creation and our role as its caretakers. God creates humans in the divine image; we reflect this image most deeply when we *see* the earth as God does—marveling at its amazing diversity of life and stone—and when we *act* as God does toward creation, with caring, compassion, and justice.

As if the richness of creation cannot be contained in just one story, the Bible provides a second Creation story, right after the first. Here God forms the first human "from the dust of the ground" (Gen. 2:7) and sets the human in a garden, asking only that the human till it and keep it. The original Hebrew brims with puns that reflect God's delight in this new creature and deepen our understanding of the story. The first human is Adam, from the Hebrew *adam,* which means "earth creature," coming from *adamah,* which means "earth" or "dust of the ground." And more: *adamah* means not only earth or dust but also arable ground or fertile soil. We are made of farmland! The Hebrew words "to till" also mean "to serve"—God sets us in the garden of the earth *to serve it* through careful tilling and keeping. Here is a human vocation that gives joy to both God and Adam: the garden's name, "Eden," means "delight."

I think of these images every fall when my neighbors and I gather for a harvest banquet at the PEAS Farm in the Rattlesnake Valley, north of Missoula, Montana, where I live. PEAS—the Program in Ecological Agriculture and Society—is a ten-acre organic farm run cooperatively by Garden City Harvest, a local nonprofit, and the Environmental Studies program at the University of Montana, where I work. Students volunteer at the farm, learning ways to keep the earth by working sustainably within our local ecosystems. The PEAS Farm weaves together care for the earth and care for neighbor, annually donating twenty to thirty thousand pounds of organic fruit and vegetables to the Missoula Food Bank.

Each fall the community gathers to celebrate the harvest. As I walk up the road from my home, I hear guitars, banjos, and a string bass. Hundreds of friends and neighbors are chatting in lines that snake through rows of cabbage, carrots, peppers, tomatoes, potatoes, and a dazzling array of native flowers, while their kids dance to the music. The tables set up in the straw-bale barn are heaped with mounds of fresh food: multicolored salads, fresh corn on the cob, and meat from free-range chickens, some of whose relatives still roam the grounds. In the fields to the north, cattle and llamas graze; on the hillsides above us, white-tailed deer keep watch. We dance into the night, nourished by the fruits of the earth and human labor and friendship.

These stories illustrate God's intentions for us: to marvel at the beauty of the natural world and to celebrate our rightful place within it as we care for and keep it. They represent a vision of how life can be for *all* God's creatures when we accept our calling to "compassionate dominion"—our responsibility to care for the planet as God cares for us: with compassion, justice, and mercy.

Increasingly we are aware that humankind does not often enough fulfill this responsibility, and that as a result the earth is in crisis. I wept the day I returned to an open field where my siblings and I spent our childhood summers chasing butterflies and collecting bugs, to find a shopping center. Such places "disappear" to development at an alarming rate, taking with them our sense of connection to the earth. And the crisis goes far beyond our loss of beloved places. Daily we hear sobering news of global warming and melting glaciers, diminishing energy sources and peak oil use, powerful hurricanes and devastated communities, species extinction and habitat loss.

Many people across the globe, aware of these environmental problems, are trying to live in ways that promote the well-being of creation. This

" I wept the day I returned to an open field where . . . I spent our childhood summers chasing butterflies and collecting bugs, to find a shopping center. "

commitment comes not only for or from Christians. But in this essay we will consider how a faithful Christian practice of caring for creation enables us to see our everyday efforts as part of a larger story, and how this practice can stretch our awareness and shape our behavior as it is interwoven with other practices, including seeking justice, peacemaking, and living as community. Caring for creation has been an important Christian witness and practice for centuries, but it has taken on new urgency today as a way of life lived *literally* for the sake of the life of the world.

Earth's complex and at times overwhelming ecological crisis can lead us to despair and inaction. But our Christian heritage and the practices of many contemporary Christian communities provide ways of living in the midst of crisis with joy and gratitude, ways of living that contribute to resolving these complex environmental issues. Acknowledging our own complicity in and responsibility for many of the earth's problems, we can practice love and care for the earth and all God's creatures in each area of our lives. Anticipating the fullness of God's reign on earth, we can live as beacons of hope. Remembering that God is the original caretaker of the earth, we can join God in affirming, "It is good. It is very good."

*Creation Care: An Ambiguous Legacy

While care for the earth long has been a part of the biblical and Christian traditions, so too have been abuse and neglect. In fact, in a famous 1967 article in *Science* magazine, Christian historian Lynn White Jr. called Christianity the most human-centered of the world's religions and held it largely responsible for the degradation of the earth hastened by Western civilization in recent centuries. Too often Christians have used the biblical text in which God gives the first humans "dominion" over other creatures (Gen. 1:28) as a mandate for domination, giving our species the right to use the earth for ourselves without regard for the effects on others in the earth community and the earth itself. In recent centuries, Christianity often has been wedded to political power and technology that pursued domination in just this way, from European colonization of the Americas, Asia, and Africa to the industrial revolution, and now in a rapidly growing global economy. Each wave of expansion and change inflicted tremendous costs on the earth and the poor. Recovering creation-care practices begins in confession and repentance for the ways we—individually and corporately—have harmed the earth and the poor of the earth.

*Creation Care: A Sacramental Vision

In the beginning God spoke all things into being—and for the rest of time all things are speaking of God. This is a sacramental vision of the world: God comes to us in and through the very stuff of the earth. "Let your mind roam through the whole creation," the influential fourth-century theologian Augustine urged; "everywhere the created world will cry out to you: 'God made me.' . . . Go round the heavens again and back to the earth, leave out nothing; on all sides everything cries out to you of its Author; nay the very forms of created things are as it were the voices with which they praise their Creator." Caring for creation sharpens our sacramental sensing: the more we live out this practice in our daily lives, the more we see that all the earth gives testimony to "a God who is ineffably and invisibly great and ineffably and invisibly beautiful."

Seeing sacramentally, we realize that as each of us gathers our first breath, we participate in the story of divine breath hovering over the waters and filling *adam* with life. Christian faith and worship—both filled with earthy symbols and gifts that bind us intimately to God, one another, and the earth—heighten our sacramental vision. Think about how each of us enters the world and is first welcomed into the Christian community: through the waters of our mother's womb and the living waters of baptism. And Christians gather regularly at a banquet filled with the fruits of the earth: in the Eucharist we share bread made from grain and wine pressed from grapes to give thanks for God's becoming flesh in Jesus. Even in death we remain connected to both God and the earth. "Remember," our final prayer goes, "that you are *adamah,* and to *adamah* you shall return" (Gen. 3:19).

In Christianity, the doctrines of Trinity and Incarnation express this sacramental vision most deeply, yet mysteriously. Although these teachings may sound like they are only about God, they are also about the mystery of life itself. Central to our Trinitarian view of God is the belief that the relationality that infuses all dimensions of the cosmos is found within the very heart of God, whom we praise (and try in faith to understand) as a single Being who is, mysteriously, also a community of three Persons. A claim of deep interrelationship also shapes the greatest discoveries of twentieth-century science: through quantum physics and ecological science, physicists and biologists began to describe the relationality of everything in the universe, from the subatomic level to the movement of galaxies through space. From his own awe-filled observation of nature, the early environmentalist John Muir, reveling in the alpine country of the Sierra Nevada, expressed something similar: "When we try to pick out anything by itself, we find it hitched to everything else in the universe." God's relational character is reflected in and throughout all of God's creation.

A second Christian conviction, Incarnation, also takes on new dimensions when linked to practices of creation care. At the dawn of creation, divine breath infused earth; and at another time of earth crisis, God became incarnate—en-fleshed—in the earth through Jesus. God became one of us and "lived among us" (John 1:14) not only for our sake but because God so loved the *whole* world. Indeed, as Paul wrote, the whole creation was groaning in labor pains for that moment, and the whole creation will participate in God's redemption (Rom. 8:18-25).

*A Cloud of Witnesses

This sacramental vision of the earth has led people of faith to love and serve creation across the ages. Consider the remarkable Hildegard of Bingen, a twelfth-century mystic and religious leader whose way of life reflected her embrace of the entire cosmos as the object of God's love and salvation. Drawing on her profound sense of the feminine nature of God and creation, she wove together many talents as musician, theologian, artist, biologist, and poetic preacher to express her love of God and the earth. Hildegard drank deeply from the beauty of the German countryside; she chose a site for the women's monastic community she led at the intersection of two rivers, a lushly beautiful place that many centuries later still strikes visitors as holy ground.

One of Hildegard's guiding images was *viriditas*, literally "greenness"— all the life-giving qualities of God's Spirit found in and through matter. This earthy, incarnational sense of God stirred visions she recorded for her community. "I, the highest and fiery power, have kindled every living spark," God says in one of Hildegard's visions. "I am also the fiery life of the divine essence—I flame above the beauty of the fields; I shine in the waters; in the sun, the moon and the stars, I burn. And by means of the airy wind, I stir everything into quickness with a certain invisible life which sustains all. For the air lives in its green power and its blossoming; the waters flow as if they were alive. . . . All these things live in their own essence and are without death, since I am Life."

Hildegard often created art and music in response to her visions. She paired her love of *viriditas* with love for liturgy—believing that the human and the divine meet in the music and light of worship—and love for those who are poor. She is among our most profound Christian witnesses to the relationship between environmental and social justice concerns.

The saint best remembered for loving and caring for creation is Francis of Assisi, who lived in Italy from 1182 to 1226. He is now widely honored as the patron saint of ecology. In Francis and the community that gathered around him, a whole way of life took shape, a way that integrated virtually all the practices described in this book. His "double conversion" to love the poor and the earth began when, as a young man, he was shaken by compassion for a leper he encountered on the road. Soon he renounced his life of wealth and comfort to live close to the natural world and among the poor and despised. Francis saw God's presence in all creatures and revered them as brothers and sisters (including a Muslim leader on whom Francis's own countrymen were waging war; see that story in chapter 10). Francis's beautiful "Canticle of Creation," which he composed and sang as his own death drew near, praises God's presence throughout creation: praise be for Brother Sun, Francis sang, and for Sister Moon, Brothers Wind and Air, Sister Water, Brother Fire, and Sister Earth. Praise be even for Sister Death, even for the creaturely mortality we humans share with all creation.

Seeing creation sacramentally, Francis's canticle reminds us, offers consolation when this life as we know it ends and our bodies return to the earth. When I was in my twenties, a dear friend was killed in a car accident. We, her friends and family, were stunned with grief that a life so full of promise and hope could end so abruptly. In a beautiful act of returning Mary's body to the earth while releasing her to God, her family members spread her ashes beneath a tall evergreen beside a rushing mountain stream near a Christian community where she had lived and befriended so many. Each time I return to that spot, I remember Mary and give thanks for her life, and for the earth that gave her life and now has welcomed her home again. And each year at the beginning of Lent, when ashes are smudged on my forehead and I hear the ancient words, "you are dust, and to dust you shall return," I think of Mary and all who have gone before us. I remember our shared trust in God's presence and loving care, from creation through birth, from life through death. Trinity. Incarnation. Redemption. Resurrection. Earth Care. Body Care. God in us and we in God.

*Contemporary Saints

Witnesses from the Bible and history testify to creation care as an age-old vocation or calling. Today, I am inspired by young people who are living this vocation in creative ways in our own time. For many of my students, the places "where [their] deep gladness and the world's deep hunger meet" involve caring for the earth.

Katie joined a class I took to Nicaragua to explore environmental and social justice issues. A skilled and sensitive videographer, she recorded the images and voices of the people we met, including many poor Nicaraguan farmers worried about the impact on their livelihoods of CAFTA, the Central American Free Trade Agreement, which was then being negotiated. When Katie returned home, she wrote an editorial for her hometown newspaper chronicling these concerns. The local radio station read her editorial and asked her to speak about her experiences and about CAFTA on an hour-long program.

Afterward, Katie met with other students to form Students for Economic and Social Justice, linking concerns for the poor in Latin America with the well-being of the land. She joined the campus sustainability committee to work on lowering the carbon footprint of our campus—part of a nationwide effort to "green" campuses. She organized student groups to help build a straw-bale house as an example of more sustainable living. She spent the summer bicycling across Montana studying renewable energy projects. In recognition of her efforts, Katie was awarded a Udall

Scholarship, given in honor of the late Congressman Morris Udall's lifelong dedication to stewardship of the environment.

*No Easy Walk

Practicing creation care is not easy. Whatever we do or do not do ripples beyond ourselves, indeed around the globe. What we choose to buy or not to buy, to eat or not to eat, to drive or not to drive, affects people, plants, and animals we will never see. Justice, poverty, and the environment present complex and interrelated issues with real human and other-than-human faces.

Care for creation is intimately linked with biblical mandates to care for the poor and to end oppression and injustice. Televised images of thousands of people left homeless and stranded by Hurricane Katrina made this connection crystal clear. As days passed and still no aid came, it was obvious that those suffering most were no random slice of humanity. They were the country's poor and oppressed, made most vulnerable to a natural disaster by years of social marginalization.

Like thousands of other young people, Anna responded by *acting*. She writes, "When hurricanes Katrina and Rita struck New Orleans, I was deep in the mountains of the Bob Marshall Wilderness in Montana. I knew nothing of the tragedy unfolding. And I did not know then all the ways in which my past would so intricately influence my future, nor that I would soon devote my life to the recovery of that faraway, flooded city." Anna enrolled in a class to study the roots of the social crisis the hurricanes exposed, then traveled with classmates to New Orleans to help people dig out and begin to rebuild. They traversed the Ninth Ward, the submerged communities of the bayou, and the center for displaced persons, lending a hand and a listening ear.

Later, back in class, they read the United Church of Christ's pivotal 1987 study on environmental racism and environmental justice, which shows that many environmental issues such as pollution and toxic wastes are most serious in poor communities of color; they analyzed the social dynamics that had led to the Katrina disaster. Inspired to do more, Anna created a youth education program about New Orleans urban environmental issues for her senior honors project. After graduation, she secured funding to return to New Orleans as an environmental justice intern with a community-based nonprofit. Like Saint Francis, Anna lives out the connection between loving the earth and loving our neighbors, both humankind and otherkind. In Anna's witness in New Orleans I see the breath of God moving again, bringing new life out of watery chaos.

Action can take many forms. For Kendra, a student on another trip to Nicaragua, issues of justice and environment became concretely and disturbingly real the morning we visited a *maquila*—a clothing-manufacturing center. The temperature in this literal "sweatshop" was over ninety degrees, and workers' stories about being forced to leave exhausted farmland for meager factory wages were powerful. After learning that such situations are replicated throughout the two-thirds world of Latin America, Asia, and Africa, Kendra returned to campus, where she and her companions in Students for Economic and Social Justice led a campaign to guarantee that University of Montana logo clothing be purchased only from "sweat-free" producers. Kendra is learning to ask questions that will shape her buying habits for the rest of her life: How was this made? Did those who made it earn a living wage? What was the environmental impact? She is asking these questions with others who share her values and who provide mutual support.

*Creation as Mystery: Suffering and Beauty

Even while celebrating creation and working to care for it, we are often reminded that the natural world is not always kind or benevolent. Suffering and death are woven into creation's fabric, as Hurricane Katrina and other disasters remind us. Sometimes the suffering overwhelms, and signs of hope disappear.

There is no more profound meditation on the mystery of the interweaving of suffering and beauty than the biblical book of Job, which belongs to the scriptural tradition Christians and Jews call "Wisdom Literature." Job is a righteous man whom God has blessed with abundance of every kind. In the divine court, Satan argues that Job worships God only because of these blessings; take away them away, he says, and Job will curse God. Accepting the wager, God allows Satan to test Job by stripping away all he has and inflicting terrible suffering, first by killing his children, then by causing him relentless physical pain. In response, Job does not curse God directly, though he does curse the day of his own birth. For Job in his suffering, creation loses its meaning and its goodness. In a powerful lament, Job begs God to reverse the creative acts by which the world came into being: light into darkness, order into chaos.

Finally, Job demands that God appear to him to explain why he—and, by extension, all innocent persons who suffer—is suffering even though he has been faithful to God. When God finally answers Job from the midst of a whirlwind, God seems to ignore Job's plea, having nothing to say about Job's suffering. Instead, God insists on the beauty and integrity of creation (Job 38–41). God describes in delight many species of animals—all of them wild animals with no need for humans—and singles out as favorites the very creatures that symbolize chaos, Leviathan and Behemoth. In marked contrast to the Creation stories in Genesis, one species is notably absent: humans. From a human point of view, it is difficult to believe that God would so callously ignore Job's suffering and his plea, choosing instead to put Job in his place: "Where were you when I laid the foundation of the earth?" the voice from the whirlwind demands.

God's response far surpasses Job's ability to understand—but it is clearly a stinging rebuke to Job and his self-concern. Although Job still does not understand suffering, he accepts the mystery and acknowledges his own limitations "in dust and ashes." God restores blessing to Job, showing in effect that Job was not wrong to ask these questions. But we readers are left with a set of contradictions: Job's relentless questioning about why the innocent suffer and his demand for justice for the innocent are affirmed by God, but the wrong Job perceives is not rectified. Creation is acknowledged to be a place of suffering, while it is also declared to be a place of beauty and delight.

Can we live with this *both-and*, where the earth is both a place of overwhelming delight and a place where many who are innocent suffer? Like Job, we cannot know why suffering persists. However, we can trust that suffering is not God's final word. That word is *hope*, with the assurance of God's sustaining presence in the midst of suffering. Christians see this reality expressed most fully in the cross and resurrection of Jesus: new life born out of suffering and death. It grounds a both-and faith that allows us to perceive and share the world's suffering while still joining the exultant prayer of the psalmist: "O Lord, how manifold are your works! In wisdom you have made them all" (Ps. 104:24). Suffering is real, but God's promise is constant, and it includes all creation.

*Creation Care in Our Own Time and Place

In the ancient story of Noah and the great flood, God displays that promise as the "bow in the clouds," a sign of covenant between God and the earth. Listen to God's words: "I am establishing my covenant with you and your descendants after you, and with every living creature that is with you, the birds, the domestic animals, and every animal of the earth with you, as many as came out of the ark" (Gen. 9:9-10). Having preserved all species of life from the destruction of the flood, God makes an everlasting covenant of life with *all* creation. Humans are included, but this promise is not for humans alone.

What might it mean to recognize a covenant with all life at a time when human activities threaten the existence of entire species? During the 1990s, certain interest groups mobilized to repeal the Endangered Species Act because it prevented development on economically desirable lands. In response, the Evangelical Environmental Network mobilized Christians to oppose repeal, calling the ESA the "Noah's Ark of our day." Calvin DeWitt, a cofounder of the EEN, framed it this way: "People in their arrogance are destroying God's creation, yet Congress and special interests are trying to sink the Noah's Ark of our day—the Endangered Species Act. Few legislative issues ought to be as clear for Christians as this one. Christian faith teaches respect for the works of God, and the Endangered Species Act offers real and fair protection of all of His creation, including us."

Many people have been moved to action by former vice president and Nobel Peace Prize–winner Al Gore and his book and film about global warming, *An Inconvenient Truth*. In response to the challenge of climate change, Christian activist and writer Bill McKibben organized the "Step It Up" campaign, a grassroots effort to obtain a pledge from Congress to reduce carbon emissions by 80 percent by 2050. Meanwhile, students such as Katie and Anna are organizing campus sustainability initiatives; one result is the American College and University Presidents Climate Commitment, where to date over 550 U.S. colleges and universities have committed to model for society ways of minimizing greenhouse gas emissions. These and many other actions represent signs of hope in a time of earth crisis.

The practice of caring for creation also takes shape in the daily rhythms of our lives: in what food we choose, how we transport ourselves, what consumer goods we live with or without—and what we do with our garbage. To be a living organism means not only consuming food but also producing waste, and our waste can create big problems. In a healthy ecosystem, one animal's waste product is another organism's food. Today we humans produce so much waste—much of it toxic—that we are overwhelming the ecosystems where we live and degrading natural habitats that other organisms need to survive. Let's face it: dealing effectively with our garbage is not always fun or energizing. It's much simpler to let someone else haul it away to parts unknown: out of sight, out of mind!

Years ago while living at Holden Village, a Christian community set deep in Washington's Glacier Peak Wilderness, I learned that dealing with garbage can become a spiritual practice. At Holden, we practice a daily discipline of "garbology": every morning, a different eight-person team collects yesterday's garbage and kitchen waste and sorts it into piles for recycling, composting, burning, or shipping to a distant landfill. Knowing that whatever we bring into the village must also leave at some point—and that every day someone we knew would be sorting through our garbage by hand—makes each villager aware of what we discard, from excessive packaging to nonrecyclable containers. This awareness in turn shapes our purchasing decisions, not only at Holden but when we return home. Now, I take this wisdom with me wherever I live.

Each of us can and must act now, in the places where we live, with the members of our communities, in whatever ways we are able. A dear college friend called to tell me about her son's upcoming bar mitzvah. In lieu of gifts, the young man, Asher, was requesting donations to a local conservation organization dedicated to preserving habitat for native waterfowl. Of the five preparing together for bar and bat mitzvahs, three were focusing on the environment in their speeches to the congregation. Asher chose to speak about the Torah passage in which Joseph interprets Pharaoh's dream as a warning that seven years of famine would follow the seven years of abundance they were currently enjoying (Gen. 41), drawing a parallel to his own country's mounting ecological concerns after a long period of abundance. Asher too is a sign of hope and new beginning in a time of earth crisis.

*Creation Care as Knowing Deeply

"In the end, we will conserve only what we love," wrote the Senegalese poet Baba Dioum. To truly love and protect something, we must know it with the kind of deep knowing that comes only over time. Knowing the earth this way was second nature for our ancestors; virtually every facet of their lives involved working with and on the earth. That kind of knowing is harder for us. Our lives seem busier and more removed from the earth, in part because technology mediates virtually every form of relationship.

Recently we tried to have a family picnic, but our teenager was present in body only: listening to her iPod and text messaging on her cell phone,

> **"** In the end, we will conserve only what we love.—Baba Dioum. **"**

she was fully present neither to us nor to the beautiful place where we were sitting. I finally asked her to turn off her cell and put away her iPod—a request not received cheerfully! Yet I too know the power of technology to distract. Since we got wireless Internet access at home, my partner and I spend less time talking to each other in the evening and more time checking late-breaking news on the Web (we're both news junkies). At work, I spend several hours a day answering email—hours I used to fill by interacting with colleagues and students or taking a walk. New technology promises endless entertainment and instant communication with loved ones, but these can come at a heavy price to our relationships and to the earth.

Our family cabin allows us to live differently for a few weeks each summer. There is no electricity, no television, no telephone, no email, no computer, no cell phone coverage—the amenities we can hardly imagine living without the rest of the year are simply not there. Yet from the oldest to the youngest in our multigenerational family, it's where we yearn to be. Instead of feeling deprived, we find rich fulfillment. Most of all, we have *time*—time for walks, for conversations, for playing games, for cooking meals, for reading books. Time to get to know one another again. My five siblings and I learned to know the earth here when we were kids—exploring meadows, building forts in the woods, watching the weather change, swimming in the lake. Today this cabin is where we introduce the earth and its wonders to a new generation. Here I have gotten to know my nieces and nephews, by getting to know them in a place.

Unstructured time, with one another and with nature, is harder to come by these days, and this reality has significant implications for how we care for the earth. We cannot care well for what we don't know. Many children today spend little time outdoors and lots of time watching television, playing video games, surfing the Web, listening to iPods. Writer Richard Louv calls the result "nature-deficit disorder." As ecologist Stephanie Mills observes, to comprehend the intricacy, authenticity, and ecological well-being of wild places requires forms of "personal, intimate, slow-paced knowledge" that most of us are losing. We face a challenge in figuring out how to enjoy the benefits of technology while keeping it in its proper place. Can we learn to use technology effectively without allowing it to displace what is most important in our lives: time for one another, for the earth, for God?

*God's Promise in the Midst of Despair

Sometimes the problems seem overwhelming. So many things we should be doing seem urgent! One afternoon, discouraged about the enormity of the environmental and social justice issues we face and wearied by my busy life, I took a walk to a nearby creek, found a familiar spot, and just sat. That long list of "shoulds" and "to do's" had drained me of the joy and delight at the biblical root of creation care.

Sit. Listen. Breathe. Gradually the quiet sounds of the creek and my own slowing breath calmed me until I could once again notice the beauty surrounding me. Somewhere behind me birds sang, and across the creek a jogger with her dog trotted by. Sunlight broke through the cottonwoods along the bank and caught the ripple of water on rock. Below the surface, mayflies were hatching, and hungry trout darted through the shallows. The gentle breeze moving across the waters and through the leaves of the trees took me back to Kintla Peak and back to scripture, to that story that grounds all our stories. The beauty of creation in Genesis, the promise of God to Noah, the humility of Job before creation's mystery, the new life coming to birth celebrated in the letters of Paul.

And then I remembered God's promise to heal the earth and all earth's members. In the last chapter of the Bible, God comes to earth in a new Jerusalem, announcing a new heaven and a new earth. And in the midst of it all flows water, bringing life to everything it touches:

> Then the angel showed me the river of the water of life, bright as crystal, flowing from the throne of God and of the Lamb through the middle of the street of the city. On either side of the river is the tree of life with its twelve kinds of fruit, producing its fruit each month; and the leaves of the tree are for the healing of the nations.—Revelation 22:1-2

"Redeemed humanity is always on a redeemed earth," writes Gene McAfee, a biblical scholar who studies the book of Revelation. "Earth, here and hereafter, is humanity's only proper habitat." Our future is here, on this earth that God loves, on this earth with whose care we are entrusted. God already is acting; we have only to answer God's invitation and join the dance.

The healing of the nations. The river of life. God's breath on the waters. I stood up from my spot by the creek, renewed, ready to return to my family and my community of faith, to think together about ways we might live more simply and more sustainably, and to pray again, in the midst of our busyness, that first prayer:

" It is good. It is very good. "

8 * Making a Good Living

Douglas A. Hicks

I n good economic times, a consulting firm hires the top students graduating from the university where I teach. Just as the seniors are beginning to think about life after college, recruiters interview dozens of candidates and extend offers to a select few. To entice them to accept, the recruiters throw in a $500 bonus and a laptop computer.

Have these students sold their inheritance for a bowl of soup, as Esau did in biblical times (Gen. 25:29-34)? At a minimum, many who take the deal later realize that they have sold themselves short. Of course, for those preparing for a career in business consulting, this is a dream job; but others have told me later that they "settled," accepting employment in a field they did not want to pursue simply because they did not know how to turn it down. In practical terms, my students were unprepared to pass up a "real job" that came with a shiny new laptop and five hundred bucks. A well-paying job promises a way out of a financial hole. And besides, during their entire senior year these students would be able to answer that inevitable question from parents, professors, and classmates: "What are you going to do next year?"

It may sound dramatic to compare these students to Esau. Esau said he was famished, and when his younger brother Jacob offered to buy Esau's privileges as firstborn with a pot of stew, Esau replied, "I am about to die; of what use is a birthright to me?" (Gen. 25:32). In the exchange, Esau lost crucial aspects of his identity. Are prospective college graduates that desperate? Difficult as it may be to get a job, they probably will not literally perish from hunger if they don't. At the same time, anxiety about finding a good job in tough financial times can be debilitating, especially for those with crushing school loans and credit card debt. In response, many sell themselves short.

"Why do you spend your money for that which is not bread, and your labor for that which does not satisfy?" an ancient Hebrew prophet asked an unhappy people (Isa. 55:2). Taking this question seriously today leads us to ask, more positively, how we can earn and use money and other economic resources in responsible and faithful ways that *do* satisfy—that is, in ways that nourish ourselves, others, and creation. Making a good living is not only about earning an income. When understood in moral and theological terms, it is the practice of using one's economic values, choices, and behaviors to shape a life focused on those goods that really do matter. Making a good living does not require removing oneself from the economic market (as if that were even possible). Rather, it calls us to engage in economic life critically, thoughtfully, and prayerfully by making choices that allow us both to develop our own capabilities and to further justice, peace, and well-being in God's world.

I have seen this kind of theological understanding bear fruit in the lives of some former students now in their twenties who have devoted themselves to work that fulfills their sense of purpose and contributes to the common good. A student with a passion for politics found her way onto the Virginia governor's staff. Another graduate remained a public school teacher after entering that field through Teach for America. A vice president of a statewide organization works to build inclusive communities across lines of race, culture, religion, and sexual orientation. What these people have in common is the ability to draw on their moral and theological convictions as they pursue lives of meaningful service. They enjoy decent but not affluent lives. They model a life of simplicity without parading the choices that allow them to live simply. And they have a sense of vocation to be doing exactly what they are doing.

Hard economic questions necessarily emerge for those who are developing economic independence from the households in which they grew up. This chapter reflects on some of these questions, drawing on both the resources of Christian faith and a critical reading of contemporary culture. Underlying the exploration is a great appreciation for the basic, urgent, material needs of persons, communities, and creation as a whole. At points, I offer ideas for making difficult decisions. I hope through these reflections to encourage you to say no to the thoughtless pursuit of material goods and yes to the joyful practices of investing your money and yourself in that which gives life.

*Dealing with Stuff

The summer I was twenty-four, I set out to travel across Europe, from Spain to Russia. I had a second-class train pass, a few hundred bucks, and a backpack. Before the trip I had found a bargain—so I thought—on a large pack with plenty of space for extra stuff, such as an additional pair of shoes and a second camera lens. My friend "Karl," who traveled with me, had a backpack a lot smaller and lighter than mine.

For six weeks Karl and I carried our possessions on our backs, from train stations to youth hostels, and often to museums and restaurants too. My back was sore every time we had to transfer from one place to the next, which was almost every day. When we sat in a small café, I had to share my allotted space with my big pack. Meanwhile, Karl's modest-sized pack continually reminded me how I should have packed. It always contained enough to meet his needs, but Karl never gloated. Sometimes he would even trade off gear with me on long treks, sharing the load.

Traveling by backpack is not how most of us live our everyday lives, of course. Yet our stuff is nonetheless burdensome. Twenty-somethings tend to move frequently, and, each time, their stuff has to be moved as well. At my college, I see new students arrive every August with huge loads of electronics and clothes to squeeze into small residence-hall rooms. Later, those who move into a house or apartment will get more stuff, and if they get married, they probably will get even more from friends and relatives. Each gift is well-intentioned and probably useful, but keeping up with all this stuff requires increasing amounts of closet space and psychic space.

Where do we put the Christmas china from Aunt Tanya for eleven months a year? Will I ever take the bread maker out of the box? How often will I use this power tool? In a figurative sense, our material goods become a giant backpack we must carry. We tend to underestimate the costs, which sometimes run so high that our possessions seem to possess us. We have to move stuff, store it, protect it, and repair it. And we worry about it.

In Matthew's Gospel, Jesus discourages such worry and warns against being a "slave" to wealth (Matt. 6:24-25). "Come to me, all you that are weary and are carrying heavy burdens, and I will give you rest," Jesus later adds. "Take my yoke upon you, and learn from me. . . . my yoke is easy, and my burden is light" (Matt. 11:28-30). Could it be that Jesus' way calls us to travel through life with lighter backpacks?

*Living in a Materialistic World

Even if we decide to live with less stuff, doing so is not a simple task. Marketing messages and advertising slogans surround us—billboards, spam, telemarketing, ads on paper and online, television commercials, and product placements. And most of these are aimed at a *target* audience of teens and people from eighteen to forty-five. The word is fitting: as potential consumers, we are targets. Even if we try to pursue the simple life, go TV-free, or spend less on Christmas gifts, ads and the desires they seek to stir still pursue us. "Where can I flee from your presence?" the psalmist cried to God (Ps. 139:7). Today we might ask the same question of the omnipresent messages of the market.

In this context, it is difficult to think clearly about what we truly need and what we merely desire. For many people in recent years, the resulting confusion has triggered a spiraling descent into debt. Collectively, Americans recently had not a *small* savings rate but a *negative* savings rate. For young adults with typically low-paying or entry-level jobs and school expenses or loans to pay, it is tough to focus on saving money. Even when we try to save, messages about what we need in order to be happy constantly distract us. Amid such pressures and distractions, desires can get so distorted that we turn away from genuine essentials and instead buy trivial toys. Meanwhile, credit card debt increases and becomes a real stumbling block to living in the present and the future. Taking on credit beyond our means played a key role in creating the most recent economic recession.

Living in an economy that runs on credit and consumerism adds challenge and complexity to our efforts to embrace the Christian practice of making a good living. Yet even if we could escape being part of the economy, we should not do so. Instead, we must engage the economy through our working, spending, saving, sharing, giving, and consuming. God made the world good, and we are creatures with bodies and material needs. We are part of this world, not some other world we wish existed. And so we are called by God to face the challenge of living in this world without being overcome by this world. Indeed, we are called to live in this world for the sake of the well-being of this world, and to discover joy in doing so. This means we are called to embrace our material nature without becoming materialistic.

*Putting Money in Its Proper Place

We cannot eat dollars, and we cannot build a house with them. Dollars are only *means* that can help accomplish *ends*—and even then only some ends, not all. During the Jim Crow era in the United States, African Americans could have had all the money in the world, but they still could not sit at drugstore lunch counters in the South. Their money was no good for that. To this day, there are societies in which a woman, no matter how wealthy, cannot own property. Indeed, she may be treated as property. In these cases, one person's money has purchasing power but another's does not.

Now consider money in a little different way. Once people have reached a minimum income level that allows them to meet their basic needs, income itself does not contribute very much to a person's happiness. In other words, absolute increases in income do not play nearly as important a role in our happiness as we might think. No matter how much they have, at whatever income level, people tend to want another 20 or 25 percent.

A far more powerful influence on our behavior, according to economic studies, is our relative status in comparison to peer groups we consider important. Six decades ago, the economist James Duesenberry gave a classic explanation of this phenomenon, which has come to be known as "keeping up with the Joneses." Duesenberry argued that a significant factor in promoting consumerism was the emotional reaction produced "by looking at a friend's new car or looking at houses or apartments better

> **❝** No matter how much they have, at whatever income level, people tend to want another 20 or 25 percent. **❞**

than one's own." "The response," he observed, "is likely to be a feeling of dissatisfaction with one's own house or car." Today such comparisons extend to how we feel when we see our neighbors using the most recently introduced smart phones or other high-tech gadgets.

Increased personal income does not make us happier for long because we can never keep up with our own ever-expanding desires. Our inability to distinguish between what we *need* and what we *want* means one more desired object always lies just beyond our grasp. This trap can be especially debilitating for impoverished persons, who may take on credit-card and payday-loan debt to own items seen as status symbols. But the cycle is ultimately debilitating for all of us. As long as we keep spending money to keep up with the consumer messages we get from neighbors and advertising, we all contribute to an ongoing economic "arms race" for more and more stuff.

It is high time we stop thinking about money as the be-all and end-all of our material lives. Don't get me wrong—money can and does open many doors and enables access to important goods. But money is just one part of a social system that allows us to meet needs. By refusing to regard money as an end in itself and learning instead to recognize it as solely a means to other ends, we can develop a new and life-giving perspective.

A Nobel Prize winner in economics, Amartya Sen, provides a better vocabulary for thinking about economic goods. Rather than emphasizing income, Sen wants us to look for what he calls *human capabilities. Capabilities* name the truly important things people are able to do and be. For example, are we nourished and healthy? Do we have decent housing? Are we able to participate in the cultural life of our community? Are we engaged in political and civic life? Are we well educated? Can we practice our religion? Do we have friends? Being able to say yes to these questions means we have attained important capabilities.

Let's consider this approach in more concrete terms. Money can be used to secure decent nutrition, health care, and housing. But even for these capabilities, being literate and numerate about food, exercise, and the housing market is at least as vital as having money to spend. Consider people who come into large sums of money but do not have the ability to convert that money into capabilities such as health or financial security; think of lottery winners and teenage celebrities who waste their money. And remember Jesus' parable about a well-to-do young man who squanders his entire inheritance and ends up living with pigs until he again becomes dependent on his parents (Luke 15:11-32).

Earning a high income may even hinder the attainment of some human capabilities. Some people with high-powered, exciting jobs become so busy that they lose their capacity to connect with other people. They do not have the time, and when they do have time, they cannot slow down enough to enjoy it. Accustomed to a "let's win" mentality, they cannot appreciate the laughter of children or the complexity and nuance of a good novel. When capabilities such as having friends and participating in community life wane, economically successful people may have gained the whole world but lost their souls (Mark 8:36, NIV).

*Choosing How to Live

"One's life does not consist in the abundance of possessions," Jesus teaches (Luke 12:15). Instead, true abundance has to do with being "rich toward God" (Luke 12:21). Over the centuries and today, some Christians have heard this good news as a call to radical simplicity and have responded by making lifelong vows to a monastic way of life that seeks freedom from the burden of possessions for the sake of service to God. Other Christians adopt such discipline for a shorter period of time, for instance during a year of service with groups such as the Jesuit Volunteer Corps or the Lutheran Volunteer Corps. Still others become part of a new monastic community like the one described in Jonathan Wilson-Hartgrove's chapter, "Living as Community."

Amartya Sen's theory of capabilities suggests a different approach, though it is also one that prizes forms of abundance that are not measured in possessions or dollars. Using this approach, individuals and communities consider what capabilities really matter to them, and why. They also ask what can be done to gain, use, and share these capabilities for the good of all. As thinking shifts, economic goals may also change: acquiring more and more stuff no longer seems as life-giving as developing human capabilities, both one's own and those of others. People learning to think this way begin to see more clearly what "a good living" actually looks like. They begin to take steps toward what will be a relatively simpler—and in many ways richer—way to live than they might have imagined.

Being faithful does not mean belittling the importance of economic needs. Instead, it means putting economic needs in the context of all that really matters. Denying ourselves basic necessities does not by itself make us more holy. Instead, the challenge most Christians in developed economies face today is ensuring that not only our own needs *but also* the needs of others are met. Addressing this challenge requires full and faithful participation in God's material creation—the kind of participation I think is best summarized in the word *moderation*.

The author of the biblical book of Proverbs describes moderation and its benefits well: "Give me neither poverty nor riches," he pleads to God,

" Being faithful . . . means putting economic needs in the context of all that really matters. "

for he knows that either could lead him astray. If he is rich, he will get comfortable and forget God. If he is poor, he will resort to stealing and cursing God. It is wise, this plea suggests, to steer between poverty and riches. What the biblical author asks for is "the food that I need" (Prov. 30:8-9), and I think he means by "food" not just what goes into the stomach but all that nourishes well-being.

*Community for Good Living in the Material World

As Jonathan Wilson-Hartgrove explains, all of us genuinely need community. Sharing our lives with others fosters a sense of belonging and also helps us achieve our individual capabilities. Because communities influence us so greatly, we need to take special care to find healthy ones. A good friend recently asked me for advice on finding a new church home, because he found that he "didn't seem to have nice enough shoes" to fit in at the affluent church he had been attending. Communities caught up in the arms race of consumer-driven happiness may not provide the encouragement we need when we are trying to develop a way of life that fosters discernment about economic well-being for ourselves and others.

At the same time, there is no market-free place on which to stand. Every community lives somewhere in the tension between materialism and material simplicity. Families, peer groups, and churches are all part of the very society on which we hope to gain some critical perspective and thus are themselves subject to the forces of consumerism. At the same time, most families, peer groups, and churches also yearn for goods that are beyond price, things that cannot be reduced to what the consumer economy supplies. Putting such yearnings on the table for conversation can lead to choices that help us make a good living.

In moving toward good choices we also discover the importance of communities that extend beyond our immediate families, peer groups, and religious congregations. Recognizing the image of God in every person, Christians are called to care about the quality of life in places nearby and far away. We have to step back from competition with our neighbors over the latest cars, biggest houses, and newest gadgets. Instead, the economist Robert Frank argues, we can begin to escape the consumerist treadmill by working with our neighbors and pooling our resources to pursue *public goods* that benefit the whole community. Parks, schools, roads, sidewalks—all these are goods that do not depend on keeping up with the Joneses and that *do* increase the happiness of people. Investing in public goods such as these changes the equation of consumer restlessness: our impulse for material goods and our impulse for communal participation are combined into one impulse that is directed to the good for all.

*Doing Justice

As global citizens and global consumers, we also belong to communities that reach across national borders. Theologically, there are good reasons to view ourselves as members of one community of human beings, each created in the image of God. In my experience, this potentially abstract understanding of "one world"—a world in which everyone should be treated with dignity—becomes really real through person-to-person encounter.

While on a young-adult mission and service trip from our church to the Yucatan region, I was with my friend "Joe" as he tried to buy a nice handmade rug in a local market. Joe's conversation with "Diego," the Mexican merchant, went something like this:

Joe: How much for this rug?

Diego: One hundred pesos.

Joe: I'll give you twenty.

Diego: How about fifty?

Joe: Twenty.

Diego: Thirty?

Joe: Twenty.

Diego (handing Joe the rug): Okay, twenty pesos.

Joe: Will you take fifteen?

You should have seen the surprise, and then the anger, on Diego's face. He had negotiated in good faith with Joe, who had refused to move his price. Diego had come all the way down to twenty pesos. Without intending to hurt anyone's feelings, Joe had thought this whole "negotiating thing" was funny. But he had broken a norm of bargaining by offering a price and then not being willing to honor that offer.

Truth be told, Joe did not really want a rug. He was in it for the fun of bargaining, the excitement of seeing new wares in the local Mexican market. Diego, in contrast, did not have the luxury of joking around about money; this potential sale would affect his livelihood. After all, the average annual income per person in Mexico was then about $1,700, less than five dollars a day.

This moment of bargaining, misunderstanding, and anger was about more than a single sale. It represented an encounter of worlds, a collision of economic realities. Joe is now a schoolteacher in Indiana; he and his family live a decent but modest life in the American middle class. I do not know how Diego is doing now. But with the average income in the U.S. now about six times that of Mexico, it is very likely that his standard of living is far below Joe's, mine, or yours.

My friend Joe encountered global inequality face-to-face during our service trip to Mexico, and in the years since that encounter, he and I have returned to it time and again. It is hard enough for Americans to make ends meet in our own fast-paced, expensive economy. Thinking about economics and faith becomes even more complicated when we place ourselves in a world where many people—billions of people—have nothing like the economic choices and opportunities we do. In this case, the issue was not about billions of people; it was about Diego. Should Joe have paid Diego his original asking price of 100 pesos? He tried to negotiate his price down to the "market" price, but was Diego so desperate that he settled for a price far below what was fair? Or, alternatively, should Joe have realized—before he ever opened his mouth to bargain—that he didn't really need a rug and so just walked right by the rug stall? But wouldn't his money help to support rug makers and rug sellers in Mexico? Thus, even if he didn't need a rug, should he still have bought at least one just to "help the economy," to help people like Diego? Or, would doing so be patronizing—as if Joe could be a sort-of savior for Diego and his country?

The Bible opposes injustice but does not always give us specific answers regarding how to address it. It does not mandate what we should buy or from whom. It does not name the "equilibrium market price" for a handmade Mexican rug. Yet the scriptures do offer some fundamental principles that can guide us.

Christian scriptures and theology devote disproportionately large attention to God's compassion for impoverished and vulnerable persons. The Roman Catholic tradition calls this God's "preferential option for the poor." In biblical texts, those who treat the economically vulnerable unjustly consistently receive God's condemnation (see, for instance, the eighth chapter of Amos); a legal code requires farmers to leave the corners of their fields unharvested so that the hungry might glean what they need to survive (Deut. 24:19-21); and economic care for widows and orphans is basic to communal economic life (Exod. 22:22-24; Acts 6:1-4). In these and other passages, a Christian ethical approach to economic life emerges that emphasizes *commutative*, *distributive*, and *social* justice. Key norms in this ethic are fairness in exchanges, the fair distribution of goods (including redistribution at times), and the call for overall economic organization that provides fairly for everyone. These rather abstract principles of justice do not make it simple to develop specific antipoverty efforts at the local, national, or global level. But they do press us to care about human capability and well-being beyond our own individual or family concerns.

As I write, some 2.8 billion people, almost half the world's population, earn less than two dollars per day. Faced with this big-picture view of a complex world, it is easy to believe that we can do little to make a difference. The mind-blowing volatility of global financial markets that came to light late in 2008 demonstrates how interdependent and fragile our economic system is. In one sense, everyone—from powerful politicians in the United States or Europe to impoverished persons in Chicago or Nairobi—shares in common the experience of living in a world that is beyond our control.

However, it is wrong to think that we can do nothing to address poverty. Take, for instance, the international movement against extreme poverty that is known in Britain, Ireland, and Europe as *Make Poverty History* and in the United States as *the ONE Campaign.* This movement is largely comprised of young, Internet-savvy folks who care about ending poverty in this generation. Global rock star Bono has become the most visible face of this movement, but millions of people in the U.S. and around the world are committed to it. Although critics contend that even Bono and all these millions cannot make a positive difference against extreme poverty, the ONE Campaign and related efforts, including the official United Nations Millennium Development Campaign, have indeed helped to place global poverty on the agenda of governments and nongovernmental agencies around the world. Together, celebrities like Bono, philanthropists like Bill and Melinda Gates, and citizens like you and me have made progress against poverty. These efforts also bring pressure on governments to direct their resources to alleviate poverty; which is significant because governments as well as individuals, churches, and a host of nongovernmental organizations will be part of the solution.

Much work remains to be done if the UN's Millennium goals for 2015 are to be met, but what has been done so far is a promising sign. What seem like small steps can make a difference. "A $30 donation to Oxfam International buys books to help 10 girls in Afghanistan learn to read and write," my former student Elizabeth Victor recently wrote. "The shelter down the street from my apartment feeds 85 formerly homeless men with approximately $75 per meal. Every dollar donated to America's Second Harvest provides 10 pounds of food and groceries to families facing hunger in our country."

*Responding to God's Providing

Although our efforts matter, none of us is God. Even together we cannot claim certainty about God's plans or purposes. And in at least one way, our limited ability to make change is a good thing: it reminds us that we are not in full control of our own lives or the lives of others. Part of the quest for economic affluence stems from the mistaken belief that we can buy happiness for ourselves and those we love, or that we can obtain economic (and physical and emotional) security through increased income or greater wealth. This is simply not so—a theological point made with great clarity in the Gospel of Luke. A rich man foolishly builds bigger and bigger barns to store all of his stuff—and then he dies (Luke 12:16-21). A ruler gives up "treasure in heaven" because he is unwilling to sell all that he has and distribute the money to the poor (Luke 18:18-25); he goes away sad. A householder feasts sumptuously while ignoring the needs of a poor man at his gate; only after both of them die does he realize that his selfish lifestyle has resulted in utter alienation from God (Luke 16:19-31).

Wealth is never completely secure, and wealth alone cannot secure what matters most to us. This might sound frightening, but when you say the same thing another way a message of comfort emerges: it is God who provides and God who will provide. This truth can be a source of great comfort, asserted John Calvin, a Protestant reformer with a profound understanding of divine providence. God's providing does not mean that we human beings should not work, that we should not give of our possessions, or that we should not persevere in our calling to serve our neighbors and work for justice. What it means is that our excessive worrying about job or economic security can be futile or even unhealthy.

The Christian practice of making a good living—not just for ourselves but for the sake of others—is rooted in joyful, grateful response to this God who provides. God gives life, and life abundant. That abundance is misunderstood when it is translated as material prosperity. Abundance is better understood as life lived in human community that enables each person to realize his or her God-given capabilities. Money and material goods can help make that possible, but possessing wealth or stuff is not the goal.

As our own capacities and capabilities develop, therefore, we respond through giving our resources and ourselves to a world in need. Our giving takes a variety of forms, including putting money into the church offering plate, engaging in public debates about social justice, and supporting domestic and international antipoverty efforts. All these express our grateful response to God, who provides.

When disconnected from God, giving can become primarily a way of making ourselves feel better. Further, giving to other people can become a way to keep them dependent or subservient. Adopting a discipline of giving regularly, as in the traditional practice of tithing 10 percent of one's income, can produce a healthier motive and effect, because its pattern gives order to our economic lives. Tithing reminds us that our giving should not be dependent on whims or on how we feel about ourselves at the moment or on what we might want to buy instead. By consistently dedicating a regular portion of income to the church and to other institutions working for God's justice, we repeatedly remember that what we have ultimately does not belong to us. What we have is part of God's own creation, intended not just for us but for all. We release a portion of "our own" resources, and through our giving, God provides for the world again.

The story of the loaves and the fishes—the only miracle story recorded in all four New Testament Gospels—offers a powerful picture of how God provides. Jesus feeds five thousand hungry people who have followed him out of town to a place where there is apparently nothing to eat. He does not turn stones to bread, as Satan once had tempted him to do (Matt. 4:3), nor does a giant, celestial loaf of bread fall from heaven. Instead, a little boy is willing to share his five loaves and two fish (John 6:9), and Jesus tells the disciples to pass this food around. Amazingly, there is enough for all—in fact, there is more than enough. A miracle indeed, and one that addresses basic human needs. But is the miracle supernatural, accomplished because Jesus makes bread and fish appear from thin air? Or is it a social miracle, accomplished by the gathered people themselves as they pull food from their satchels and throw it into the common supply? Either way, this story suggests that when people respond to Jesus' call to share with one another, there is enough for all. Just as important, in this sharing there is joyful celebration.

*Investing Ourselves for Good

"Why do you spend your money for that which is not bread, and your labor for that which does not satisfy?" we heard the prophet ask at the beginning of this chapter (Isa. 55:2). The question unmasks the confusion and emptiness behind so much of contemporary economic life. At the same time, the question suggests that real, nourishing bread *is* available and that there are some things to work for that *do* satisfy our genuine needs. "Listen carefully to me," God continues, speaking through the prophet, "and eat what is good, and delight yourselves in rich food. Incline your ear, and come to me; listen, so that you may live" (Isa. 55:2-3). As in Proverbs, we sense that more is at stake than the kind of food that goes into the stomach. At the same time, within a way of life where we eat at Jesus' miraculous table the kind of food that goes into the stomach will never be unimportant, and it will always be shared.

> " When people respond to Jesus' call to share with one another, there is enough for all. Just as important, in this sharing there is joyful celebration. "

The practice of making a good living provides opportunities to invest for good in many ways, both locally and globally. Entering this practice, we find the good news in unlikely places, such as in the work of an economist who tells us that we can all improve our well-being by investing together in public goods such as schools, parks, and roads. And we learn that some of those unlikely places extend far beyond our national borders. As Bono puts it, "In the Global Village, distance no longer decides who is your neighbor, and 'Love thy neighbor' is not advice, it's a command."

What we invest through this practice is not only our time and our money. We invest ourselves. We invest ourselves through commitments to friends, families, and churches. We invest ourselves in the work we do and in the patterns of spending, saving, and giving we adopt. We invest ourselves in the communities we help to create. We invest ourselves by serving others and by doing justice.

You need not use your gifts and talents as consumer culture expects. You have the power to shape your life and our common future. Let there be no doubt about it, though: those who take this path face an uphill battle against marketing forces and the desires they foster. In addition, our society's failure so far to address gaps in access to basic goods such as health care is also an impediment. Do not let anyone tell you that living a relatively simple lifestyle is an easy practice of faith. It is one of the most difficult.

At the same time, certain questions will not go away: why do you spend your money on that which is not bread, and your labor for that which does not satisfy? Why do you sell your inheritance for a bowl of soup? Why do you neglect the poor? As hard as these questions are, ignoring them is even harder. We need to forge the disciplines and habits that enable us to engage critically in economic life every day. We need to decide what we need to live on, how we will spend our time and talents, and how we can support work for justice that allows others to live more fully. Making a good living for ourselves and for our local and global neighbors is a matter of our money. But it is also a matter of our very selves and the choices we make in joyful service to the God who provides.

9* Honoring the Body

Evelyn L. Parker

One Friday morning last spring, my mother called to tell me my father's condition had worsened. I packed a few things, made arrangements to miss an important meeting, and booked a flight from Dallas to New Orleans, the closest major airport to my hometown of Hattiesburg, Mississippi. I was on my way to the airport within two hours, but traffic was very heavy. At the airport, flights were delayed by weather and overbooked by fans heading to the New Orleans Jazz Festival. I pulled my luggage from gate to gate, desperately seeking an earlier flight after learning that my scheduled flight would not get to Houston in time for my connecting flight. Finally I pleaded with an agent, "Please, I must get on this flight, my father is dying!" She looked at me with compassion, printed boarding passes to Houston and New Orleans, and sent me on my way with gentle words. "I'm sorry about your father," she said.

New Orleans was rainy and crowded, and my cousins Nathan and Verdeen were delayed in picking me up. We drove across Lake Pontchartrain toward Mississippi through blinding rain, staying the course with only the white center line as a guide, unaware of tornado warnings in the area. We arrived at my parents' house a little before 11:00 PM.

My father was lying in a hospital bed in the guest room, his six-foot three-inch body crammed into its metal frame. He was reaching upward and pointing with his right hand, mumbling words we couldn't understand. "It's Evelyn," I said, touching his arm in greeting and blessing. "I'm home." Nathan slept in the chair next to his beloved uncle all that night, while my mother and I retired to bedrooms nearby. Twice, my mother heard my father call out and, thinking he was dying, summoned me to come quickly to his bedside.

Early the next morning, my cousins and mother joined me around my father's bed for our traditional family devotion. My dad's parents had had devotions every Sunday morning with their children and later their grandchildren, kneeling in a circle before a breakfast of hot biscuits, fresh churned butter, syrup, rice, bacon, eggs, and fresh milk. My parents had continued this with my brother and me each Christmas morning. Now, while my father continued to move and mumble restlessly, we sat around his bed and sang one of his favorite songs, "He Understands, He'll Say 'Well Done.'" We took turns reading Romans 8:18-39, the wonderful passage about how *nothing* can separate us from the love of God in Christ Jesus. Then we knelt around his bed, each of us touching his body, each of us praying aloud. I had complete confidence that he was praying too.

A stream of visitors that would last all day started around 9:00 AM. In midmorning, the hospice nurse arrived. My father's pulse was eighty-three, she said, but she could not get a blood pressure reading. This usually meant that a patient would die within seventy-two hours, she told us as she began to cry. Seeing our love and care for my father moved her to tears, she said.

At eight o'clock that evening, my mother and I decided that my dad might be more comfortable if we gave him a bath. My sister-in-law, Yvette, once a hospice social worker, and my nephew's wife, Johnnita, a former nurse's assistant, offered to help. When we lifted my dad to place a turning sheet under his hips, he began to struggle. Cradling his long legs in my arm as I lifted them, I told him I would not let him fall. My mother washed his face; my task was to wash his body.

I prepared warm sudsy water in a basin and wet a small white towel. After his tee shirt was lifted over his head, I washed his chest, neck, and arms, being careful not to rub too hard. Then using the same pattern I washed his legs. While I was concerned to clean his body, I avoided washing his groin. It seemed disrespectful for a daughter to see the private parts of her father; I was ashamed to look at him. Yvette and Johnnita admonished me to get on with it or they would have to bathe him themselves. Determined to fulfill that responsibility, I took a deep breath and lifted his underwear. As I began to wash between his legs, my fear, shame, and embarrassment subsided. We turned him over, and he relaxed as I gently rubbed the warm wet towel over his back, hips, and legs. Yvette suggested that I put a little baby powder on him, and he seemed to enjoy the way it felt. We dressed him in clean bedclothes and turned him on his left side. He became more peaceful, no longer struggling. "Pop just wanted to be clean," commented Yvette. "Yes," I agreed. "My dad has always been a sharp dresser."

> **Caring for my father as he died helped me to understand God's love, and the love of my father, more fully.**

We left his side when four friends arrived. One, a preacher who walked the track with my dad at the YMCA, began to pray; I could hear his passionate words from the dining room. As soon as the men left, someone said, "I think he's gone." I ran into the room and sat in the bed beside my father. I checked the pulse on his wrist and then his neck. Nothing. I placed my hand over his eyes, but there was no response. Frantically, I asked everyone to sing, once more, "He Understands, He'll Say 'Well Done.'" As we sang, I felt a calming peace.

When we finished singing, it was 8:45 PM on May 3, 2008. The man who played basketball when he was a teen and exercised at the YMCA until it became too painful for him, the man who loved to wear stylish suits, the man who rested from hard work in the garden with a tall glass of ice water, the man who loved to eat at full buffet restaurants, the man who often enjoyed deep belly laughs but was not afraid to let others see him cry—this man had now passed on to the great realm of saints, to be among our cloud of witnesses.

All my life, my father had helped me to know God's unconditional love toward me. Caring for my father as he died helped me to understand God's love, and the love of my father, more fully. Love, I now saw, is not just an emotion. Love is also tangible—touchable and embodied. God's love for us, and ours for one another.

*The Human Body as God's Tangible Grace

Grace becomes tangible through God's gift of the human body. This gift is also what allows us to be in relationship with others. Our bodies, given out of God's own goodness and created in God's own image, house the essence of who we are as beings of body, mind, and spirit. Our bodies hold the characteristics that make us unique: our values, beliefs, attitudes, hopes, dreams, fears, identities. Our bodies are an intricate design of DNA, RNA, chromosomes, ribosomes, and all the organelles inside each of our billions of cells which orchestrates the touchable organ we call "the body." Praise God for the gift of the human body, God's artistic creation of flesh and bones, muscle and connective tissue, systems and structures.

Our bodies also have the capacity to hold and reveal the Holy Spirit. "Do you not know that you are God's temple and that God's Spirit dwells in you?" the apostle Paul asked the bickering congregation in Corinth not once but twice. So then, "glorify God in your body," he urged, hoping his readers would honor God by honoring their bodies and the bodies of others as the dwelling place of the Spirit (1 Cor. 3:16; 6:19-20). The human body was created to shelter the Holy Spirit, who yearns to dwell in communion with our spirit, the two together in our bodies.

When the Holy Spirit comes to dwell in us, Jesus says in the Gospel of John, we receive an "Advocate," which means one who speaks on behalf of another. This Advocate speaks for Jesus, bearing witness about God's saving love to each of us, and also through us to others. The indwelling Spirit is also the Spirit of Truth, who teaches and reminds us of everything Jesus has said (John 14:26), leading us in the way and truth of Jesus (John 16:13). And the Spirit imparts Christ's peace (John 14:27). Imagine what it might mean for our bodies to be "temples" of all this! It would mean that we too would become advocates, and truthful ones, and sources of comfort, peace, and encouragement to others. It would mean empowerment for wholesome human relationships.

The sense that advocacy, knowledge, and care for others go hand in hand differs from the sense that truth is best gained by detachment, which is the dominant view in modern Western culture. This connection between knowledge and loving relationship resembles what feminist theoreticians call "women's ways of knowing," which emphasize relationality and care rather than distance and "objectivity." Faithful participation in practices like those described in this book requires both truthful

> **"** Our bodies are an intricate design of DNA, RNA, chromosomes, ribosomes, and all the organelles inside each of our billions of cells which orchestrates the touchable organ we call 'the body.' **"**

knowing and caring relationship, seamlessly woven together. Consider those who practice justice or peacemaking. In recent years, student activists have been moved by both empathy and research as they become advocates on behalf of those whose bodies are at risk of mutilation and slaughter. For example, a Harvard student group advocating on behalf of people harmed by Sudanese genocide persuaded the Harvard Corporation to divest $4.4 million in holdings of stock in PetroChina Company Limited, which was supporting the violence in Darfur. Advocacy against crimes that destroy human bodies is a form of relationship that goes beyond face-to-face contact, a form of the practice of honoring the body as it emerges in public life.

Wholesome relationships, empowered by the Spirit and shaped by the practice of honoring the body, enable us to share God's love by becoming means of tangible grace to other human bodies. Such relationships invite unity in purpose among friends, colleagues, and team members, and even with those who were only recently strangers. I learned this during a ropes-course exercise with a group of teenagers attending a program at Perkins School of Theology, where I teach. On this course, challenging games require an entire group to work together to complete a difficult physical task rather than setting individuals against one another in competition. On the day I am remembering, some participants shouted "you can do it" or "way to go" and cheered each time a team member took a step on the wires thirty feet above the ground. Others untangled ropes and kept them accessible, while leaders made sure safety hooks were properly attached. All of us used our bodies, in one way or another, to support, catch, and brace the others; and our voices encouraged and guided them. Each person's body was important as we built community and reached our goals.

Handshakes, hugs, pats on the back, and kisses communicate affection and affirmation. All of these are acts of tangible grace, small ways our bodies bear God's grace to others. So are the high fives, belly bumps, and hip slaps shared by athletes, or the handshakes and occasional hugs offered by opposing teams in counterstreaming single-file lines.

Such gestures are not shared equally with all, and sometimes they carry subtle disrespect. A firm handshake can express the giver's confidence and her respect for the receiver, while a limp handshake can express diminished confidence or a lack of affirmation. And when one person refuses to shake the extended hand of another, it might be a sign of rejection or disapproval, possibly reflecting differences in race or class. I've heard hurt or outrage from African Americans who extended their hands to European Americans who refused to take their hands in response. And I've noticed that homeless people never offer a handshake while sharing moments of fellowship with those who volunteer in shelters and soup kitchens. Like other marginalized people, those who are homeless usually wait for the extended hand of those more fortunate. By simple gestures one body can bear, or deny, grace to another.

*The Body of Christ

Christians speak of the church as "the body of Christ." This image, drawn from the letters of the apostle Paul, describes us as "members" (as in legs and arms) of one whole and unified entity. Moreover, this image reminds us that the church—with all its members—is God's body in the world, called to bear God's grace to others through appropriate touch.

When I served on the staff of Northaven United Methodist Church, a reconciling congregation in Dallas, I learned a valuable lesson about the importance of touch and how touch can express the gift of God's love. Several persons in the congregation had shared that they had AIDS or were HIV-positive. As head of the youth ministry program, I worked with some of these individuals who had volunteered as youth counselors. While I did not hesitate to touch them, I would slip away to wash my hands after shaking the hands of those who were suffering from full-blown AIDS. I did this knowing that one cannot contract the virus from a handshake.

One Sunday morning, immediately after my ritual of hand washing, I hurried into the sanctuary to assist in serving Communion. When worshipers gathered around the table, I moved around the circle, breaking off a portion of the Communion bread and pressing it into the palm of each person's hand. As I did this, I looked into each person's eyes and said, "The body of Christ, broken for you." Soon I came to a parishioner I knew had AIDS; in fact, less than an hour before, I had washed my hands after shaking his. I looked into his eyes and began to repeat the words assuring him that Christ's body was broken for him. At that moment, I heard the Holy Spirit's words of conviction: "Will you deny me, Evelyn?" I wept, ashamed that I had set conditions on touching those people the world labels as untouchable.

Serving Communion to those suffering from AIDS was transforming for me, but for a time the transformation remained incomplete. I stopped secretly washing my hands, but I still made assumptions about people who had HIV/AIDS. A year later, I moved away to go to graduate school. During my first semester I received the sad news that one of my youth counselors, as well as two other members of the congregation, had died from AIDS. During the weeks that followed, I dealt with the shock of losing this friend, but I never truly grieved his death or the deaths of the other parishioners. Then I saw the movie *Philadelphia*, which tells the story of a man who lives with AIDS and finally dies of it. As that powerful film ended and the credits began to roll, I found myself sobbing. My body could no longer suppress the release of bottled-up grief. Alone in the theater, I felt as if I had been crying forever and would never be able to stop. Those tears carried me the second step as I learned truly to honor the bodies of those living, and dying, with AIDS.

The people of Northaven United Methodist Church blessed me with transformative grace. As years pass, I am more and more thankful for this congregation and others like it. When it stands without shame or apology in solidarity with human beings who have been rejected and marginalized by society, the church becomes a sign of God's tangible grace in and for the world. When this happens, the church, the body of Christ, opens its arms to the homeless, the sick, the poor, and all who suffer. The early church did this, ministering to the needs of widows and orphans and caring for members of the community—"If one member suffers, all suffer together with it; if one member is honored, all rejoice together with it" (see 1 Cor. 12:25-27).

We share God's tangible grace every day in face-to-face, hand-to-hand ways. We also share it through action and advocacy for political, economic, and social policies that aim to promote the well-being of those in physical need. Some denominations make policy statements on hunger, health care, housing, and other issues. When members live out these stands through their way of life and worship, the policies become living documents made of flesh and blood, and we see that working in feeding programs and advocating for policies that address the root causes of hunger go hand in hand. Finally, in humility, we lift all of our efforts to God in song and prayer, trusting God to make of us signs of tangible grace in our communities and throughout the world.

In the doctrine of the Incarnation, Christians speak of the flesh-and-blood body of Jesus, whom we worship as Christ ("the anointed one"). Our creeds declare that this body was conceived and born, suffered, died, was buried, and was raised from the dead. Jesus was and is God's grace in utterly tangible form, God's grace in the flesh, God's Word made flesh:

> In the beginning was the Word, and the Word was with God, and the Word was God. He was in the beginning with God. . . . And the Word became flesh and lived

among us, and we have seen his glory, the glory as of a father's only son, full of grace and truth.—John 1:1-2, 14

This is the in-carnation, the en-fleshing, of the second Person of the Trinity, who became a human being in Jesus of Nazareth. Enfleshed, Jesus lived with human beings. Enfleshed, he modeled all the practices discussed in this book.

Christians know God's gift of tangible grace, then, through the Incarnation of Jesus Christ, through the church, and through our own bodies in relationship with other human bodies. At the same time, all of these can be sites of suffering. Being enfleshed, being embodied—for us and also for Jesus—includes vulnerability, suffering, and death. Sometimes, awareness of such limits makes us treasure the human body even more, as I did when giving my father his last bath. But sometimes we feel overwhelmed or frightened and don't want to look at or be near those who are suffering; we want to wash our hands of them, as I did at Northaven United Methodist Church.

Jesus stays close to those who suffer throughout his ministry, and at the end of his life he suffers alongside others who are also being shunned and tortured as they die. With the resurrection of Jesus, however, God insists that suffering is not the end, that life is stronger than death, and that the body is deeply important to true life and relationship. "Touch me and see," the risen Christ says, "for a ghost does not have flesh and bones as you see that I have" (Luke 24:39). New life in Christ is not only a spiritual reality, the disciples learn, and Christians now insist; it is a life received in the body, in a world full of many other beautiful, broken, and often suffering bodies. And we live this life not only for ourselves but also as tangible grace to others, even though we are wounded and vulnerable and so are they. "The Christian practice of honoring the body," says Stephanie Paulsell,

> **Being enfleshed, being embodied—for us and also for Jesus—includes vulnerability, suffering, and death.**

author of this book's chapter on friendship and intimacy, "requires that we view the world through the lens of Jesus' wounded but resurrected body." Jesus' broken body, she continues, "brings into focus the bodies of the sick and the wounded and the exploited. His resurrection shows us the beauty God intends for all bodies. As we love and suffer, as we seek God and each other, with our bodies, we remember that every body is blessed by God, deserving of protection and care."

When we offer one another protection and care, we communicate God's blessing to each other, even in the midst of the brokenness that we also experience. When we honor actual bodies, our own and those of others, we express gratitude to God for being with us, in the midst of suffering and mortality, as tangible grace. We practice this blessing, this grace, in many large and small ways, as part of our everyday life.

*Clean or Unclean?

Some of my fondest memories of bathing come from when I was about six years old, and my parents and I lived with my maternal grandmother in the rural area of Covington County, Mississippi. We didn't have indoor plumbing, so I bathed in a large round galvanized tub set in the middle of the bedroom floor. My mother would mix hot water from the kettle with cold from the well until the temperature was just right, and stepping into the tub was a very pleasurable experience. I washed my face and ears as my mom instructed, and then she washed my back and worked on the rough skin of my tomboyish elbows and knees. I would sit and soak a while, then ask for more warm water so I could enjoy being there a little longer.

When I make time to enjoy a leisurely bath today, the pleasure never equals what I remember from my childhood. Perhaps my mother's presence reminded me of being in the waters of her womb. Perhaps I miss the love and care I received each time she touched my body or combed my hair. Her hands taught me the meaning of appropriate touch, and her massaging my scalp and curly tresses in shampoo was sheer delight. In these acts, my mother was God's tangible grace to me, and in a way I was (and I am) God's tangible grace to her as well. She expressed her gratitude to God for the gift of her girl-child by bathing my body and washing my hair.

"Cleanliness is next to godliness," she sometimes said, justifying her relentless scrubbing of elbows and knees. This common saying actually reflects a major pattern in ancient and contemporary religious practice. Cleaning up has long been one of the ways in which human beings prepare to enter the presence of God—a pattern we see, for example, in Leviticus, a biblical book that includes laws defining "clean" and "unclean" and mandating specific rituals of cleansing. In a sense, my own childhood baths were also rituals meant to prepare me for worship. They came on Saturday evenings, timed to prepare my body for Sunday services at our little country church, Mt. Pleasant Christian Methodist Episcopal (C.M.E.) Church. I was being made clean so that I could worship God in the sanctuary.

In spite of my pleasant memories of bath time, the distinction between "clean" and "unclean" has some disturbing overtones. My sense of well-being was often shattered when the congregation sang hymns that included quite different images of what it meant to be washed. I remember one with great clarity: "Nothing but the Blood." The images in this hymn troubled me deeply when I thought in the concrete way that children do, and they still cause cognitive dissonance when I listen with the abstract thinking of an adult.

> What can wash away my sin? Nothing but the blood of Jesus;
> What can make me whole again? Nothing but the blood of Jesus.
> Oh! precious is the flow that makes me white as snow;
> No other fount I know, Nothing but the blood of Jesus.

Where was the logic in this—that something red and gross could make anything white and pure? And did some of those singing with me actually desire to become "white as snow"? How does a young African American come to terms with the meaning of these words? The metaphor of blood making one white as snow never worked for me and many others. These words contradict affirmation of the black body as a gift from God.

The notion that black bodies are "unclean"—not just with dust from the playground but in a larger sense that defines black bodies as unholy—has a long history, and notions of black bodies becoming white through the uncleanness of blood are not new either. I'm glad my mother never tried to persuade me to embrace the theology of that song. What I did embrace was the care of my body by a beloved parent.

Later in life, I realized that my Saturday-night baths did connect to my parents' pledge before God and the congregation to nurture their baby girl in the love of Christ as a baptized Christian. In my denomination, the sacrament of baptism is extended to infants and children as well as adults. During the ritual act of sprinkling, pouring, or immersion, parents, guardians, godparents, aunts, uncles, and a host of caregivers pledge to keep the child close to the ministry of the church until she, by the grace of God, publicly accepts the gift of salvation and receives confirmation and full membership in the Church of Jesus Christ. The congregation also pledges to be a living example of Christ through the power of the Spirit and to love and teach the child. Every time I witness a baptism, I remember with thanksgiving my own baptism, even though the memory lives in my spirit rather than in my mind.

For those who remember baptism, water can bring comfort too deep for words. Kay Northcutt, a pastor and writer, tells of assisting her dying mother to bathe. "The water," Kay recalls, "sounded like baptism. Holy, quiet, small splashes." Water comforts in part because it brings the satisfaction of being physically clean, as my father seemed to feel after his last bath. But such washing also restores to relationship those who are marginalized, who are made "unclean" and separated from others because they are old and sick. As in baptism, God's grace is in the water and in the loving touch of others upon bodies created in God's image.

*Getting Dressed for Church, and for Life

When babies are baptized, some parents dress them in white heirloom dresses and bonnets trimmed with delicate embroidery. Baptismal garments, though varying in different Christian communities, express the new identity of becoming a member of the household of Christ. In Eastern Orthodoxy, a baptismal robe symbolizing light and the fullness of divine grace is worn by the newly baptized for eight days after the adult or child's baptism by immersion in a pool of water. This robe declares that the new Christian has "put on Christ" and is now clothed in his goodness and love. The apostle Paul wrote, "As many of you as were baptized into Christ have clothed yourself with Christ" (Gal. 3:27).

Clothing protects our naked bodies from exposure to heat, cold, and the gaze of others. Clothing can also reveal identity. Hip-hop break dancers adorn themselves in sagging jeans and oversized tee-shirts—clothing that allows freedom to tumble, spin upside down, or moonwalk across the floor. Punk rockers wear black denim pants, jackets decorated with metal studs, and spiked hair in green, black, purple, or any combination of colors. Sorority sisters or fraternity brothers boast shirts or jackets sporting Greek letters. And sometimes adornment goes right on the skin, in tattoos, body piercings, and body art.

Many religious communities have also placed great importance on clothing. Some have set their members apart by adopting clothing to identify their community and show their values, such as habits for monks and nuns or plain clothing for the Amish. In other traditions, "Sunday-go-to-meeting" clothes have expressed respect for the presence of God. Clothing helps to shape identity, all these groups have sensed.

In some African-American church traditions, adorning one's body for Sunday worship follows a strict cultural code. Women are instructed to wear modest long-sleeved dresses that are long enough to fall to or below the knees. Bright colors such as red or hot pink and, in some places, pants have been prohibited for women. My paternal grandmother, a church mother in the Baptist tradition, followed this practice to the letter. When her daughters or granddaughters came to visit, we were not allowed to wear pants at all, let alone to church.

Some African-American women have resisted such dress codes in creative ways, while others have rebelled and abandoned them. Those who do like to dress up often adorn their heads with hats or (for younger African-American women) creative hairstyles. "Sundays are a precious gift to hard-working women who have labored unceasingly through the workweek," notes the poet and novelist Maya Angelou. "And then Hallelujah, Hosanna! Sunday morning comes. If the woman is African American, she has some fancy hatboxes on a shelf in her closet. . . . She may try on each hat two or three times before she dresses, just to see which one goes with her most recent hairdo." Some black women do not feel fully dressed until they adorn their heads with a precious crown (hat). Some reject this notion—but almost all black women appreciate a stunning hat or hairdo. These hairdos are permed, natural, long or straight, and black, blonde, brown, or red, standing high above the head in artistic design or close to the skull like a cap.

How we dress and groom ourselves can be empowering, but it can also engender self-doubt and financial problems. Our desire to look good can lead us to allow media to dictate what we need to "be beautiful"—something few people can match. Peers influence our ideas of beauty as well, often in ways that make us feel doubtful and self-conscious. Many thus spend more on appearance than they can afford; the creation of elaborate hairdos is big business, and getting a new hairdo plus a manicure and pedicure can be expensive. Worrying too much about these things can result in hardship and heartbreak. We do best to remember Jesus' words: "And why do you worry about clothing? Consider the lilies of the field, how they grow; they neither toil nor spin, yet I tell you, even Solomon in all his glory was not clothed like one of these" (Matt. 6:28-29).

In my church and in many others, younger members are prompting the rest of us to become more easygoing about apparel. Not so long ago,

" How we dress and groom ourselves can be empowering, but it can also engender self-doubt and financial problems. "

some people said they didn't go to church because they couldn't afford to get their hair done or because they didn't like to get dressed up and feared they would be shamed if they wore what they had. Now I know more people who reject such thoughts and come to church just as they are, because they want to be among people who accept them without regard to how they dress. These influences can even encourage people in the church to control their consumer habits and to resist dressing to impress. People are reminded that we are created in God's image and clothed in Christ. What could be more beautiful?

*Rest and Recreation

Our bodies follow rhythms, as does all the created world. Our bodies need both recreation and rest if we are to maintain wholeness of mind, body, and spirit. For me, dancing is the most renewing form of recreation. I still enjoy dancing the Lindy Hop and the jitterbug moves I first learned from my dad at my eighth-grade formal, all dressed up in a hot-pink organza dress. Sometimes I'm brave enough to attempt hip-hop moves, just shy of break dancing. Dancing refreshes and relaxes me—and it brings together a community of people in the shared effort and pleasure of coordinated movement. I am most accountable to staying with the exercise my body needs when I exercise in the community of my jazz aerobic and salsa classes.

Rest—especially sleep—complements the recreation that comes through exertion. The proper amount of sleep heals wounds, helps with weight loss, maintains a healthy immune system, optimizes memory, and encourages emotional health. Few activities honor our bodies as richly as does sleep. Although sleep does not literally re-create our bodies, it does allow us to release our bodies into God's care. This too is part of what it means to live faithfully in and with the body God has provided each of us as tangible grace.

God's gift of tangible grace became real to me as I grew up under the doting gaze of my father, and it took on deeper meaning in the final hours of his life. What a wonderful blessing to cradle my father's legs in my arms, stroke his forehead, and bathe his body as he transitioned from life to death. What a marvelous gift to touch his warm dying body and yet not fear the cold finality of death. What an amazing gift to discover in my father's dying a renewed sense of what it means to sing with others in worship:

> For all the saints, who from their labors rest,
> who thee by faith before the world confessed,
> thy name, O Jesus, be forever blest.
> Alleluia, Alleluia!

It is God's intention that all children, whether young or grown or of ripe old age, should offer and receive such care, and in the end be given such rest.

Living a whole life attentively . . . together . . . in the real world . . . *for the good of all . . . in response to God

10* Knowing and Loving Our Neighbors of Other Faiths

Scott C. Alexander

At first, I couldn't get the images out of my head. I still can't. Angry faces with gaping mouths. Clenched fists. Women draped in black. Young men with beards as black as the women's clothing. American flags set ablaze in the street. And the sound—a chant in a language I had never heard of—expressing a sentiment I had never conceived: "*Marg bar Amrika!*"

TV news commentators told us it meant "Death to America!" They also told us why a group of university students in Tehran, Iran, had stormed the U.S. embassy there and taken the embassy personnel hostage, just weeks after the Iranian people had risen up against and ousted the U.S.-backed Iranian king and his cronies. "Experts" informed television viewers that the cause was a tidal wave of "religious fanaticism" that was sweeping through the Iranian body politic. When asked how this fanaticism could take hold in a society as modern and Westernized as late-twentieth-century Iran, some contended that these events represented the death rattle of traditional religion as Iran was wisely giving itself over to Western secular modernity. Both the revolution and the hostage crisis, they insisted, could be best understood as a function of what they perceived to be the dark essence of the people's religion, namely the "Shiite mentality."

This sounded to me a bit like the racist attempts to blame the Watts riot of 1965 on the "black mentality." Were there no important historical or socioeconomic factors at play in this major political upheaval in a major Middle Eastern nation state? I had a hunch that there was more to all this than met the eye of the television camera, but what did I know? It was November of 1979 and I was a freshman in college. Almost every night, my suitemates and I were huddled before the sorry excuse for a television in our sorry excuse for a living room, watching what I would one day learn was a sorry excuse for in-depth network news coverage of the Iranian Revolution and its central drama known simply as "the hostage crisis." This drama, destined to last more than a year, would indelibly etch negative images of Middle Easterners onto the psyche of most U.S. Americans and topple President Jimmy Carter's administration after one term.

About eight months later, I found myself in a very different place. Almost daily, I was visiting Boston's renowned Children's Hospital, where my girlfriend's younger sister was recovering from surgery to correct a chronic medical condition. Directly opposite her room was a quarantined room where only authorized medical staff and immediate family, properly gowned and gloved, were allowed to enter. On my second or third visit, I noticed a slightly chubby, dark-complexioned man of medium height sitting quietly with his head in his hands on a small bench under the windowsill at the end of the hallway. I'd like to think it was compassion that made me first sit next to him and introduce myself. Truth be told, it was probably boredom. "Hi, I'm Scott," I said as I extended my hand. He looked up at me with a face that had gone unshaven for a couple of days and smiled politely. "My name is Ahmad. I am pleased to meet you." That encounter initiated a three-week relationship that would literally set the course of my life over the next three decades. If someone had told me that back then, I would have said he or she was crazy.

Ahmad, in his late twenties, had come to Boston from Dhahran, Saudi Arabia, to accompany his seven-year-old brother for what his family and doctors back home hoped would be life-saving surgery to repair a severely ruptured intestinal tract. Now that the surgery was over, he was keeping vigil as his little brother fought the massive sepsis that had resulted from the rupture. Over long summer afternoons, Ahmad and I conversed about many things—from his brother's progress to Boston's muggy summer heat to Middle Eastern politics. With time, our conversations turned more personal. Ahmad diplomatically expressed surprise that my girlfriend's father would let her dress "in so very few clothes" (on most days, a halter-top and shorts, if I recall correctly). He expressed even more surprise that, though she was not my sister, she would go to and from the hospital with me and not her father. I had no explanation for these aspects of my own culture, to which I had barely given any thought. My new friend did not intend to put me on the spot; he just wanted to understand the strange culture

> " My new friend . . . wanted to understand the strange culture that now enveloped him, so different from his own. "

that now enveloped him, so different from his own. I asked him if he were married. He said he was not, but that one day he hoped to marry, "*in sha'a Allah*" ("God willing"). For the present, his responsibility was to care for his beloved brother.

Then something happened that gave me a chance to look into my new friend's soul. Whenever I visited the hospital cafeteria and suggested that he join me, he politely refused. Worried that he wasn't eating enough, I brought him a piece of fruit and some water, insisting he eat or drink something. He gently gestured me to sit beside him. He gave my knee a pat, bowed his head, and very softly said: "I will drink and eat after sunset, *in sha'a Allah*. It's Ramadan and I am fasting." He asked if I knew anything about Islam, and I mumbled something about fasting's being one of the "five pillars," along with testimony, prayer, almsgiving, and pilgrimage. His face lit up with a joy I had not yet seen there: "So you know something about my religion!"

After that, we spent hours talking about God, prayer, and the moral life. He asked me questions about my Christianity that I had never before asked myself. I had taken my faith very seriously ever since I palpably felt the call of Christ a few years earlier. Yet somehow I had never felt so spiritually alive in conversation as I did when I was talking to Ahmad. I asked him questions about Islam in order to learn more about this religion from the perspective of an actual believer rather than the mass media coverage of the hostage crisis. I also had discovered that Ahmad never seemed happier or more animated than when talking about his faith.

Over time I realized that as significant as the Iranian Revolution was in shaping my academic interest in Islam, the revolution that had the most profound impact on my life began quietly inside of me in the hallway of that hospital as I made a new friend. What I could not see then but do see clearly now is that Ahmad—whether conscious of it or not—was tutoring me (and perhaps I him) in knowing and loving my neighbor of another faith. What I had no way of knowing then but try to thank God for every day is that this practice—a practice we Roman Catholic Christians usually call "interreligious dialogue"—would become my life's ministry.

In simplest terms, knowing and loving our neighbors of other faiths, like the other practices in this book, is rooted in the practice of Christ Jesus himself. Specifically, it is the practice of crossing cultural boundaries in humility and grace, as Christ so often did. The Christian purpose for crossing these boundaries is to engender greater solidarity within the human family, and thus to realize more fully the reign of God on earth by means of sincere witness, increased mutual understanding, mutual respect for human dignity, and the exercise of a love that knows no limits.

Jesus forged relationships with a stunningly diverse array of people—especially those whom many of his fellow first-century Jews considered outcasts beyond redemption, such as tax collectors, Samaritans, and pagans—in order to share with them the unsurpassable gift of God's presence and healing love. As his disciples, we are called to do the same with one important caveat: we are not Christ. Although we may be witnesses to Christ and the healing power of God's love, we are not its source, and thus it is not ours to give. When we cross boundaries in Christ's name, be these boundaries religious or otherwise, we do not bear Christ as a gift for us to bestow on others. Rather, we bring our relationship with Christ into our other relationships. The Holy Spirit brings new, even unimagined possibilities for healing and transforming the human family in solidarity and love. Practiced in this Spirit, knowing and loving our neighbors of other faiths—especially in an age of increasing globalization, conflict, and unavoidable religious diversity—is interwoven with other practices explored in this book, especially seeking justice, living as community, and making peace.

Unfortunately, our Christian forebears have not always recognized the value or fully understood the scope and implications of this practice. Indeed, across the centuries many have labored under the erroneous impression that a Christian crosses any kind of cultural boundary mainly to destroy it or render it irrelevant in pursuit of a false "unity" imposed by domination. By doing so, they, and we, too often miss the sacred mystery at the heart of this practice.

*A Sacred Mystery

Meeting Ahmad helped me discern part of my vocation: I knew I wanted to major in comparative religion. My encounter with him made me more interested in studying my own religion and the religion of others than I ever had been before. Knowing Ahmad made me want to learn as much as I could about an Islam that had less to do with political upheaval and more to do with twenty-four-hour vigils at the bedside of a sick brother thousands of miles from home; an Islam that gave a man the strength and courage to abstain from all food and drink, including water, for nearly nineteen hours a day, for thirty days straight; an Islam that taught him to respect and befriend a stranger whose culture and beliefs could hardly be more different from his own. I was hungry for these insights and also for something more. I had encountered a sacred mystery that would take years for me to begin to fathom.

The sacred mystery at the heart of interreligious dialogue is this: in trying to understand and appreciate another's very different relationship with God, we somehow come to understand more deeply and cherish more dearly our own. This mystery unfolds not in the context of a competition over which religion is superior but in the context of humility. In the humility of dialogue we develop what the Lutheran bishop and biblical scholar Krister Stendahl called "holy envy." In recognizing life-giving elements in the faith of another that are not apparent or that have lain dormant in our own tradition, we come to yearn for a deeper relationship with God and others that sometimes leads in new, rich directions. For example, my friend and colleague Dan Spencer, who wrote the chapter on care for creation, says that he and other North American Christians were inspired to search their own tradition for sources of creation spirituality after experiencing "holy envy" for the deep respect accorded the sacredness of the natural world among practitioners of indigenous American religious traditions.

> **"In trying to understand and appreciate another's very different relationship with God, we somehow come to understand more deeply and cherish more dearly our own."**

In the humility of dialogue we also develop what Lee Yearley, a Western scholar of Chinese religions, calls the virtue of "spiritual regret." Sometimes, we come to recognize that certain elements of our various religious traditions are ultimately, at least as far as humans can see, incompatible with each other. Here, as persons of faith, we can do nothing other than stand firm, all the while recognizing that the Truth to which we are bound to give witness by our words and deeds is not something any of us can possess, much less use as a stick for beating those who believe differently than we. Those of us who are Christians can do this by remembering always that the Truth to which we give witness is not a set of propositions. This Truth is the person of Jesus Christ crucified and risen, the One who is constantly calling all humanity into a deeper relationship with God the Father, in the power of the Spirit.

*Jeremy, Rosa, and Bao

After a recent interreligious conference in Chicago, three Christian participants sat down to "dinner"—leftover pizza from a party two nights before and soft drinks. They were amazed at the variety of people they had met in just one day: a bunch of mainline Protestants and Roman Catholics; a handful of Evangelicals; two Mennonites; a Native American practitioner; three or four Mormons; a female rabbi and two members of her Reform congregation; six or seven Muslims (with all but one of the women wearing a head scarf); one Hindu; a Buddhist monk and a Buddhist nun; and a Jain.

All three of these friends had attended the conference because they wanted to commit themselves, as Christians, to knowing more fully their neighbors of other faiths. They wanted to enter the Christian practice of crossing cultural boundaries for the sake of the solidarity of the human family and the realization of the reign of God. Even so, each of them responded very differently to what they had encountered that day.

Jeremy came away feeling deeply disappointed and frustrated. Most of the discussion that day, with the exception of a lively but respectful exchange between the rabbi and one of the Muslim participants over the Israeli-Palestinian conflict, was not very "hard-hitting." He thought some of the speakers compromised or toned down their beliefs in order to present a more irenic face to their dialogue partners. He believed that such "timidity" and "compromise" demonstrated the weaknesses of interreligious dialogue.

Rosa believed Jeremy's concerns were valid. She had a strong sense that the integrity of interreligious dialogue could be undermined if parties consistently avoided difficult issues or felt pressured to soft-pedal their faith instead of freely offering sincere testimony to what they believe and practice. However, Rosa felt that what Jeremy was reading as timidity and compromise were actually forms of prudence and respect. Rosa reminded Jeremy that meaningful dialogue, like any other meaningful relationship, cannot be rushed. Without the requisite level of trust, Rosa argued, candor and the eagerness to tackle the "hard stuff" can very easily lead to debate, which is very unlike dialogue. Debate is a contest of ideas oriented toward

> **" Dialogue cultivates mutual understanding through attentive, receptive, and compassionate listening. "**

discovering truth. Dialogue cultivates mutual understanding through attentive, receptive, and compassionate listening—without winners or losers.

Bao listened to all of this quietly but with a growing sense of despair. Raised in a very religious home, he knew how hurt and angry his parents would be if he decided to leave their church. He believed *in* God; he just wasn't sure anymore exactly what he believed *about* God. Then, today alone, he had heard three intelligent and spiritual people talk about Jesus in three different ways. One described him as "God incarnate" and the "greatest act of divine love the world will ever know." Another said that "Jesus" was the name under which generations of his ancestors had suffered marginalization, persecution, and ultimately genocide. A third said that, for her, Jesus was a great prophet and teacher whom she respected but nothing more.

Somewhere deep inside himself Bao took refuge in the orthodoxy of his parents' beliefs. He had gone to the conference with Jeremy and Rosa because he wanted both to hold on to his Christian identity and to be open to the religious beliefs and practices of others. But he now felt a deeper ambiguity about the nature of his own Christian faith and an overwhelming confusion in the face of what struck him as a troubling cacophony of dissonant worldviews. When Rosa asked Bao what he thought about the conference, he shrugged his shoulders and answered, "There's a lot to think about, isn't there?"

*The Four Modes of Interreligious Dialogue

Jeremy, Rosa, and Bao can teach us several things about the practice of knowing and loving our neighbors of other faiths. First, even those who belong to the same tradition come to the practice from different perspectives. Second, no two people interpret the same words or set of events in the same way. Third, interreligious dialogue can be frustrating, slow-moving, or overwhelming, just as it can also be exhilaratingly transformative and enlightening. As with other Christian practices, the experience of these three individuals teaches us that *one size does not fit all.*

Bao was not ready for the day of dialogue that had such different but largely enriching effects on both Jeremy and Rosa. If the exchange of theological perspectives that shaped so much of this particular interreligious encounter were the only way of building relationships with people of other faiths, then Bao's reaction would suggest that, although it may be a practice that some Christians can and should take up, interreligious dialogue is not a practice for every Christian at every point in life. One could even argue that, because it's not a lifelong practice open to all Christians, it cannot be a practice integral to the Christian faith.

This, however, is not the case. Theological exchange is one indispensable *mode* of being in relationship with people of other faiths, but—thanks be to God—there are other modes of dialogue as well. Are any of them more accessible and democratic than the *dialogue of theological exchange?* According to Roman Catholic theology, at least three additional modes of dialogue are more important and accessible to a wider range of believers than the dialogue of theological exchange.

One of these modes is the *dialogue of social action,* in which Christians and people of other faiths act together for the benefit of the human family and the planet it inhabits. Bao, who may not be ready for a broad exchange of conflicting theological ideas, would eagerly work at the local interfaith food pantry, side-by-side and in solidarity with the other Christians and people of other faiths he met at the interreligious conference. Although he may be confused about certain aspects of Christology, he has never doubted the centrality to Christian discipleship of service to the poor. He would find great spiritual and intellectual nourishment talking with those companions about the values that impel them to work for greater social justice.

Bao might also greatly enjoy the *dialogue of spiritual experience.* Growing up, he said the rosary as part of a daily family ritual. Now that he is away at school, he's pretty much neglected the practice. He didn't give it much thought until he saw the Buddhist monk and one of the Muslim participants at the interreligious conference with what looked very much like rosary beads. When he asked the Buddhist nun about the beads, she smiled, said she used them for meditation, and then offered them to him as a gift. When he said he couldn't accept them, she again smiled and said, "Okay." Since then, Bao has thought he would like to talk to a Buddhist and a Muslim about his own experience praying the rosary and theirs with their own special beads. Bao would be a perfect candidate for a dialogue of spiritual experience in which any sincere practitioner can share the meaning and power of her spiritual practices and experiences with any other sincere practitioner.

The most important mode of dialogue is the *dialogue of everyday life*. In many ways, it is the framework in which all interreligious dialogue ideally takes place and the end toward which all practices of dialogue should lead. It is also the simplest and yet most difficult to define. Those who practice the dialogue of everyday life quite simply and literally try to know and love one another by striving "to live in an open and neighbourly spirit, sharing their joys and sorrows, their human problems and preoccupations," as an important Roman Catholic statement on dialogue puts it.

When a Jewish mom offers to watch the children of her Muslim neighbor while that mother takes her eldest to a doctor's appointment; when a Christian man, aware that his Hindu coworker does not eat meat, orders vegetarian fare for the upcoming office retreat; when the Buddhist family living down the street from Grandma visits her in the hospital and comes to the church for her funeral; when the local Islamic center offers space to the local Jewish community that just lost its synagogue to a fire; when a Muslim man far from home gently instructs an inquisitive Christian teenager who is clueless about Ramadan and is worried that he's not eating— all these are living examples of the dialogue of everyday life.

The dialogue of everyday life lies at the heart of any and all genuine efforts to develop good relationships with people of other faiths. This kind of profound dialogue has been at work in the lives of countless and nameless Christian individuals and communities throughout the ages—as well as in the lives of exemplary individuals like Francis of Assisi and the Reverend Dr. Martin Luther King Jr. and in the movements they inspired.

Even so, it has yet to emerge across the vast cultural and denominational spectrum of contemporary Christianity as an explicit and uncontested hallmark of Christian living.

*The Jericho Road

A Christian practice, by definition, meets a basic human need. Knowing and loving our neighbors of other faiths meets at least two. The first is the human need for dignity: every human being must come to recognize herself—and be recognized by others—as a beloved child of God, made in the image of the Creator. The second, distinct but closely related, is the need for reconciliation. Given the pervasive brokenness of our selves and our world, the healing that comes with reconciliation is essential to living out our basic dignity as human beings. We need to be reconciled with God through and in a loving communion with our fellow human beings and all the rest of creation.

Many stories in Christian sacred scripture speak of humankind's need for dignity and reconciliation. One well-known parable speaks especially powerfully and explicitly about how these needs are met through loving encounters with people of other faiths. "What must I do to inherit eternal life?" a legal scholar asks Jesus, testing to see if this charismatic preacher has what it takes to be a respected teacher of the divine law (Luke 10:25). Jesus answers that he must obey the two central commandments of the Torah—to love God unreservedly (Deut. 6:5) and to love one's neighbor as oneself (Lev. 19:18). But the scholar wants more. Like an ambitious journalist at a presidential press conference, the scholar seizes the opportunity to ask a follow-up question: "And who is my neighbor?" Jesus responds with a story that takes place on the hilly, rock-strewn road from Jerusalem to Jericho (Luke 10:30-35).

In first-century Palestine the Jericho road was as rough a setting, topographically and socially, as it is today. Imagine a narrow, winding version of an unpaved interstate highway, which many people travel on foot or on slow-moving pack animals. Imagine that this is the only artery connecting two important cities. Imagine all the types of people one might come across as fellow travelers—some of whom you might know, some who might know you, many who are complete strangers, and some you would never care to know in a million years. It's a place where fear and apprehension are the dominant ethos.

Jesus tells a story about a man—presumably Jewish—who was robbed, beaten, and left for dead on the Jericho road. A priest and a Levite, fellow children of Israel and members of the same covenant community as the victim, both have the opportunity to come to his aid. For some reason, most likely a superficial interpretation of the law and an equally superficial concern for their own ritual purity, this particular priest and this particular Levite avoid the victim by walking past him on the other side of the road. In contrast, a Samaritan—a religious pariah, whose group is absolutely despised by the victim's covenant community—is "moved with pity." Counterintuitively, especially for Jesus' largely Jewish audience, a consummate outsider cleanses the victim's wounds with his own precious resources, places the victim on his own mount, spends the night caring for the victim at an inn; and the next day, he provides the innkeeper with money for the victim's continued convalescence, promising to reimburse the innkeeper for any additional expenses when he returns.

After telling the story, Jesus turns the scholar's question back to him, asking, "Which of these three, do you think, was a 'neighbor' to the man who fell into the hands of the robbers?" If the scholar were to answer this question strictly in a demographic sense, he could reply, "the priest and the Levite," who were the victim's fellow Jews. In this answer the term "neighbor" carries with it no real moral obligations. The scholar, however, answers the deeper question: Which of these three *acted* like a neighbor? Which of these three actually obeyed the divine law of which the priest and Levite are supposed to be exemplars? The scholar responds, "The one who showed [the victim] mercy" (Luke 10:36-37).

Were this the end of the interaction between Jesus and the scholar of the law, the lesson might be to appreciate those neighbors who share one's own values, regardless of their political or religious identity. This scriptural passage then could serve as the basis for loving neighbors of other faiths whose values are most like our own. But the passage does not end here. To the one who asked, "Teacher, what must I do to inherit eternal life?" Jesus says, "Go and do likewise." In other words, Jesus instructs him not to ask, "Who qualifies as my neighbor?" or "Who is worthy of my compassion?"

> **"** Our world is filled with Jericho roads— places marked by violence and traversed by a stunning variety of people, including folk with sharp religious and political differences. **"**

but rather, "Whom am I obliged to treat like my neighbor?" and "How can I best love my neighbors, especially those least like myself?"

Our world is filled with Jericho roads—places marked by violence and traversed by a stunning variety of people, including folk with sharp religious and political differences. Like the Samaritan of the parable, we too encounter violence in the context of religious difference and wonder what we should do. Jesus' answer warns against making the mistake of the priest and Levite by indulging in a superficial understanding of our religious identity; such a superficial understanding can prevent us from living out the core values of our tradition. Instead, Christ calls us to dig deep into what it means to follow the way of the Cross. Following this way, we speak a resounding no to the violence and alienation we encounter in the human family. Further, we speak this no by entering into relationships of compassionate care and concern, especially with brothers and sisters whose religious ways seem strange and different from our own.

*The Witness of the Saints: Francis of Assisi

Francis of Assisi faithfully embodied many Christian practices, including living simply, doing justice, and caring for creation. Most people do not know that Francis also embodied—in his own way, and shaped by the circumstances of his own time—the practice of knowing and loving our neighbors of other faiths.

This story begins nearly eighty-five years before Francis was born, at the dawn of a particularly dark chapter in the history of the human family. In 1095, Pope Urban II preached the First Crusade to wrest the Holy Land from the hands of those he called "the Saracen infidels" (read Muslims) who, by that time, had ruled Jerusalem and its environs for well over four centuries. Historians have disputed what motivated the pope, but whatever the reason, the Crusades introduced a virulent heresy into Christian thinking and practice.

Ever since the time of Augustine, the church had understood that, even though acts of violence ran counter to the central teachings of the Gospel, there were times when violent confrontation with one's enemies could be morally justifiable and even imperative for a Christian society. (This understanding, known as just war theory, is discussed in depth in chapter 11 on peacemaking and nonviolence.) With the Crusades, however, came the theological proposition that war could be sanctifying and redemptive; if it were in the service of God, war could actually be "holy." The great Cistercian monk and mystic Bernard of Clairvaux, who in 1146 preached what would come to be known as the Second Crusade, had written some years earlier that when a knight kills an evildoer or a pagan (that is, a Muslim), "he is not the killer of a human being, but, if I may so put it, a killer of evil."

A century later, as the Crusades continued, Francis fiercely resisted the heresy of "holy war." The Christian response to Muslims and Islam should not be violent confrontation, he believed, but courageous evangelical witness. After two failed attempts to journey to Muslim lands in order to preach the gospel, Francis finally succeeded in 1219. According to Franciscan lore, he journeyed to the port of Acre with Italian reinforcements for the Fifth Crusade and then made his way, with a small company of fellow friars, to the Crusaders' camp in the Nile delta. Here Francis questioned the legitimacy of the Crusades in his preaching to the troops. After spending several days there, he finally crossed enemy lines with one other friar and entered the camp of the Muslim Sultan Malik al-Kamil.

There are many versions of what transpired once Francis reached the court of the sultan. The truth is, we don't know what exactly happened. We do know that they parted amicably and that Francis returned, unharmed. One Christian source records that the two parted with the sultan saying,

"Pray for me that God may deign to reveal to me the law and faith which is more pleasing to Him." A gesture of politeness? Most likely. But perhaps also an expression of the two men's mutual recognition of the integrity of each other's faith and relationship with the living God, in spite of the significant differences that divided them. In any case, by virtue of their meeting, both Francis and Sultan Malik al-Kamil bore *countercultural witness*. They witnessed against the dominant ethos of Christian-Muslim violence, and they witnessed to the heart of their respective traditions' foundational teachings of peace and of the inherent dignity of all God's creatures, especially human beings. The story of Francis and the sultan demonstrates that God raises up saints as "good Samaritans" who encourage and inspire us to travel today's Jericho roads as Christ's disciples.

*Dialogue and Evangelization

When I was discerning my vocation and preparing for it through many years of schooling, I never imagined I could land a teaching job at a Catholic institution that would value both my baptismal commitment to Christ and his church *and* my longstanding intellectual and spiritual love affair with Islam and Muslim peoples. But I have found a professional and spiritual home at the Catholic Theological Union in Chicago. Here the practice of knowing and loving our neighbors of other faiths—or interreligious dialogue—is considered an essential part of the evangelizing mission Christ fulfilled and then entrusted to the church. In fact, in my eight years at CTU, I have come to believe that *interreligious dialogue is the only truly workable framework for evangelization—for living the gospel and giving witness to Christ—in a religiously plural society and an increasingly globalized world.* It is critical, however, that my Christian sisters and brothers not misunderstand me when I use this language. Building relationships with people of other faiths can never be legitimately used as a strategy for Christian or any other kind of proselytism. It absolutely cannot. Evangelization does not mean proselytism. In fact, these two are subversive to each other.

The difference between *proselytism* and *evangelization* is that between conquest and partnership, between denigration and respect, between genocide and life together. It's the difference between a legacy of sin in God's name (manifest in things like the Crusades and European colonial decimation of native peoples and their cultures in the Western hemisphere) and love in God's Spirit (manifest in the work of countless missionaries who truly loved and gave their lives for the people they genuinely sought to serve). It's the difference between, on one hand, seeing oneself as the agent of "conversion" and the other as its object, and, on the other hand, understanding that the Holy Spirit is the true agent of transformative, sanctifying, and redeeming grace, and that all of humanity, indeed all of creation, is the permanent object of this grace.

Not too long ago I was on an airplane bound for a largely non-Christian country. A few rows behind me sat a group of young Christian missionaries—most in their early twenties and traveling outside of the United States for the first time. Even through my minimally adjustable seatback, I sensed their exuberance over their adventure; they were going "to bring people to Christ." I chatted with a few of them and asked if they knew anything about the culture and religion of the people to whom they would be witnessing. They were honest: they knew nothing. All they really needed to know, one woman explained, was that they would meet "good people with bad ideas." Their mission, she said, was to show them just how "bad" their ideas were, and to offer them the good news of Christ instead.

Whether by coincidence or providence, this group and I met again on the flight back to the U.S. The young people were visibly worn, tired, and without a trace of the infectious exuberance they had exhibited just five weeks earlier. They spoke soberly about what a "difficult time" they had had. They did not realize that what they had wanted so desperately to dismiss as a people's "bad ideas" was actually a venerable and rich culture and religion that grounded this people's dignity as human beings. As a result, they left with noticeably hardened hearts. They were headed home with stories of obstinacy and confrontation that would cover the real truth: as victims of their own arrogance born of theological and cultural ignorance, they squandered countless opportunities for dialogue. They missed every chance God gave them to build relationships of mutual respect and trust—relationships in which both missionaries and hosts could have been transformed by sharing their respective faiths with one another in sincerity, humility, and love.

I would say their mission failed because it lacked the spirit of dialogue. Dialogue is grounded in uncompromising respect for the dignity of others—fellow Christians, people of other faiths, and people of no faith. It is a practice of love that admits no attempts to coerce, dominate, or take advantage of the weakness of others. In the words of a 1984 Roman Catholic statement, dialogue "is thus the norm and necessary manner of every form of Christian mission, as well as of every aspect of it, whether one speaks of simple presence and witness, service, or direct proclamation. Any sense of mission not permeated by such a dialogical spirit would go against the demands of true humanity and against the teachings of the Gospel."

*Some Words of Caution

The Jericho road is filled with pitfalls. One is illustrated by the young missionaries' failure to realize that true evangelization first and foremost involves our own transformation. Being in dialogue with people of other faiths might have deepened their own faith, revealing that evangelization is not the work of human beings but of the Holy Spirit. We can neither take credit when our efforts "bear fruit" nor despair when they "go awry." Our role is to dedicate ourselves to loving our neighbors, not to causing some change in them that we deem to be the goal.

The practice of knowing and loving our neighbors of other faiths can also lead to difficult encounters with other Christians. Amidst the brokenness of our selves and our world, this one faith has splintered into many manifestations, across differing denominations and various leanings within each denomination. As we build relationships with people of other faiths, we should try also to sustain a dialogue of hope and reconciliation among different communities of Christ's fractured body. As a practice of our faith we need to exercise dialogue with every bit as much strength *ecumenically* and *intra*religiously as we do *inter*religiously. Just as we learn not to demonize those of other faiths, we must be careful not to demonize sisters and brothers in Christ who do not, for one reason or another, share our vision of friendship across boundaries of faith. Instead we are called to know, understand, and love them more fully, trusting the Spirit is at work transforming and healing the whole body of Christ.

A final danger arises when we begin to think that because words like *love, relationship,* and *dialogue* sound pleasant, they refer to work that is easy and safe. It is neither. As both history and personal experience demonstrate, would-be peacemakers and bridge-builders often threaten the status quo—and the status quo rarely, if ever, changes without a fight.

My own relatively short career in interreligious dialogue includes a painful experience that took me by surprise. In doing what I thought was the right thing in relation to one set of dialogue partners, I deeply offended and hurt another set of dialogue partners; the two are currently locked in conflict with each other. During this difficult time, I felt what it was like to be maligned as an outcast. Hate mail arrived every day, and nightmares disturbed my sleep every night; and even now, several years later, some people still exclude me from personal and professional gatherings. The experience made me desperately aware of my own sinfulness and weakness, and I considered giving up my ministry. At the advice of a spiritual director, however, I took my doubts and anxieties to the foot of the Cross. There I heard Christ saying three things to me. The first was, "Yes, I did call you to this work." The second was, "No, I never said it would be easy." His third word to me, as I envisioned him hanging on that tree, was: "And I *never* said you would not get hurt."

*That We May Have Life and Have It Abundantly

For Christians, the mystery of coming to know God by entering into right relationship with our fellow human beings and with the rest of creation lies at the heart of our faith. When we confess that the one God is a Trinity of divine persons in relationship, we are expressing this same mystery. Through our baptism into Christ's death and Christ's life of radical love for God and neighbor, we have become reconciled as adopted daughters and sons to the One whom Jesus called "Father." In and through the only-begotten Son we are invited into an ever-deepening communion with the Father by entering into relationships of reconciliation and love, not only with our sisters and brothers in Christ but with all humanity. This includes, in a very special sense, those who relate to God in ways that are very different from our own, but in whom we can see and marvel at the work of the Holy Spirit which "blows where it chooses" without our knowing "where it comes from or where it goes" (John 3:8).

When Christians trust that we are held in this relationship with the Triune God, we become free to embrace the practice of knowing and loving

> **"** Although I am not a very good Christian, I know that in and through my encounter with the Spirit in the holy practice of knowing and loving my neighbors of other faiths, I am a much better. Christian than I would have been otherwise. **"**

our neighbors of other faiths as part of our uncompromising commitment to Christ. We do not stray into relativism, which supposes that truth does not matter, and we do not adopt absolutism, which makes an idol of a single truth known only to a few. Instead, we experience a more profound humility before the triune God who, we discover, is revealed in ever new ways and in constantly surprising places—including the lives of people of other faiths.

My Muslim friends—through the distinct goodness and holiness of their devotion to *the Merciful, the Compassionate, the Sustainer of the Universe*—have taught me about my own relationship with God and what God expects of me. Although I am not a very good Christian, I know that in and through my encounter with the Spirit in the holy practice of knowing and loving my neighbors of other faiths, I am a much better Christian than I would have been otherwise.

Only when we genuinely desire to understand the ways in which God lives in the hearts, minds, and circumstances of our sisters and brothers of other faiths can we begin to act as true and effective ambassadors for Christ. Without such a desire, we cannot pretend that we wish to love them as Christ did: by sharing both their suffering and their joy. In the dialogue made possible by this desire, however, we may begin to work together against all the forces—be they greed or deprivation, pride or fear, anger or indifference—that prevent the entire human family from having the life won for us by the great Shepherd of the sheep, and having it abundantly.

11 * Peacemaking and Nonviolence

Mary Emily Briehl Duba

One dripping cup of clover honey, one-half cup of extra virgin olive oil, and water, warmed like a child's bath: my sister whisked these together and poured the warm, sticky mixture into a bowl filled with whole wheat flour and yeast, adding a sprinkling of salt. When we were in high school, my sister and I often shared the task of baking communion bread for Sunday Eucharist. Baking it this time, however, something was different.

For six weeks, members of our congregation had met on Wednesday evenings to study the practice of peacemaking. We learned to name the sources of violence within and around us, to confess our failure to live fully into God's reign of peace, and to hear more clearly God's promise to accompany us in the radical work of nonviolence. After the culminating session, we held a worship service in which those who felt so called stood before the community to take a vow of nonviolence. Almost half the congregation took the vow that evening, including my sister and me. We spoke the vow together, knowing that we could not live out such an audacious promise alone: "Recognizing the violence in my own heart, yet trusting in the goodness and mercy of God, I vow for one year to practice the nonviolence of Jesus. . . ." We each symbolically sealed our vow by sprinkling a bit of yeast into a wide-rimmed bowl of flour. The reign of God, Jesus told his disciples, is like yeast that a woman mixed into enough flour for dozens of loaves of bread. Just a little yeast, he reminds us, gives life and leaven to the whole batch (see Matt. 13:33).

Taking a vow of nonviolence, adding our yeast, was an act of hope. We knew that some days anger would seize our hearts and our words would harm others rather than heal. We knew that our lives are tangled up in webs of violence bigger than ourselves and that no struggle against these forces would ever overcome them completely. But greater than these truths was our trust in Jesus' word: the reign of God in and among us, small as it may seem in a violent world, will give life that is enough and more.

A Vow of Nonviolence

Before God the Creator and the Sanctifying Spirit, I vow to carry out in my life the love and example of Jesus

- by persevering in nonviolence of tongue and heart through an openness to personal conversion;
- by continually working to create just relationships in the world, my community, and my personal life;
- by striving for peace within myself and seeking to be a peacemaker in my daily life through prayer and acts of forgiveness and reconciliation;
- by refusing to participate in acts of violence or to retaliate in the face of provocation, and by seeking creative responses to conflict;
- by living conscientiously and simply so that I do not deprive others of the means to live or harm the earth;
- by actively resisting the evils of oppressive structures and the causes of war;
- and by embracing the redemptive suffering of Jesus and believing in the transforming power of the cross.

After the service, my sister and I carried the bowl of yeasty wheat carefully through the wet spring snow, sensing it already bore a kind of sacrament. On Sunday, we brought it back to the congregation as bread, where it was blessed and broken and shared. Leavened with our promises, signs of God's new creation already taking shape in and around us, we tasted the truth: This is the Body of Christ.

*The Beginning of Peace

In response to the horrific violence of World War II, Albert Camus wrote, "Hope remains only in the most difficult task of all: to reconsider everything from the ground up, so as to shape a living society inside a dying society." A secular French philosopher, Camus nonetheless articulates for me the meaning of the Incarnation: Jesus is God reconsidering everything from the ground up. Seeing our world of violence, God reconsidered the whole creation. Choosing not to act with wrath or terror, God imagined a way of making peace with humankind. God entered the dying world from the ground up as the new *Adam*—a being of the earth—the firstborn of a new creation. God entered human life to bring us the yeasty presence of the reign of peace, to be life and leaven so that the whole earth might rise.

The Incarnation—God dwelling among us in Jesus—is God's supreme and subversive act of peacemaking. Into a world that looks to military might to secure the peace and save the people, into a region of the Middle East occupied by the Roman army, God entered human life as a dependent, vulnerable infant. This confounded the ancient expectation that God would send a warrior-king and that Israel's salvation would take the form of military victory over its enemies. God subverted the occupying powers with the weakness of a baby.

> " God entered human life to bring us the yeasty presence of the reign of peace, to be life and leaven so that the whole earth might rise. "

For Christians, peacemaking begins with the body of Christ, as God invites us to join the work already begun in Jesus (Eph. 2:14-16). In him, love transforms enemies into friends; the poor, the meek, and those who suffer are blessed with abundance; violence is exposed as too weak to bring peace; peacemakers are called children of God. When we enter this work, our assumptions about the world, our knowledge of ourselves, and our sense of the unfolding future begin to shift. As imitators of an incarnate God, we use our bodies, minds, and imaginations to resist all that causes and perpetuates violence, and to cultivate all that invites and sustains peace.

*The Great All-Is-Well

Think of a time when everything felt *right*. Maybe you were home with your family for the first time in a while. Maybe you got accepted for a job, a college, or a graduate program, and suddenly everything started falling into place. Maybe it was a first date or the freedom of a newly recovered singlehood. For me it was a backpacking trip with my husband of three weeks through the Cascade Mountains where I had grown up. After the joyful pandemonium of our wedding and the disarray that precedes a move across the country, four days of hiking through subalpine forests felt like a wide-armed homecoming and a true sabbath.

As powerful as such experiences of "rightness" may be, they are but an ephemeral foretaste of God's shalom, the great All-Is-Well. Shalom is peace lived in community, rooted in justice, and inclusive of all. It is the peace that God desires for us. When shalom reigns, everyone has access to the abundance of life. This includes freedom, the dignity of work, health, and right relationships with the earth, God, and one another. Shalom is not simply a happy life; shalom has room for grief. I have known no peace greater than that of my grandfather's last breath. God intends this all-embracing peace for the whole creation—children, adults, animals, the earth itself—not just for those with the means to establish security for themselves. We can't experience shalom independently of our neighbors or our enemies. No form of violence, from derogatory jokes to preemptive wars, will bring shalom, for the fleeting laughter or security it may bring belongs to some at the expense of others. Peace is not shalom if its means violate life.

Since peace is more than a cease-fire, peacemaking is more than disarmament. Since peace is lived in community and practiced over time, peacemaking cannot be done in isolation or accomplished in a single act. Since peace requires justice, peacemaking is more than a feeling, more than a starry night and songs around the campfire. Most importantly, peacemaking is not only the work of select people called to vocations of international relations, counseling, or conflict resolution. As imitators of Christ—whom Father John Dear has called "the revolutionary face of the God of nonviolence"—we are all called to be peacemakers.

*The Subversive Imagination

If you can envision what shalom might look like in the world today, then you're already using the best tool for the practice of peacemaking: imagination. *Imagination*, as I am using it here, is the capacity to envision a future unlike the present and a present different than it is. Imagination is subversive when the future it envisions challenges the unjust and violent realities of the present. Envisioning such a future prepares us to live into it in concrete ways.

Unlike fantasy or utopian dreaming, imagination requires that we honestly face hard realities. But instead of succumbing to them as though they were inevitable, we imagine a way beyond them and begin to take steps toward a new future. Subversive imagination gave my congregation, my sister, and me courage to admit our own propensity for violence, to face the violent reality of the world, and—trusting in God's goodness and mercy—to commit ourselves to nonviolence. Peacemakers wear God's gifts of mercy and freedom like corrective lenses that allow us to see the world more truly and clearly. These lenses are not rose-tinted, magnifying, or distorting. They bring into focus the world as it is: brimming with possibilities for peace that are otherwise blurred by sin. This new vision undermines the authority of those who tell us to fear our neighbors, our enemies, and even our own motivations for peacemaking. Through the lens of the child Jesus, who threatened the power of King Herod, we see that shalom overwhelms violence, and mercy confounds revenge.

On the night of October 1, 1943, the subversive imagination of the Danish people saved the lives of more than seven thousand Jews. Two days prior, Georg Duckwitz, a German who worked closely with Denmark ·

in the shipping industry, had learned that Nazis were planning to round up and deport Denmark's Jews to concentration camps. Moral outrage gripped his conscience. He leaked the information quickly, and the news spread so rapidly that by the next day nearly the entire nation knew. Recognizing the impracticality of mounting violent resistance to the Nazis, the Danes devised a creative, nonviolent plan of action.

That night, when Nazi troops broke into their homes, the Jews were gone. Of the roughly eight thousand Jews living in Denmark, the Nazis found less than three hundred. The rest had found sanctuary in their

> **Peacemakers wear God's gifts of mercy and freedom like corrective lenses that allow us to see the world more truly and clearly.**

neighbors' homes and summer cottages, in hospitals, university dorms, and churches; even complete strangers walked up to Jews on the street offering keys to their apartments. However, the Jews could not stay safely hidden for long. And so Danes and Swedes sent fishing boats back and forth across the Sound between them for a month, bringing the Jews to a lasting refuge in Sweden. When Germany surrendered in the spring of 1945, the refugees began a steady migration home. Upon arrival, most found that while they had been away, neighbors had cared for their homes and gardens in anticipation of their return. The Danes disabled imminent violence with their collective imagination. Wearing the lenses of love, the Danes did not see the Jewish people as the Nazis did, but as citizens of the same country, children of the same God.

We share this vision any time we become allies to marginalized groups and individuals. Offering sanctuary and services to illegal immigrants, joining a queer-rights group or a church that openly affirms all sexual identities, and working for restorative justice for those in prison are all acts of peacemaking. We cast strangers as enemies when we condemn whole countries as "evil," when we teach that homosexuality is the ruin of marriage and family, and when we circumvent "bad" neighborhoods as we drive through town. A subversive imagination sees an alternative vision: strangers, enemies, and people of other faiths becoming our friends.

The Old Testament prophets had this kind of imagination. Rarely popular in their hometowns, they challenged the status quo and offered alternative visions. Isaiah envisioned a "peaceable kingdom," in which the vulnerable are protected by their former enemies and no one has cause to fear (Isa. 11:6-9). Micah spoke of a time when the common battle cry— "Prepare for war! Beat your plows into swords and your pruning hooks into spears!"—would be reversed and nations would beat their weapons into tools for an abundant harvest (Mic. 4:3-4). Joel saw God's peace restoring earth's bounty and beauty: "In that day the mountains shall drip sweet wine, the hills shall flow with milk, and all the stream beds of Judah shall flow with water" (Joel 3:18). The prophets help us to see the world around us and to ask critical and creative questions about how to practice peacemaking in embodied, from-the-ground-up ways.

*When There Is No Peace

A few months before our college graduation, my best friend and I had a terrible falling out. Though a believer in the power of reconciliation, I did not know what to do with the pain and anger seething inside of me. Never before had I felt such a profound inability to forgive, or that terrible hatred that eats you from the inside, leaving you hollow and hopeless. My campus minister reminded me of Thomas Merton's wise comment that the desire to please God does in fact please God. When I could not find in myself even the desire to forgive, she suggested that I try praying for this desire. I could not do even that. Instead, I took as many steps back from forgiveness as I could, praying, "God, give me the desire to desire to pray to you for the desire to desire to forgive."

Then my friend Mary gave me an incredible gift: freedom from the obligation to make peace. She proposed that I take one whole year of grace time, time in which I wasn't allowed to even think about reconciliation. I didn't have to pray for him or for the desire to forgive—she would do that for me. When that year was up, Mary gave me a second year in which to begin remembering the humanity of my friend—to tell stories about adventures we'd shared, to put pictures of our escapades into photograph albums, to reconnect with mutual friends from whom I had distanced myself as well. Very slowly, I began to realize that over the course of those years, Mary had not been helping me to avoid the hard work of peacemaking. She had been disarming my heart. She had been living as community with me, reminding me that we never do the difficult work of peacemaking alone.

Jesus teaches his disciples, "Don't react violently against the one who is evil." This word necessitates that we disarm our own hearts before confronting someone with whom we have a conflict, no matter how long that process takes. Allowance for periods of grief and anger applies not only to instances of interpersonal conflict but to community-wide and international conflict as well. Shalom—the Great All-Is-Well—has room for grief and anger because it is not a state of perfection but of diligent communal affirmation of each and every member's humanity. What shalom cannot accept is peace declared when there is no peace.

*Disturbing the Peace: Nonviolent, Active Resistance to Violence

Jeremiah, one of the Hebrew scriptures' toughest social critics, decried the false prophets, saying, "They have treated the wound of my people carelessly, saying, 'Peace, peace,' when there is no peace" (Jer. 8:11). He critiqued professional prophets hired by the king to tell him what he wanted to hear. When Jeremiah put his inconvenient truths in writing for all to read, King Jehoiakim burned his words, scroll by scroll. Jeremiah knew, as all peacemakers must, that disturbing the so-called peace of the status quo is the first task of peacemaking. Therefore, in an act of nonviolent defiance of the king, he instructed his scribe Baruch to transcribe the whole manuscript again (Jer. 36:27-32).

Truth telling is central to each of the many forms of nonviolent, active resistance. These forms can include everything from public protests, community boycotts, and civil disobedience, to parenting, art, and scholarship. Each of these actions, done with honesty for the sake of peace, can expose the falsified peace that masks injustice or violence. The form of nonviolent resistance chosen by peacemakers depends on the situation they are confronting, the means available to them, and the effect they seek.

> **"** They have treated the wound of my people carelessly, saying 'Peace, peace,' when there is no peace.—Jeremiah 8:11 **"**

The civil rights movement used boycotts to make visible the economic and civic power of an oppressed people. War-tax resisters withhold all or part of their taxes as a form of civil disobedience, directing the money withheld to organizations that work for peace. Artists and authors give shape to color and clay, words and rhythms, enabling hard truths to slip past our rational defenses and into our hearts.

Exercising our subversive imaginations, we ask, *What would happen if Christians devoted the same discipline and self-sacrifice to nonviolent peacemaking that armies devote to war?* When Christian Peacemaker Teams (CPT) reflect on this question, they hear a call to literally "get in the way" of violence. They use their loving and persistent presence in militarized areas to deter violence and, when it does occur, to document it as eyewitnesses. The Nonviolent Peaceforce has an equally audacious mission: training civilians from around the world to enter areas of conflict at the invitation of struggling local peacemakers and human rights workers. By accompanying local groups in their daily work and monitoring adherence to cease-fire agreements, the Peaceforce stabilizes volatile regions and empowers local action. Such nonviolent direct action, notes Walter Wink, a scholar of Christian peacemaking, promises our adversaries that we will lay down our own lives rather than commit violence against them.

With this same promise, Jesus practiced nonviolent, active resistance in his public life and teachings. He disobeyed both the laws of civil society and religious purity codes by breaking bread with outcasts, touching the "untouchables," speaking with women and children, and keeping company with the poor. Jesus upset social standards of rank and association. He committed civil disobedience by healing on the sabbath, thereby exposing the way people were misusing the sabbath law to keep the infirm afflicted, the poor hungry, and the widowed powerless. Because his small, local deeds undercut the fundamental religious and social structures of his day, they threatened the whole system.

Jesus also taught his followers ways of responding to violence or injustice without either violent retaliation or submission. He taught them creative ways to convert situations of oppression into opportunities to preserve the humanity of both the oppressed and the oppressor. In a society where Roman soldiers could order conquered people to carry their packs for one mile, Jesus instructed his followers to volunteer to carry them for two miles. Doing so preserved their agency in the situation. When they were demeaned by a backhanded slap across the face, Jesus told them to offer their other cheek as well. Because the left cheek cannot be struck backhanded in a right-handed society, this peaceful confrontation would force the aggressor either to back down or to lose status by fighting the person as an equal.

Perhaps you have been on the receiving end of discrimination. Perhaps you have been the victim of economic or social power plays. Perhaps you have felt "backhanded"—treated by others as if you were a person of lesser worth or lower status. Creative interpretations of Jesus' teachings may serve you and your communities well.

We all, however, must consider the ways in which we play the role of oppressor, whether wittingly, carelessly, or by our participation in unjust social structures. To build a peace rooted in justice, we must recognize our privilege and learn to use it in ways that do not perpetuate injustice but counter it. Our society systematically keeps some people powerful and others powerless by perpetuating the myth that those with power have earned their position or deserve it more than others. Identifying the ways such factors as race, class, sexual orientation, and gender contribute to privileged status is the first step toward actively resisting our own capacity to use that privilege unjustly.

Active, nonviolent resistance is the work of every peacemaker. Each of us has different gifts to bring to this work, however. For every person who commits an act of civil disobedience, a whole community of peacemakers offers related gifts in support. Some help the person discern whether or not God is calling him or her to this act. Some accompany the person, in order to bear witness to the act. Some visit the imprisoned one in jail; others care for his or her home or children; while still others defend him or her in court, write articles to publicize the issue, and remember him or her in prayer. Each role is necessary, and none is more important than another.

No matter what form nonviolent action takes, its goal is transformation. Our hope is not to defeat an opponent but to transform the fear and hatred that lead to violence into love and openness to the other. Even as we work for the transformation of volatile situations, we must be open to having our own hearts and minds challenged or changed. The greatest danger in peacemaking is that we will cease to love our enemies, to desire life and wholeness for them, and to long for transformation—theirs and our own. Knowing this, many Christian peacemakers gather regularly for confession, prayer, and discernment. These acts are elements in congregational worship every week.

*Conscience

Knowing how to respond faithfully in violent situations is hard. Sometimes we fail even to notice violence—racial slurs in the newspaper, sickening movie scenes that have become run-of-the-mill entertainment, conflicts erupting in countries we've barely heard of. Discerning an appropriate response begins when we listen to our conscience. The phenomenon of conscience has fascinated human beings for centuries, though no one can quite agree on what it is or how it works. The speeches of Dr. Martin Luther King Jr. call upon "the conscience of this nation," suggesting a communal element of conscience. Saturday morning cartoons, on the other hand, interpret conscience as an individual phenomenon, picturing it as a miniature harp-toting angel perched on the shoulder of a befuddled Daffy Duck. Many church bodies have claimed that conscience is the voice of God welling up from within us, or the law of God written on our hearts. The Roman Catholic Church offered a description of conscience in 1966: "In the depths of his conscience, man detects a law which he does not impose upon himself, but which holds him to obedience." These depictions share a common theme: confidence in the ability of conscience to lead you to act rightly.

Dietrich Bonhoeffer, a theologian and peacemaker in Nazi Germany, took a radically different position. Because of sin, he argued, the human person has no infallible core, no pure and perfect place within, where God's laws remain unadulterated. In fact, what we take to be the voice of conscience may be our self-interest in disguise. Bonhoeffer worked out these ideas on scraps of paper in his jail cell as he watched the firebombing of Berlin from a small window. He was imprisoned for having made one of the hardest decisions of his life: whether to override his conscience (which told him that killing is wrong) in order to assassinate Hitler and potentially save the lives of millions of innocents. He concluded that since "Jesus took the guilt of all human beings upon himself, everyone who acts responsibly becomes guilty." Yes, killing is wrong, but sometimes, Bonhoeffer believed, God calls us to sacrifice our own moral purity for the sake of others.

Reflect on your own understanding of conscience. It will shape when and why you get involved in potentially volatile situations, how you deliberate your role in that situation, and how you explain your motivation to those who ask. As important as your understanding and decisions are, however, peacemaking is not finally about choosing rightly. It is about living into the reality that God has chosen us. We are peacemakers because we are recipients of the same Spirit the resurrected Christ breathed into his disciples on the first Easter, when he sent them into the world as emissaries of peace and reconciliation (John 20:19-23).

Since the time of Christ, Christians have struggled to know how to live as recipients of that Spirit. In these next few sections, we will explore two ways of interpreting peacemaking that have developed in the church over the years: pacifism and just war. As you read, consider which interpretation of this practice sits best with you. Reflect on your preconceptions of the words pacifism, just war, and conscientious objection. Do not be afraid to reconsider from the ground up the value or problems inherent to each.

*The Nonviolent Church

Had you been a member of the early church, your first act as a newly baptized person would have been to lay down your weapons. "From the end of the New Testament period down to [the decade] 170–180 we have no evidence of any Christians in the army," wrote Roland Bainton, a church historian. For them it was a matter of keeping the first commandment: "I am the LORD your God . . . ; you shall have no other gods before me" (Exod. 20:2-3). Confessing Jesus as Lord meant that nothing else and no one else could rule their lives: not the king, not his likeness cast in gold, not the occupying military. Submitting to fear, looking to weapons to save them, and obeying the mandates of a soldier's life amounted to idolatry.

Almost two hundred years after the birth of Christ, the theologian Tertullian taught that Christians ought to refuse military service, since Jesus had "disarmed" the whole church when he told Peter to put his sword back in its sheath (John 18:10-11). Origen, another early Christian teacher, wrote that the government could not require Christians to fight in battle but that Christians are called to "put on the whole armor of God" (Eph. 6:11) and to form a special army, one that prays for peace. It would be anachronistic to describe the early church as "pacifist," but the teachings of Jesus to love the enemy, to resist not evil with evil, and to pray for persecutors were indispensable to the Christian life.

As followers of Christ in this century, we too must contend with false gods. We make violence a false god when we put our ultimate trust in it to save us. This happens most often in times of great fear. Fear, though a good and natural response to danger, makes us vulnerable to the manipulations of those who seek power over us. Corporations can use our legitimate fears to persuade us to purchase their products. Politicians can use our legitimate fears to persuade us to relinquish our rights and to spend

❝ The alternative to fear is not bravery but hope. ❞

tax dollars on weaponry rather than on nonviolent peacemaking strategies that history has proven effective. The alternative to fear is not bravery but hope. The angel Gabriel appeared to Mary, saying, "Do not be afraid." He then gave Mary reason to hope, telling her that she bore in her womb God's peace given to transform the world (see Luke 1:26-38). We bear witness to this same hope when we renounce the false gods of fear and violence.

*Onward Christian Soldiers

The nonviolent church of Christ, initially a marginalized sect of the poor, grew during the first and second centuries, a time of relative peace and stability. Missionaries traveled the roads the Romans had built to spread the gospel throughout the empire. When war broke out on the empire's perimeters, Christians began to wonder about their proper role in maintaining Rome's security, and by 200 CE they were joining the military in greater numbers. Over the next two hundred years, the Roman Empire saw its first Christian emperor (Constantine), the declaration of Christianity as the official state religion, and a dramatic shift to an all-Christian army.

Recognizing the disconnect between the church's peaceful beginnings and its warring present, church fathers Ambrose and Augustine developed an ethical method for discerning when war is justified. Just war theory, as this still-evolving approach is known, operates on "the presumption which binds all Christians: we should do no harm to our neighbors; how we treat our enemy is the key test of whether we love our neighbor; and the possibility of taking even one human life is a prospect we should consider in fear and trembling." In short, espousing just war theory means viewing war and violence as an evil, but accepting that under certain stringent conditions, it may be necessary to take the guilt of that evil upon ourselves. The conditions for just war are intentionally strict and not meant to be used to justify a war when the decision to wage it has already been made. Some scholars propose that Augustine meant to describe an impossible scenario.

Jus ad Bellum

1. Just cause
2. Just authority
3. Last resort
4. Just intention
5. Probability of success
6. Proportionality of cost
7. Clear announcement
8. Capacity for just means

Jus in Bello

1. Protection of noncombatants
2. Reassessment of proportionality of cost and probability of success

Just war theory concedes to a war that has a just cause, which is limited to humanitarian interventions such as stopping a massacre or the systemic violation of human rights; that is waged by a just authority, which means that those who declare war have been granted authority by the people they represent and that those people were not coerced by fear, untruths, or threat to grant that authority; that has a just intention, which means that the ultimate goal is to create a lasting peace; that has probability of success, which forbids entering a war if there is little probability for a lasting peace; that maintains proportionality of cost, which means that the total good achieved by the war will outweigh the total suffering caused, including the suffering of the enemy; that is preceded by a clear announcement, which gives the enemy one final chance to enter negotiations and prohibits governments from waging secret wars; and finally, that uses just means.

Just means—or *jus in bello*—include the principles of discrimination and proportionality. *Discrimination* means protecting noncombatants and preserving the sanctity of enemy lives, which rules out the use of torture. *Proportionality* means continually reassessing whether the good accomplished is still outweighing the harm done and whether success is still probable.

I do not know of an American war that the contemporaneous commander in chief did not justify according to these criteria. However, the Revolutionary War and World War II are the only American wars around which there is notable consensus regarding status as a just war. Many people argue that no modern war could ever be just because of the disproportion of evil to good caused by modern weaponry. For these reasons, peacemakers learn to be skeptical of the motivations of leaders who try to justify a war using these criteria. When applied wisely, however, just war theory potentially can reduce the number of wars in which we engage and encourage us to look first to every form of nonviolent, active resistance we can imagine.

*Conscientious Objection to War

You've heard the arguments for Christian pacifism and for just war theory. You've considered how you understand the voice of conscience. You know that Jesus calls us not to passive-ism but to active, nonviolent resistance. What do you believe about war?

Do not answer this question hypothetically, but ask yourself whether your commitment to Christian peacemaking would or would not allow you to participate in war making. Identify the privileges and particularities your social location contributes to your discernment. Perhaps you attended or are attending college on an ROTC scholarship and have loyalty (contracted or not) to the military for this opportunity. Perhaps you have a cousin, sibling, parent, or friend in the armed forces whom you do not want to dishonor. Or perhaps—because the U.S. does not currently have a draft—you have the privilege of opposing or supporting war purely on principle. Whatever your particular situation, keep it in mind as you grapple with the question of your participation in war.

Entire Christian denominations, including historic peace churches like the Mennonites and the Society of Friends, are devoted to nonviolence. Partly as a result of their witness, laws in the United States now grant citizens the right to obey their conscience in matters of military service. All citizens—soldiers and civilians—whose religious or philosophical convictions prohibit them from serving in the military at any level have the right to apply for status as a conscientious objector to war (CO).

Pacifist: One who makes peace through nonviolent means; from the Latin *pax facere*, "to make peace"

Passivist: One who is inactive or disengaged

Conscientious objectors must make this claim: "I am a conscientious objector opposed to war in any form." This claim ensures that a person takes responsibility for opposition to war and to the results of that opposition and also that the claim has been shaped by a longstanding conviction rather than a sudden fear of a draft. A CO opposes all wars (not just nuclear or preemptive wars, for example). A CO does not have to disagree with historical wars such as the American Revolution or World War II, or with a hypothetical war such as a Canadian invasion of the United States. A CO need only oppose war as it would be fought today.

Many COs are pacifists and oppose all violence; others support self-defense and the use of force to defend a weaker person in a one-on-one situation. Since conscientious objection is not civil disobedience but an American freedom, CO status legally cannot be used to prevent someone from working in public schools, being a weapon-bearing law enforcer, or holding a government position. Nor does it prevent a person from receiving FAFSA money for school, unless a male refuses to register with the Selective Service.

In the case of a draft—or if you are in the military, in the case of a "crystallization of conscience," a CO should be prepared to answer these three questions, which reflect those asked by draft boards and military courts:

- What beliefs form the basis for your conscientious objection?
- How did your beliefs develop?
- How do your beliefs shape the way you live day by day?

If you think you would ever want to identify yourself as a CO, it's worth articulating your beliefs now and gathering letters of support from teachers, pastors, and employers. Reflecting on the questions a draft board might ask forces you to consider aspects of your objection that you might not otherwise. Bringing your CO file to your pastor or priest is itself a powerful witness and may be a catalyst for starting a peacemakers affinity group or Lenten study series in your congregation. For me it is a way to honor and stand in solidarity with those who do serve in the military, because it takes my commitment to nonviolence out of the theoretical realm and makes me physically accountable for my position. Not all peacemakers are conscientious objectors; not all conscientious objectors are pacifists. It is a commitment worth considering, but ultimately your decision must be true to your gifts and sensibilities.

*Life and Leaven

In the years since I took the vow of nonviolence, I have broken it too many times to count. Hurtful words escape my mouth too easily. I settle for less-than-creative responses to conflict. I participate in systems of violence larger than myself, and because it's easier and to my advantage, I believe it when I'm told these systems are inevitable. Over the centuries, the church also has participated in systems of violence, sometimes even creating or promoting them. From the Inquisition to imperialism, the church is complicit in the violence of the world.

In every century, however, peacemakers have followed another way, the nonviolent way of Jesus. Still today, faithful communities choose to practice peacemaking as a way of life. I long to be part of communities like these, where peacemaking is a way of moving through the world every day—a way of seeing strangers, choosing language, raising children, and navigating relationships, a way of being a creature of the earth, a citizen of this world, and a member of the in-breaking reign of peace. When practiced in this way, nonviolence is the spirit in which we engage each of the other practices described in this book.

> **" I long to be part of communities like these, where peacemaking is a way of moving through the world every day. "**

And so, letting hope subvert fear and all the other forces that might lead me to do otherwise, every year on the anniversary of my baptism I find a group of friends to join me in taking the vow. It is a small act, small as yeast in a bowl of flour, but it guides our daily living throughout the year and binds us to a community struggling to live into that promise together.

We live in a world at war, in a time of torture, in a church that struggles to know how to speak prophetically, in an age desperate for imaginative leadership. We confess the reality of violence in and around us, and yet we boldly proclaim the equally real possibilities of shalom. Our common vocation is to be the disarmed and disarming body of Christ, leavened and living, broken and blessed, given to the world that it might taste and see the goodness of God.

12* Doing Justice

Joyce Hollyday

During orientation week on a college campus in Washington State, a lavish welcome buffet was spread. A new student piled his plate with food—more than he could eat. He turned to the young man sitting next to him—a student from the African nation of Namibia—and commented, "I guess my eyes were bigger than my stomach." The Namibian looked at the other student's eyes—and then at his stomach—and was clearly confused. So the American said, "Don't you have a word that means taking more than you can eat?" The Namibian thought a moment and then said, "Yes. We call it stealing."

At the most basic level, doing justice means living in a way that takes into account the common good. It means caring about the needs of others and, in whatever ways we can, acting to ensure that everyone has access to such benefits as food, shelter, education, freedom, and safety. Those of us who intend to practice doing justice as Christians find guidance in the Bible's rich accounts of the critical importance and ethical character of this practice. Doing justice, we learn, is at the heart of our life with God and others. "What does the LORD require of you," the prophet Micah asks, "but to do justice, and to love kindness, and to walk humbly with your God?" (Mic. 6:8).

*God's Justice Reaching Out to Humanity

The Jews of Jesus' day suffered under brutal occupation by the Romans. Exploited and despised, they longed for a messiah who would establish a reign of justice. They had in mind a godlike warrior on a thundering steed who would break the chains of their oppression with a sweep of the sword. What they got was a poor, naked, vulnerable baby, born on straw in a drafty stable to an unwed, impoverished young woman—Jesus the homeless one, whose journey took him from feeding trough to cross, born a refugee and executed a criminal. He spent the years in between hanging out with simple folk and outcasts: fishermen, prostitutes, and beggars; people bent over, bleeding, and blind; people impaired in body, spirit, and mind. Hardly what the Jews expected. Imagine.

In his first sermon, given in his hometown of Nazareth, Jesus quoted the prophet Isaiah:

> The Spirit of the Lord is upon me,
>> because he has anointed me
>>> to bring good news to the poor.
>> . . . to proclaim release to the captives . . .
>>> to let the oppressed go free,
> to proclaim the year of the Lord's favor. (Luke 4:18-19)

The "year of the Lord's favor" refers to the Jubilee year, which God had commanded our early ancestors in the faith, the Israelites, to observe every fifty years (Lev. 25). During this special year, all debts were to be forgiven, all slaves set free, and all land returned to its original owners. In other words, people were supposed to live justly again, turning away from accumulation

❝ What does the LORD require of you, but to do justice, and to love kindness, and to walk humbly with your God?—Micah 6:8 **❞**

and wealth generated at the expense or exploitation of others. This need was one the Israelites understood, for their own ancestors had been slaves in Egypt until God set them free in a dramatic exodus (Exod. 14).

Their first place of freedom was, to their surprise, a wilderness, a desolate place where they would wander for forty years, many of them spent, scripture tells, in complaining. But in that place, they learned to trust God and one another. They had to; they had nothing else. In the wilderness, God formed them into a community based on equality and committed to the common good. In that barren spot, they survived on manna provided every morning by God. Everyone got as much as he or she needed—and only that much. If people hoarded, scripture reports, the manna "bred worms and became foul" (Exod. 16:20).

Once the Israelites were out of the wilderness, however, they began hoarding and accumulating. Some went into debt, and others enslaved those who were in debt to them. Some among them grew rich; others became destitute. Some were satiated; others died of hunger. That's why God established the Jubilee year: to set things right again. But the lesson never really took hold. Things got worse.

So God sent prophets to remind the people, chastising them for their greedy and exploitive ways. "They sell the righteous for silver," charged Amos, "and the needy for a pair of sandals—they who trample the head of the poor into the dust of the earth" (Amos 2:6-7). Addressing those who accumulated property while consigning the poor to homelessness, Isaiah admonished those who "join house to house, who add field to field, until there is room for no one but you" (Isa. 5:8). Over and over, the prophets called the people to share their bread with the hungry, take in the homeless, and care for aliens, widows, and orphans, the most vulnerable and most easily exploited ones among them.

Today, thousands of years after the Israelites left the wilderness, the injustices and divisions in our world boggle the imagination. Millions of people in our country—and many more millions around the globe—lack safety, housing, food, and health care. Children bear the brunt of injustice. How shall we, in our own time, try to break the spiral of slavery and injustice that again prevails?

Perhaps we too, the Old Testament theologian Walter Brueggemann asserts, need to go to "wilderness school." Just as the early Israelites

> **"** Just as the early Israelites needed forty years of practicing a way of life based on trust and sharing before they could enter the promised land, so too must we figuratively make the journey from enslavement in Egypt to freedom in the promised land again and again. **"**

needed forty years of practicing a way of life based on trust and sharing before they could enter the promised land, so too must we figuratively make the journey from enslavement in Egypt to freedom in the promised land again and again. And for us, as for them, the only way is through the wilderness. We have to keep moving *out of* our captivity to an empire that runs on violence, greed, gluttony, and most of all anxiety. And we have to keep moving *into* a wilderness community based on trust. There we will find not "prosperity"—the enrichment of a few—but "abundance"—the enrichment of all through the sharing of goods.

*Practicing Just, Kind, and Humble Living

In his Sermon on the Mount, Jesus points to the birds in the air and the lilies of the field, which are fed and clothed by God, and says, "Therefore I tell you, do not worry about your life, what you will eat or what you will drink, or about your body, what you will wear." God knows we need all these things. Therefore, Jesus says, strive first for God's realm and God's righteousness, "and all these things will be given to you as well" (Matt. 6:25, 32-33).

When I read these words, I want to protest, "But people starve—even good and faithful people." And then I am reminded that "righteousness" means "right relationship." It means living justly and generously with one another. This promise of God is not directed to solitary individuals. It's a promise to the community, to the whole body of Christ. We have all that we need. The only question is whether we will share it, so that all are recipients of the bounty. If so, the promise holds.

I grew up in Hershey, Pennsylvania—"Chocolatetown, USA." I was raised in the First United Methodist Church on Chocolate Avenue, where the streetlights have domes in the shape of Hershey's kisses. My sisters and I spent the summers swimming, riding the roller coaster in our town's amusement park, and sipping chocolate Cokes at the drugstore at the corner of Chocolate and Cocoa Avenues. As an upper-middle-class white kid in a wealthy town, I was following a script of privilege that could have lasted my whole life. (We all have such figurative scripts, based on factors like our skin color, economic class, gender, and education.) When I was thirteen, however, something happened that changed the script for me. The day after the great civil rights leader Martin Luther King Jr. was assassinated, I sat in my comfortable living room in Hershey and watched on TV as people in Harrisburg, thirteen miles away, burned parts of the city in response to the tragedy. That's when I learned that not every child in America grows up in a town with a chocolate factory, an amusement park, four swimming pools, and nine golf courses. That summer I ventured into Harrisburg to volunteer at a vacation Bible school in an inner-city church. I was shocked to discover that most of the children we served lived in crumbling tenements infested with violence and drugs. Almost all of them arrived hungry, having had nothing at home to eat for breakfast. That experience launched me on a lifelong journey to try to understand injustice.

In an email that circulated after the attacks of September 11, 2001, an author wrote of taking a walk in the woods with his young daughter. She was pretending that there were monsters in the woods ready to eat them. Her father asked, "What should we do if we see them?" "Feed them," she replied. "If we feed them, they won't want to eat *us*." The author then suggested that we take the billions of dollars about to be spent on waging war and invest it in people instead. Bob Alberti, of the First Unitarian Universalist Church in Minneapolis at the time, echoed this sentiment by encouraging us to "unleash our weapons of mass construction"—to go about digging wells, laying roads, building hospitals and schools. "Let us scour the earth clean of terrorism through the merciless application of knowledge, compassion, hope, and tolerance."

Some politicians tell us that "the terrorists hate what we have." But I believe that those who have targeted us *want* what we have: access to food, health care, education, and employment; freedom from violence; options for the future. In too many places, our nation's foreign and economic policies have deprived people of these basic rights in order to ensure a high standard of living here. U.S. materialism and militarism have alienated and angered much of the rest of the world, raising the need for a dramatic shift in priorities and posture. Perhaps it's time to consider whether redistribution would be a more secure path than retaliation.

*Will We Know It When We See It?

For most of my life, if you had asked me what my work has been devoted to, I would have answered "social justice." But my view of justice got completely undone and reworked when I spent time in South Africa. I first visited there in 1988, when that country was still in the stranglehold of the system of racial hatred and separation known as apartheid. Blacks were forced to live crowded into the worst parts of the country. They worked under slavelike conditions and suffered from inferior education and lack of health care. The white-supremacist government enforced the injustice with terror—imprisoning, torturing, and even assassinating people who tried to bring change.

I was invited to South Africa by church leaders. The week before I arrived, they had led a march on the capital to demand an end to apartheid. They were hosed with water cannons, just as civil rights marchers in my own country had been in the 1960s, then arrested and imprisoned briefly. On March 13, my first day in South Africa, I was taken to a church service in St. George's Cathedral in Cape Town. While riot police massed outside, people streamed into the cathedral, filling the pews and aisles, taking up every space in the choir loft, on the floor, and around the pulpit. Despite police blockades put up around the black townships, young people got through and surged together into the sanctuary like a river of hope, chanting and dancing the freedom dance known as the *toyi-toyi*.

Archbishop Desmond Tutu preached his hope that day, addressing the defenders of apartheid: "You may be powerful, indeed, very powerful. But you are not God. . . . You have already lost! Come and join the winning side . . . because if God is for us, who can be against us?" The applause in the cathedral was deafening, but the hope felt unrealistic to me. I couldn't imagine apartheid ever releasing its death grip on South Africa. Just two years later, however, anti-apartheid activist Nelson Mandela was freed from prison. Within a few years, apartheid was declared illegal and Mandela was elected as South Africa's first black president.

Among the millions who had worked boldly and peacefully for this change was a young man named Jam-Jam. In 1988 he showed me around the black township of Duncan Village, his home. After we had walked for about an hour, a large, armored personnel carrier approached us. Eight members of the South African army surrounded us and ushered us at gunpoint past rows of razor wire to an interrogation room in the military tower at the center of the township. An officer of the security police wagged his finger at Jam-Jam and said menacingly, "If you don't give up your subversive activities, you'll be back in before long." He was referring to the fact that Jam-Jam had just been released from ten months in police detention, where he had been abused and tortured. Jam-Jam's only response to the threat was to reach calmly into his back pocket and take out his small New Testament. Holding it up, he said, "Sir, I am a Christian." A brief moment of silence descended as the arrogance of evil met the quiet power of the gospel.

We were released, and Jam-Jam made plans to go into hiding. When I asked him why he had risked showing a white American stranger around his township, he said, "Now is not the time to be afraid. We are moving forward." And then he offered the stunning observation that P. W. Botha—at that time the president of South Africa and the chief enforcer of apartheid—was "just another worker oppressed by the system." Jam-Jam added, "We are not fighting against whites but against an unjust system." He understood that the New Testament he had shown to that security police officer contained Jesus' command: love your enemies.

After political power shifted in South Africa, the command to love our enemies undergirded an unprecedented process known as Truth and Reconciliation. Millions of black South Africans had been detained and tortured, or had witnessed bombings, assassinations, and massacres carried out by the government and pro-apartheid forces. To a much smaller degree, anti-apartheid activists had committed acts of violence in their freedom struggle. In similar situations of regime change, other nations have convened truth commissions that have investigated atrocities, meted out punishment, and sent societies into unending spirals of vengeance and counter-vengeance. In South Africa, however, President Mandela and Archbishop Tutu insisted that both truth and reconciliation were needed. Their approach was grounded in the belief that all human beings—even the worst perpetrators of violence—bear the image of God and are members of the human community. They knew that the nation would be unable to move toward healing without a widespread recounting of the truth, but they also understood that the deepest healing would also require reconciliation—the gift of forgiveness, mercy, and amnesty to those who had perpetrated atrocities. Indeed, when Nelson Mandela made a very public witness to this belief at his presidential inauguration on May 10, 1994, one of the dignitaries on the platform was James Gregory, Mandela's jailer for more than two decades.

For a year and a half, members of the Truth and Reconciliation Commission traveled throughout South Africa, hearing the testimonies of more than twenty thousand victims of human rights abuses—only a fraction of those who had suffered. South Africa's bold and amazing approach prevented what many people there and around the world predicted would be an inevitable nationwide bloodbath when power shifted.

Forgiveness was at the heart of the proceedings, and it resided in the hearts of many South Africans as well. I met Maude at a residence for senior citizens outside Cape Town. More than forty years before, when South Africa's Group Areas Act declared all desirable neighborhoods "white areas," Maude, her mother, her husband, and their five young children were pushed out of their home at gunpoint and dumped on an isolated stretch of bush. Such "forced removals," as they were termed, created massive squatter camps containing millions of black South Africans. When I asked Maude what she felt toward her persecutors, she answered with tears in her eyes, "I don't know if I have forgiven them. But I believe that if I want God to forgive me, I have to forgive them." I couldn't imagine that anything she had done in her life came close to the injustice that had been done to her, and I resisted accepting her words. But Maude's view was common among South Africans. As one person put it, "There's a little bit of perpetrator in each one of us, evil in all of us. . . . And even in the most evil perpetrators, there's a dimension of humanity."

In the United States, where *retributive justice* is popular, such expressions of shared humanity seem to exert less influence. The building of prisons outstrips the construction of schools and hospitals, and we spend far more on punishing those who commit crimes than we do on efforts to rehabilitate them. The U.S. is the only Western industrialized nation that still applies the death penalty for capital offenses. *Restorative justice*—which asserts that we would all be better off if we worked to restore perpetrators to the community rather than isolating and punishing them—provides a different approach. It is making headway here, but it's a hard sell.

*Restorative Justice in My Own Backyard

The Cape Town friend who took me to meet Maude was Courtney Sampson, an Anglican priest. When he spoke the truth about the United States in very pointed terms, he helped me to connect what was happening in his country to what is happening in my own. "I have become aware," he said, "of how evil slavery—the ownership of another human being—really was. You had 'forced removal' not up the road, not to a hill far away, not across the river, not across the railway line—but from one continent to another." I agree—and I believe we are still paying the price today for our refusal to confess our racism and address the harm it has done and continues to do. We have never told the truth as a nation about our genocidal policies toward Native Americans, our enslavement of Africans, our history of lynching, our establishment of legalized segregation, and continuing race-based violence and discrimination. Without a process for telling the truth, the divisions that plague us cannot heal. But could such a process happen in the United States?

Yes. In the summer of 2005, the first large-scale Truth and Reconciliation process in the United States was convened in Greensboro, North Carolina. It focused on an event that took place on November 3, 1979. That morning, a group of people gathered in a low-income neighborhood for a rally to demand racial and economic justice in the city. Soon after all the police escorts were called away to an early lunch break, members of the Ku Klux Klan and the American Nazi Party arrived in a caravan of cars, pulled out guns, and opened fire on the demonstrators. Five people were killed, and ten were wounded, in what has come to be known as the Greensboro Massacre. Among the wounded was the Reverend Nelson Johnson, a longtime leader in Greensboro's African American community and one of the march's organizers.

On July 16, 2005, Gorrell Pierce and a cadre of white young men walked into the auditorium where the Truth and Reconciliation hearings were under way. Mr. Pierce had been the Grand Dragon of the Federated Knights of the Ku Klux Klan in November 1979. When Rev. Johnson saw Pierce, he got up from his seat, walked across the auditorium, and made his way down that row of white men, thanking each one for coming and

> **❝** In the United States, . . .the building of prisons outstrips the construction of schools and hospitals. **❞**

shaking every hand—including Mr. Pierce's. Rev. Johnson confessed later that it wasn't his first impulse, but that as a Christian he knew he needed to bring his best self to that encounter and to reach out to the best self inside Gorrell Pierce.

Later, a former American Nazi Party member who had participated in the massacre learned that he was dying of cancer. He asked Nelson Johnson to visit him, and he asked for forgiveness. Rev. Johnson said, "I forgive you." The man replied, "But can God? I don't believe God can forgive me." Rev. Johnson assured him of God's forgiveness and offered a prayer of absolution.

The Reverend Bongani Finca, one of South Africa's Truth and Reconciliation commissioners, made several visits to Greensboro to support the process there. "Where we could have called for revenge, we decided to call for forgiveness," he said of South Africa's decisive moment. "Where we could have called for retribution, we decided to call for reconciliation. Where we could have called for the blood of those who had shed our blood, we decided to call for a new beginning based on mercy, compassion, and forgiveness. The miracle is that what is noble in humankind triumphed over what is natural; what is special triumphed over what is ordinary. It was the triumph of love over hate, reason over passion, peace over war."

*How Do We Get There?

God intends peace on earth. But everywhere we look, we see storms of conflict—gale-force winds of war that destroy everything in their path, tornadoes of terrorism that touch down and spin off into perpetual cycles of vengeance and counter-vengeance, hurricanes of hatred that divide us one from another. A bumper sticker tells the truth: "Without justice, there is no peace." It's easy to feel overwhelmed by it all, and hard to know where to begin to make a change.

The world belongs to those with wealth and power—unless some of us are hopeful and bold enough to believe otherwise. Unless some of us follow Jesus, who turns all the assumptions about power upside down and gives his followers this promise:

> Blessed are you who are poor,
>> for yours is the [realm] of God.
> Blessed are you who are hungry now,
>> for you will be filled.
> Blessed are you who weep now,
>> for you will laugh. (Luke 6:20-21)

Before helping to distribute groceries every Saturday morning to about three hundred families in her DC neighborhood, Mary Glover prayed, "Lord, we know you're coming through this line today, so help us to treat you right." Mary Glover understood Jesus' words, "Just as you did it to one of the least of these who are members of my family, you did it to me" (Matt. 25:40). She knew where Jesus lives, who he claims as family. The beginning of justice is compassion, and compassion starts with going to the places where we can find Jesus' sisters and brothers. That generally means leaving our "comfort zones" and meeting people whose paths we wouldn't otherwise cross. If we have our eyes and ears open, we will begin to see and hear the stories. And if our hearts are open as well, we may move from kindness and compassion to solidarity. Then the struggles of those who are victims of injustice become our own. Those of us who inherit privilege and affluence as a birthright can use our power for enormous good when we join with those who are working for justice.

A few years ago, as our government was preparing to launch the war against Iraq, a young woman's eyes and ears and heart were being opened: Kate Foran wrote about her experience:

March 15, 2003. I'm fresh out of college, and I'm standing outside the Federal Building in Hartford, Connecticut, arm-in-arm with others who are blocking its doors in protest. On the news, they say we're gearing up to "shock and awe" the people of Iraq. It makes me think of what they first declared when we went after Afghanistan following 9/11—Operation Infinite Justice. It smacks of comic book superheroes. It shocks like blasphemy.

I am standing in protest, surrounded by the cast of characters—activists in handcuffs, police in riot gear, journalists behind cameras. Above me, carved in stone on the government building, stands Justice in her blindfold. The president is speaking of Saddam Hussein and 9/11 in the same breath. And it looks to me like blindfolded Justice is playing some game of Pin the Tail on the Donkey. She just stuck her tack in a map of Iraq.

That's the last glimpse I have of Justice, and then I'm in a jail cell with a frail young woman of color. She's been arrested for a domestic disturbance. Defending herself against the fists of her boyfriend. Maybe Justice is blind, but God is not. God sees all, and the God of the Bible is on the side of my cellmate and the Iraqi boy I later meet whose body is riddled with radioactive shrapnel.

I grew up in the white suburbs where the streets are clean and suffering is covered by new vinyl siding, but now I'm living at the Catholic Worker house in the middle of the ghetto, and we're giving hospitality to this Iraqi boy and his family. He learns basketball from the neighborhood kids. Some of them have lost siblings in drive-by shootings. They go to schools with bars on the windows. Then they go to jail. I went to schools with plate glass windows and a view of a bright future.

If doing justice starts with being able to see injustice, I'm praying, God, help me take my blindfold off.

" If doing justice starts with being able to see injustice, I'm praying, God, help me take my blindfold off.—Kate Foran **"**

Churches can lead the way in removing our blindfolds and inviting us to do justice. Some things are relatively simple: making sure the coffee served after the worship service has been fairly traded with growers and pickers, designing mission trips that give an eye-opening experience of a different part of our country or the world. My congregation has a sister church in Cuba, which has enabled us to experience the daily life and worship of a faith-filled congregation in a country our government has declared an "enemy." Young people of my generation were involved in the movement for sanctions against apartheid South Africa; today another generation is leading in such efforts as the Save Darfur and Sudan divestment campaigns, eco-justice efforts around global climate change, and workers' and immigrants' rights struggles such as the Smithfield Justice Campaign.

In July 2007, I visited the Smithfield plant in Tar Heel, North Carolina, the world's largest hog-processing plant. Every day thirty-two thousand hogs are slaughtered there. Workers at the plant—most of them African American or undocumented immigrants—suffer a multitude of injuries related to the speed of the line, the use of knives, heavy lifting, and a slippery floor covered in the blood and waste of the hogs. I was part of a clergy delegation that went to the plant to confront its managers about the injuries and abuses the workers are suffering. We were turned away at the door and threatened with arrest if we didn't leave the premises.

Afterward, we convened a Bible study that included some injured former Smithfield workers. Teresa had been severely wounded when a three-hundred-pound hog carcass fell on her. Rafael, who had worked in the sweltering heat of the livestock yard, had suffered a back injury. Elsa had sustained a repetitive-motion injury and lost her job; as a result, she had to send her seven-year-old daughter, who has asthma, back to Mexico because she can't afford medical care for her here. Tears flowed freely as the stories were told.

We read together the parable of the persistent widow and the unjust judge, a story Jesus told about the need to pray always and "not to lose heart." The judge in the parable has no respect for God or for anyone. A widow in the city comes to him again and again to demand justice. The judge refuses several times, but the widow keeps coming. Finally the judge, tired of her bothersome pleading, grants her justice, "so that she may not wear me out by continually coming" (Luke 18:1-8).

Before the great biblical exodus from slavery, Moses had to keep going back to Egypt's pharaoh, demanding, "Let my people go." It took plagues of bugs and frogs and blood before Pharaoh relented, but ultimately he did. It took persistent peskiness on the part of the widow of the parable to get justice—but finally she did. It took more than four decades of resistance for South Africans to overthrow apartheid—but eventually they did. As Martin Luther King Jr. said so eloquently, "The arc of the moral universe is long, but it bends toward justice." So we need to keep knocking at Smithfield's door—and at all the doors that hide injustice.

As the prophet Micah insists, God calls us to pursue justice with kindness and humility. God invites us to be part of changing the world. We cannot do it alone, but we can each play a part, relying on God and one another, trusting that others will come after us to continue the work. "Living in faith is knowing that even though our little work, our little seed, our little brick may not make the whole thing, the whole thing exists in the mind of God, and that whether or not we are there to see the whole thing is not the most important matter," wrote Vincent Harding, a historian and theologian who worked with Martin Luther King Jr. "The most important thing is whether we have entered the process."

I hope that you will enter the process and find a door on which to knock. If enough of us embrace this practice, then one day the prophet's beautiful vision will come true:

> **Let justice roll down like waters, and righteousness like an everflowing stream.**—Amos 5:24

Living a whole life
attentively . . .
together . . . in the
real world . . . for
the good of all . . .
*in response to God

13* Living in the Presence of God

Susan Briehl

When my siblings and I were children, my father charged us money to see what he called "natural wonders." A dime— the price of a full-sized candy bar—was the going rate. The youngest paid a nickel, our introduction to the sliding-scale fee. "Who wants to see a natural wonder?" he would call, drawing us from our books or chores or Saturday cartoons, sending us scrambling in search of coins and one another. Who could refuse?

Occasionally these wonders were in the basement: a nest of newborn mice in a box of old cloth diapers. Usually they were outdoors: the puzzling paths of bark beetles suggesting some indecipherable ancient script; the first avalanche lily of spring rising through the sodden leaves and snow; a papery wasp nest, the whole story of a colony's life together told in its elegant geometry. Intricate patterns and delicate structures fascinated him. He bid us come close, then closer, to watch, to listen, sometimes to touch, carefully, reverently, and often, as he said, "to smell of it."

Death and decay fascinated my father too, things dark and dank and rank with rot. He once gathered us around an old garbage can, and lifting the lid slowly to heighten our anticipation, exposed the inside crawling with hundreds of fat white maggots. Horrified, and frugal to a fault, I wanted my dime back, as well as the nickel I had given my brother. But a deal was a deal, and my father figured this wonder was well worth a quarter. I sashayed back into the house, arms crossed against my chest, while he did a joyful little jig beside the garbage can. Who could refuse this joy? I could.

We paid a dime, but my father was offering us something much more valuable, and more costly: he was schooling us in wonder. Childhood was fleeting, and forces already were at work making us—and him—too busy or bored or self-absorbed to consider the lilies—or the larvae or lichen—in our own backyard and to see in them "all the wonders" God has done (Ps. 78:4). While there was time, he was kindling our curiosity and sparking our imaginations. He was opening our eyes to the mysteries of the universe and widening our hearts to receive the beauty of the world and its suffering. He was inviting us into the practice of living together, everywhere and always, in the presence of God.

"The world is charged with the grandeur of God," writes the poet-priest Gerard Manley Hopkins. "The heavens are telling the glory of God," the psalmist sings (Ps. 19:1). And Paul writes that from the beginning, God's "eternal power and divine nature," though invisible, have been "understood and seen" through the things God made (Rom. 1:20). All these—poet, psalmist, and apostle—invite us to live wide-awake and aware of God's presence all around us. Look closely, they say; what is visible makes the Invisible known; the finite speaks of the Infinite. Kneel on those sodden leaves, thick with the smell of decay, for there the Holy Spirit broods, summoning life from death. Bend toward that tiny wild lily, where the wisdom of God calls you more deeply into life.

*Knowing Where We Come From

Bending earthward is the best way to appreciate many natural wonders; it's the only way to watch a team of red ants carry a crumb six times their combined weight. But this simple movement also embodies the essence of being human, *merely* human. Bowing low puts us in our proper place;

it grounds us. The first human is called Adam, or earth creature, from *adamah,* the Hebrew word for earth or dust of the ground. The words *human* and *humus,* meaning rich soil, are related in a similar way. From the same Latin source we get *humility,* which at its root means knowing where you come from and what you are made of. "You are dust," God reminded the first human beings, "and to dust you shall return" (Gen. 3:19).

God's Grandeur

The world is charged with the grandeur of God.
    It will flame out, like shining from shook foil;
    It gathers to a greatness, like the ooze of oil
Crushed. Why do men then now not reck his rod?
Generations have trod, have trod, have trod;
    And all is seared with trade; bleared, smeared with toil;
    And wears man's smudge and shares man's smell: the soil
Is bare now, nor can foot feel, being shod.

And, for all this, nature is never spent;
    There lives the dearest freshness deep down things;
And though the last lights off the black West went
    Oh, morning, at the brown brink eastwards, springs—
Because the Holy Ghost over the bent
    World broods with warm breast and with ah! bright wings.

—Gerard Manley Hopkins

Humility, in this sense, roots us in the blessed truth about who we are and who we are not. We are not the center of the universe or its creators. While discerning God's call, walking the path to "I know not where" searching for "I know not what," we at least can remove "being God" from our list of possible vocations. We are creatures: bound by the limits of time and space, the laws of gravity and entropy. In curiosity and wonder, we

lack of order
or predictability

> **"** When our heads are up and our eyes wide open, we see the grandeur of God flaming out from every seed and stone, and the image of God shining in every human face. **"**

rightly test and press against these boundaries, seeking deeper knowledge and wider wisdom. But the sweetest fruit of our exploration is gratitude, because the mystery at the heart of our finite lives, we discover, is the gift of God's infinite love. Our attempts to earn this gift or to prove we are worthy of this love are futile. Our mounting anxiety over failing or about disappointing others literally constricts our hearts and takes our breath away. Humility lets us catch our breath and sets us free to laugh together at our foolish efforts to do it all and do it perfectly.

If a person bending or bowing toward the earth signifies the *merely* human being, then a person standing upright facing the wider world signifies the *fully* human being. Standing, we breathe more deeply and sing more heartily, we dance with abandon and hasten in compassion to those who are in need. Our arms freely welcome the stranger and embrace our beloved. Our hands gratefully receive and generously share every good gift. And when our heads are up and our eyes wide open, we see the grandeur of God flaming out from every seed and stone, and the image of God shining in every human face. Fully human beings, we flourish in community with one another and in communion with God as we tend the earth and delight in its wonders.

Consider another familiar human posture described in the Latin phrase *incurvatus in se,* "curved in upon yourself." Babies sleep in the fetal position, and mothers curl around them. Lovers spoon each other. Battered women cringe. Abused children cower. For better and for worse, we know this posture.

The phrase *incurvatus in se,* however, describes more than a bodily posture; it is the best definition I know of that overused, underestimated three-letter word *sin*. Time and again we fall for the old lie that we can be more than merely human, or the equally deadly lie that we are less than fully human. Both lies disfigure the image of God in which we were made. Not trusting God's good intention for us, we turn away from God. We turn our backs on one another and a blind eye toward the world. We curve inward—as persons, friends, churches, or countries—and make ourselves the center of a very small universe. Who can refuse God's invitation to the fullness of life? We can.

And yet, while we are still curved in on ourselves, the invisible, immortal, and infinite God bends earthward and comes close, then closer to us in Jesus, who is bone of our bone, flesh of our flesh, bound by time and finite as breath. In him the grandeur of God gathers to a greatness— like juice filling grapes, nearly bursting the skins—and is crushed. Christ empties himself. He pours out his life and love, fine wine upon the thirsty earth, even unto death (Phil. 2:6-11). But look closely. In his dying "there lives the dearest freshness deep down things," the power and promise of God raising us—uncurled, upright, and fully human again—with Christ, so we might "walk in newness of life" (Rom. 6:4).

"Peace be with you," the risen Christ says to all who would walk this way, breathing into them the Holy Spirit and sending them to embody God's love in the world. Abide in me as I abide in you, he tells them. Love one another as I love you. Forgive as I forgive. Bend to serve one another, pouring out your life, as I have done among you. This is life, authentic and abundant.

*Receiving New Life, New Eyes

Singing filled the candlelit church as a young man walked toward the center of the gathering. After months of discernment and prayer, reading scripture, and learning the way of Jesus, he was taking the next step in the journey toward that great bath Christians call baptism. He stepped into a pool of water and into a stream of stories: the Spirit brooding over the waters at creation; an ark harboring earth's future through the flood; a people crossing the sea to freedom; Jesus being baptized in the Jordan; the woman at the well receiving living water; the man born blind washing, then seeing Jesus. Water was poured over the young man's head— in the name of the Father and of the Son and of the Holy Spirit (Matt.

28:19)—and with it came God's promise: Matthew Ervin, child of God, I am with you always. You are my beloved. Nothing can separate you from my love.

In those waters, by that promise, Matt was joined to Christ whose death and resurrection became Matt's own dying and rising to newness of life. Matt was knit into the body of Christ, the community of servant friends who know the biblical stories to be the story of their life together. As on the day Matt was baptized, so it is every day for this community. The Spirit broods among them bringing forth a new creation. In Christ the Ark they harbor through every deadly flood. With Christ they cross to freedom, released from the powers that bind them. From Christ they drink the water of life. Day after day Christ washes them in mercy, giving them new eyes. Eyes open to wonder. Eyes filled with compassion. Eyes to see God in unexpected places and unlikely people.

Nearly twenty years ago, two college students knocked at our door. They were all wrapped up in themselves—consumed by the demands of their work and studies, obsessing over their relationships or the lack thereof, anxious about the future. They needed a refresher course in the childlike joy of being merely human, and they had come looking for teachers (Matt. 18:1-5). "May we borrow your children?" they asked. "We've forgotten how to play." Off they went to the park, a couple of book-weary guys, a second grader, and a four-year-old.

Erik, twenty-seven, volunteers at a food bank, is active in his local church, and knows by heart every song from *The Phantom of the Opera*. He always will be something of an irrepressible—and irresistible—child. His mother has helped him become quite independent, but he will never live on his own or support himself; Erik was made for community. Recently he was invited to join Daybreak, an eclectic group of people in Portland, Oregon, creating an extended family in a cohousing experiment. Erik will have his own small condo, but he will share the evening meal, the common rooms, his music, and his life with the others. Some of these people want to help Erik, his mother says, but others see the deeper truth: they would not be whole without him and his special gifts and needs.

Rachel lives in a little apartment in the city. Trained as a social worker, she works full time, arranging services for poor elderly and disabled persons. She barely makes enough to cover rent and necessities, but she wants to stay in this neighborhood with its funky shops and sidewalk vendors, its students and street kids, gay bars and bag ladies. Life feels honest here, heartbreaking and beautiful. So she made a deal with her landlord: in exchange for lower rent, she cleans the apartment building, including picking up liquor bottles, needles, and condoms left in the parking lot. She sees Jesus all the time: he is the guy rifling through the dumpster, the woman on the bus with her three small children, the young gay man disowned by his parents, the veteran crippled by invisible wounds, her clients, her friends.

A small church within walking distance of Rachel's apartment is home to a community of faith that made the same decision she did: to do whatever it takes to stay in this part of the city, worshiping and serving. Every Sunday morning the community gathers as Christians have done for two millennia to sing and pray, to hear the Word of God, and to share the bread and cup of Christ's holy meal. They gather again each Wednesday night for supper and for evening prayer. On both Sunday and Wednesday they set the table as Jesus would, making room and providing food for all who come, including those who have no table of their own and those not welcomed at other tables. They bring simple food and grateful hearts to both tables. They offer the Wednesday meal as Christ offers the Sunday feast, as a gift freely given to all who hunger and thirst.

> **She sees Jesus all the time: he is the guy rifling through the dumpster.**

This little band of the baptized come to both meals as beggars, empty-handed and needing to be fed. They come to meet Jesus in their hungry neighbors and to receive him in the breaking of the bread. This congregation, like Rachel, Matthew, the Daybreak community, and the students at our door, practices seeing the world with new eyes, eyes opened to God's presence in the little and the least, including themselves.

*Facing the Heart of Darkness

There are some places so dark that we cannot see, even with our eyes
wide open. Inside the Cave of the Mounds in southwestern Wisconsin,
for example. One hot August afternoon we walked single file through a
narrow tunnel in the side of a grassy mound into a cool, damp cavern.
Millions of years ago, this part of the continent was a warm, shallow
sea. Caverns formed beneath a fault line, a fracture in the earth's surface,
through which acidic water had flowed. This fissure is called the lifeline
of the cave.

Long after the sea was no more, the alchemy of time and chemistry
turned a billion seashells into colorful gems. "Like walking into a jewel
box," the guide said, shining a flashlight on the ceiling and walls covered
with calcite crystals. We turned a corner, then another, meandering like
the streams that once flowed there. We descended a stairway into a cave
seventy feet below ground and stopped.

The guide switched off the electricity. He turned off his flashlight. "We
are standing in total darkness," he said. "If we stay, some of us will lose
our balance; others will become nauseous. Eventually, we all will be disoriented and lose our way."

Human history includes even darker places; the human heart holds
deeper caverns. I knew this the day I stood before a pile of shoes in the
Holocaust Memorial Museum: the shoes of starving men, of mothers and
the children from whom they were torn, of brothers and sisters and lovers.
Human beings, feared and hated, stripped of their homes, their families,
their dignity, their lives. Their shoes. We are standing in total darkness.

Gas chambers. Killing fields. Lynching trees. How does one live in the
presence of God in the face of such evil? Where is God? What good is
being wide-eyed and awake in a world where people are bought and sold,
murdered and tortured, degraded and ignored? What does "practicing
faith" mean when your own church, your own people, your own way of
life are complicit in such horrors?

I wrestle with these questions. But not every day. Most days I am too
busy or bored or self-absorbed to think about these things. It's easy. Like
you, I know a thousand ways to distract myself. But standing before those
shoes, dizzy and disoriented, my body remembered the posture of humility, bending toward the earth in weakness.

My body bowed before the shoes, and as if dislodged by that move-ment, words I have known all of my life appeared: *Kyrie eleison.* Lord, have mercy. I could not speak them, but again they came. These words are my inheritance, handed down through centuries by people of faith. This long has been the church's song, begging for the fresh water of God's mercy to fill each fractured heart with grace and peace: Lord have mercy. Christ have mercy. Lord have mercy.

When I returned to the hotel and tried to wash away the day, more words welled up—and music, another gift from my ancestors. I began to sing. For every shattered soul, every victim and abuser who cannot sing or pray, I sang. For everyone everywhere who knows the darkest places in human history and the deepest caverns of the heart, I sang:

> Create in me a clean heart, O God,
>> and renew a right spirit within me.
> Cast me not away from your presence
>> and take not your Holy Spirit from me.
> Restore to me the joy of your salvation
>> and uphold me with your free Spirit.—based on Psalm 51:10-12

Before, beneath, within these words came God's promise: I am with you always; I will not cast you away. You are my beloved; I will renew you. By their gifts of these ancient prayers and songs, my community of faith had led me back to the water of life. On a flood of grace Christ bears us to the heart of God, a heart wounded by human cruelty, fear, and pain; a heart wide enough to cover this wound with compassion. The wound remains in God's heart, like a deep fracture in the earth's surface. It is our lifeline. Through it flow streams of healing mercy.

*Opening the Treasury of Scripture

"Your word is a lamp to my feet and a light to my path," the psalmist sings (Ps. 119:105), but sometimes God's Word sheds light on the very thing we have tried to hide from ourselves or others. Sometimes God's Word reveals that we are on a path heading toward our own dead end. Certainly on that day in the Holocaust Memorial Museum, *Kyrie eleison*—"Lord, have mercy"—was not first a word of comfort but a word that brought me face-to-face with the worst that human beings can do to one another, and the fault that runs through my own heart. Only then, bowed low in utter helplessness, did *Kyrie eleison* shine as a welcomed light to my path. It was as if all the people who had uttered these words before me had lighted little lamps to guide my feet back into the way of life. Whenever we become disoriented and lose our way, when we have no words of our own to pray, scripture offers us the words we need to speak, and sing, to God.

Through liturgy and song, whether ancient chants or new hymns and praise choruses, Christians pray and sing the scriptures. "Like walking into a jewel box," the tour guide said as we stood in the crystal-encrusted cave. One could say the same thing about opening a Bible, that ancient treasury of stories and histories, prophetic visions and parables, poetry, liturgies, and letters that we have inherited from our ancestors in the faith. And if the Bible is a jewel box, the book of Psalms is its loveliest pearl. Here countless joys and sorrows are compressed into crystalline poetry. Over time, layer upon luminescent layer is added, as voices in a thousand tongues sing these songs.

Jesus knew the Psalms; they were the songs of the synagogue, the prayers of his people. God's covenantal relationship with the children of Israel engages them in a bold, passionate conversation with God. No topic is taboo, no emotion forbidden. The Psalms voice every aspect of human life to God—praise and thanksgiving, longing for healing, anger over injustice, even the desire for revenge. When Jesus cried out from the cross, "My God, my God, why have you forsaken me?" (Ps. 22:1), he joined his plea to the pleas of those before him who had prayed this psalm as they faced life and death in the seeming absence of God.

We never pray the Psalms alone, even when we are praying them in a room by ourselves. We pray with Jesus, with our Jewish brothers and sisters, with the young church in the catacombs, and with all the others who have found in these now-ancient words the songs and sighs of their own hearts. When the Psalms become our song, we join this ongoing, life-giving conversation, adding our voices—another luminescent layer—to the treasure. So we sing them at worship and we pray them at home.

It is good, says the psalmist, to declare God's love in the morning and God's faithfulness at night (Ps. 92:1-2). Receive this wisdom. Read a psalm in the morning. When its words or phrases come to mind during the day, let them turn you in openhearted gratitude toward God and in openhanded generosity toward others. And when night comes, pray again this psalm, or another one, placing your day and your deeds in God's hands.

Scripture is indeed "the richest of mines which can never be sufficiently explored," as Martin Luther wrote. Whenever the baptized gather for worship, we are led through the portal into the wealth of this inexhaustible mine, to sing its songs and pray its prayers, to hear its wisdom and heed its warnings, but above all to listen together for God speaking to us. From this mine, this jewel box opened in the midst of the worshiping community, we receive God's dearest treasure: the presence and the promise of Christ Jesus, God's living and life-giving Word.

*Practicing in Doubt and in Death

"Faith's a tide, it seems," the poet Denise Levertov wrote; faith "ebbs and flows." Raised by faithful parents and nurtured in a Christian community, Levertov composed poems rich with images from scripture, the language of the Psalms, and the cadences of the liturgy. But she struggled with doubt and unbelief for most of her adult life. Her poetry reflects that too. She writes of the dry season of doubt when the tide of faith has gone out so far it seems as if the sea is no more: "Where is the Giver to whom my gratitude rose?" her poem "The Tide" begins. "In this emptiness there seems no Presence." The beach, once sparkling with life, is now littered with the wreckage of the world. "Blown sand stings your face, anemones shrivel in rock pools no wave renews." The horizon holds only the silence of God. In such times we are wise to ask a trusted friend or mentor to walk beside us through the blowing, stinging sand.

Though centuries or continents may separate us from them, writers can be cherished companions on this journey. Their ordinary words, like natural wonders in our own backyard, astound us by widening our hearts to receive the beauty of the world and its suffering. When your soul shrivels like an anemone without water, Levertov says, "clean the littered beach, clear the lines of a forming poem"; use the gifts you have been given, tend the strand of sand beneath your feet. When doubt overwhelms you, welcome the stranger, feed the hungry, do the things that make for peace. Remember that faith does not give us the answers to life's most perplexing questions but invites us to engage them without fear. Imagination is an act of hope; working for the common good is an act of peace; faith is an alternative way of seeing and being in the world. In other words, when in doubt, practice living in the presence of God.

Seek out the community of faith. Join them in attending to the Word, praying for the world, and breaking the bread of life. If nothing else, this will draw you out of your self and turn you toward others in need. But it also keeps you on the beach, the last place you saw the sea, because when "the waters flood inward," as the poem concludes,

> Dull stones again fulfill
> their glowing destinies, and emptiness
> is a cup, and holds
> the ocean.

I have known such grace, the refreshing return of the gift of faith. Not voices in my ear as some testify to hearing, nor signs I can describe, but the quiet, persistent presence of the One whose heart is love, whose will is mercy for me and for the whole creation. On rare occasions I have known the complete surrender that comes at high tide when the struggle over what—or if—I believe gives way to trust. Then, through no effort of my own, like a swimmer who knows the water will hold her, I rest in God's embrace. We know songs for these days too:

> Bless the Lord, O my soul
> and all that is within me,
> bless [God's] holy name.—Psalm 103:1-2

Faith's a tide, Levertov writes: it ebbs and flows. "And emptiness is a cup, and holds the ocean." When my father was dying, our family kept watch beside his bed. We filled the sterile emptiness of his hospital room: we told stories, sang songs, read Psalms, and prayed. We massaged his long narrow feet, which were growing cold from lack of circulation. We thanked him for loving us. We shared one last meal with him. A crumb of bread: "This is my body." A drop of wine: "This is my blood." An unbreakable promise: "Given for you." As was done eighty years earlier at his baptism, we traced a cross upon his forehead, placed our hands upon him, and spoke the deepest truth about him: You are a child of God.

Finally, when death seemed but a breath away, we commended my father into God's keeping. But death did not come. Another day of shallow breathing passed, another night of vigil. Then another. Outside this small room, clocks numbered the passing hours; the sun rose and set. Inside this room, around this bed, time held its breath. As a tiny lily holds the promise of the whole earth springing to new life, so a single moment widens to hold things seen and unseen: daylight and darkness, grief and gratitude, memory and hope, life and death.

Death is a mystery. It is release to those who suffer, blessed rest to the weary, a benediction upon a full life. But death also is a thief, stealing life bit by bit or snatching it swiftly, violently. Death is personal, taking those we cherish most, claiming us. It is impersonal. Whole villages slide into the sea; cities are bombed from above. Death is natural, part of earth's faithful rhythms. It is unnatural, the deadly fruit of human sin: murder, genocide, war.

But for all that death is, it is not God's last word. God's lasting word is life. Emptiness, even the emptiness death brings, is a cup and holds the ocean. Death invites us to witness this wonder: God's creative Spirit brooding—"with warm breast and with ah! bright wings"—over the graves of our beloved dead, over our broken hearts and our weak faith, over the whole creation, summoning life that is stronger than death.

*Gathering to Receive Grace

Week after week, amid the ebb and flow of faith, in the midst of life and in the face of death, Christians gather to remember who they are and where they come from, to be raised again—uncurled and upright—with Christ, and to be reoriented by grace toward life. This gathering embodies the church's deepest wisdom about what it means to be human in this world, how to best practice living together in the presence of God. We call it worship or liturgy.

In the second century of its life, rumors swirled around the church in Rome. What were those "followers of the Way" doing when they got together on "the day named after the sun"? Why were they caring for orphans and widows who were not even part of their own community?

Why did unrelated people—Jew and Gentile, slave and free—call each other sister and brother? Were they a threat to the empire?

Around the year 150 a Christian named Justin wrote to the Roman Emperor Antoninus Pius describing the community's worship and defending its way of life. His description of their Sunday meeting looks like an amplified version of an earlier description in the New Testament: the baptized "devoted themselves to the apostles' teaching and fellowship, to the breaking of bread and the prayers" (Acts 2:42). For that matter, it describes what happens in a lot of churches around the world today, because much about Christian worship has remained the same for nearly two thousand years.

What happens? First, the people come, bearing gifts—the fruit of creation and the work of their hands. These are for the poor, the hungry, and immigrants, including those in their company. In Justin's time people brought not only bread and wine to share but things like milk and cheese, honey, figs, and olive oil. Today the gifts come mostly in the form of money and checks but sometimes also canned goods and fresh food, school supplies and clothes.

The people gather as one to sing their lives to God and to open the treasury of scripture, letting God's Word dwell in them richly. They pray for the sorrowful and the sick, for the newly baptized among them, and for everyone everywhere who is in need. They set a table with simple food: bread and wine. One from among them takes the bread and gives thanks, remembering all the wonders God has done. The people lift their hearts and voices in praise and thanksgiving. The bread is broken; the wine is poured. With eyes washed by grace, the community sees in these ordinary things the mystery of God's love, Christ Jesus, crucified and risen, feeding them. They eat and drink. They taste and see: God is good. Finally, the people are sent back to their daily lives to practice what they have seen and heard and tasted: the gift of God's shalom coming to earth.

Everything about this gathering is a gift: the water that washes, the word that frees, the peace that unites, the bread that nourishes, the wine that heals. Christ is present in all of these and in the community itself gathered as his body. But not only in these things. Christ is also present—God's love given to us and to a hungry world—in our daily bread, and in the sun, rain, soil, trees, and bees that gave life to the wheat and yeast, the oil and honey.

> **In worship we become what we receive: the very body of Christ, blessed, broken, and given for the sake of the life of the world.**

*Becoming What We Receive

"Humanity at full stretch before God." That is how one theologian describes Christian worship. That is difficult to imagine in churches where the community seems more curved in on itself than at "full stretch." Where the people look bored or self-absorbed and the liturgy feels more dead than alive. Where the real world, broken and heartbreakingly beautiful, seems like another world, far away. But even here, in the places and among the people you might least expect, the Spirit is brooding. God in Christ is raising us all until we are once again what we were created to be: merely, fully human.

On Sunday morning the little church near Rachel's apartment is bright with light streaming through stained-glass images of the life of Christ. On Wednesday evening, along the walls of the church basement, one also sees scenes from the life of Christ, not in stained glass but in real people. A paramedic takes blood pressures. A woman—fresh from her visit to the methadone clinic—teaches children to knit. One man shares information about ESL classes; another plays his guitar. A family with enough zucchini to feed a multitude shares bags of vegetables from their garden. Rachel sits with a friend at a table helping people register to vote.

In worship, Saint Augustine wrote, we become what we receive: the very body of Christ, blessed, broken, and given for the sake of the life of the world. Imagine that. We are sent as Christ's body into the world: caring for creation, honoring one another's bodies, nurturing the gifts of friendship and intimacy, making a living that is good for us and for others, knowing and loving our neighbors, making peace, doing justice, sharing our bread, singing our lives, and living as the community God created us to be. Our whole lives become our response to God's call, as we attend to the Word and the world, learning and unlearning along the Way.

This is a natural wonder: humanity at full stretch, living and dying together in the presence of God.

Living a whole life
attentively . . .
together . . . in the
real world . . . for
the good of all . . .
in response to God

*On Our Way

Jesus tells a parable about yeast. A woman mixes just a little into a great quantity of flour, and gradually the yeast leavens it all. The reign of God is like that leaven, Jesus says. Though it seems small when first stirred in, it changes the world.

The faith and grace that come to us by God's Spirit work in the same way. These do not leaven the whole lump at once, but gently, gradually, they do their work in our lives. Eventually we become bread, God's bread, sent to nourish a hungry world.

A whole life is made not of godliness but of the process of becoming godly. A whole life is known not by health but by getting well, not by being but by becoming, not by rest but by exercise.

We are not now what we shall be, but we are on our way. The process is not yet finished, but it is actively going on. We have not reached the goal, but we are on the right road.

At present, everything does not gleam and sparkle. But everything is being made new.

—based on Martin Luther's comment on Matthew 13:31,
as he explained the character of the Christian life

The Authors

TONY ALONSO
serves as minister of music at Loyola Marymount University in Los Angeles, California. He has composed several collections of liturgical music, and he is a noted speaker and writer on prayer and worship.

SCOTT C. ALEXANDER
a Roman Catholic layperson, teaches Islamic studies and Christian-Muslim relations at Catholic Theological Union, a graduate school in Chicago with students from over forty countries.

DOROTHY C. BASS
directs the Valparaiso Project on the Education and Formation of People in Faith (www.practicingourfaith.org). She is a member of the Evangelical Lutheran Church in America and the author or editor of several books on Christian practices.

MATTHEW MYER BOULTON
is a Disciples of Christ minister who teaches at Harvard Divinity School. His wife, Liz, and children, Jonah and Maggie, are the best teachers and fellow students he knows.

SUSAN BRIEHL
a Lutheran pastor who lives in Spokane, Washington, works with the Valparaiso Project. She writes hymn texts, liturgies, and books about worship.

MARY EMILY BRIEHL DUBA
studies theology and ethics at Yale Divinity School. With her husband, Jason, she convenes a chapter of the Beatitudes Society, where emerging Christian leaders find strength for lives of peacemaking.

JENNIFER GRANT HAWORTH

an Episcopal laywoman who is in the process of discerning a call to the priesthood, is an associate professor in the graduate programs in Higher Education Administration at Loyola University Chicago.

DOUGLAS A. HICKS

is associate professor of leadership studies and religion at the University of Richmond, and a Presbyterian minister. He is author of *Money Enough: Everyday Practices for Living Faithfully in the Global Economy*.

JOYCE HOLLYDAY

is co-pastor of Circle of Mercy, an ecumenical congregation in North Carolina, and an ordained minister in the United Church of Christ. Her work for social justice includes writing, editing, and work against racism and domestic violence.

EVELYN L. PARKER

is a member of the Christian Methodist Episcopal Church. She teaches at Perkins School of Theology, Southern Methodist University, where she participates in the wellness program at the center for lifetime sports.

STEPHANIE PAULSELL

is a Disciples of Christ minister who teaches at Harvard Divinity School. She is married to Kevin Madigan, with whom she has enjoyed friendship and intimacy for more than twenty years.

DANIEL SPENCER

is a pastor in the United Church of Christ and teaches environmental studies at the University of Montana, where he links social and environmental justice concerns while reveling in the beauty of the Rocky Mountain West.

JONATHAN WILSON-HARTGROVE

lives with his wife, Leah, their son, JaiMichael, and other friends at the Rutba House in Durham, North Carolina. He directs the School for Conversion (www.newmonasticism.org) and is an associate minister at St. John's Baptist Church and the author of several books.

References

AN INVITATION

I have written about Christian practices in a number of other books and articles. If you wish to explore additional practices or learn more about this approach to the Christian life, I encourage you to turn to these. The first was *Practicing Our Faith: A Way of Life for a Searching People,* ed. Dorothy C. Bass (San Francisco: Jossey-Bass, 1997; second, revised edition 2010), which explores the practices of honoring the body, hospitality, household economics, keeping sabbath, saying yes and saying no, discernment, testimony, shaping communities, forgiveness, healing, dying well, and singing our lives to God. As with *On Our Way*, thirteen authors formed a community of writers that discerned which practices to write about and encouraged one another throughout the process. Later, Don Richter and I convened another group of writers who worked together in a similar way; this group, which included both teenagers and adults, wrote *Way to Live: Christian Practices for Teens*, ed. Dorothy C. Bass and Don C. Richter (Nashville: Upper Room Books, 2002). Much information about all this work, including study guides and additional writing, is available at www.practicingourfaith.org.

The way of thinking about faithful living that informs *On Our Way, Practicing Our Faith,* and *Way to Live* developed over many years of conversation and collaboration with Craig Dykstra, a practical theologian who is senior vice president, religion, at Lilly Endowment. Craig and I have gathered two other groups of writers who have further explored the theology of Christian practices and their role in fostering abundant life in and for the world. These groups created *Practicing Theology: Beliefs and Practices in Christian Life*, ed. Miroslav Volf and Dorothy C. Bass (Grand Rapids, MI: Eerdmans, 2003), and *For Life Abundant: Practical Theology,*

Theological Education, and Christian Ministry, ed. Dorothy C. Bass and Craig Dykstra (Grand Rapids, MI: Eerdmans, 2008). The chapter Craig and I wrote for *Practicing Theology*, "A Theological Understanding of Christian Practices," provides a succinct and comprehensive account of this approach.

STUDY

"Beware the *grammateon*" (Luke 20:46) is most often translated, "Beware the scribes." In the New Testament scribes are rabbis who belong to a highly trained, elite cadre of theologians. Jesus criticizes them for using their education as a form of power over others, and for being arrogant, selfish, legalistic, and hypocritical. Beware the scribes, Jesus warns, who are very knowledgeable but neither wise nor compassionate.

To explore this curriculum yourself, see Matthew 6:25-34 and Luke 12:22-31 for the lilies; Mark 12:41-44 for the widow; Luke 10:25-37 for the Samaritan; Luke 18:9-14 for the tax collector; and Matthew 18:1-5; Mark 9:33-37; and Luke 9:46-48 for the child.

Rowan Williams, Archbishop of Canterbury, quotes Martin Luther's statement about the Bible, *de te loquitur*, "it's talking about you," in *Tokens of Trust: An Introduction to Christian Belief* (Norwich, UK: Canterbury Press, 2007), 121. Jonathan Edwards wrote about finding types and images of divine things in nature, human history, and current events in "Images of Divine Things" and "Types of the Messiah," published in *Typological Writings*, vol. 11, *The Works of Jonathan Edwards* (New Haven, CT: Yale University Press, 1993).

DISCERNING GOD'S CALL

Frederick Buechner defines vocation, or calling, in *Wishful Thinking: A Seeker's ABC,* rev. ed. (San Francisco: HarperSanFrancisco, 1993), 119. Father Michael J. Himes describes a calling as a "particular way of self-gift" in *Doing the Truth in Love: Conversations about God, Relationships, and Service* (New York: Paulist Press, 1995), 55.

"[A] world filled with voices. . ." is from Henri J. M. Nouwen, *Life of the Beloved: Spiritual Living in a Secular World,* 10th anniversary ed. (New York: Crossroad Publishing, 2002), 31. "I have called you by name . . .," Nouwen's poetic weaving of images from several biblical passages, including Isaiah 43:1; 49:16; and Psalm 139 is from the same volume, pp. 36–37.

James Martin, SJ, discusses the role of desire in the spiritual life in *Becoming Who You Are: Insights on the True Self from Thomas Merton and Other Saints* (Mahwah, NJ: HiddenSpring, 2006). "What God wants for us and from us . . ." is from *Weaving the New Creation: Stages of Faith and the Public Church* (San Francisco: HarperSanFrancisco, 1991), 123, by James W. Fowler.

Margaret Silf wrote about those whose heart's desire is "in tune with God's dream for them" in *Companions of Christ: Ignatian Spirituality for Everyday Living* (Grand Rapids, MI: Eerdmans, 2005), 51. She said every believer's vocation is to bring that dream to birth in *Inner Compass: An Invitation to Ignatian Spirituality* (Chicago: Loyola Press, 1999), 3.

St. Ignatius wrote his autobiography in a formal-sounding third person. It covers seventeen years, beginning at the time of his life-changing battle injury, continuing through his season of discernment, and ending soon after founding the Society of Jesus. The phrase "dry and discontented" is from Joseph F. O'Callaghan's translation, *The Autobiography of St. Ignatius Loyola: With Related Documents*, ed. John C. Olin (New York: Fordham University Press, 1992), 24. In *The Discerning Heart: Discovering a Personal God* (Chicago: Loyola Press, 1993), Maureen Conroy, RSM, uses Ignatius's story to explore the spiritual experiences of contemporary people. She recasts sections of his *Autobiography* in the first person, including the quotation "I paid no attention. . ." from page 6. Father William Barry, SJ, examines the human longing for "I know not what" in *Letting God Come Close: An Approach to the Ignatian Spiritual Exercises* (Chicago: Loyola Press, 2001), 58–61.

"Nobody sees a flower—really . . ." is from Georgia O'Keeffe and Ansel Adams, *Natural Affinities: Essays by Barbara Buhler Lynes, Sandra S. Phillips, Richard B. Woodward* (New York: Little, Brown and Company, 2008), 32. Michael Himes makes a critical connection between our "particular way of self-gift" and what brings us joy, what we're good at, and what others need us to do in *Doing the Truth in Love*, pp. 55–59. Dennis Linn, Sheila Fabricant Linn, and Matthew Linn make fresh and accessible the ancient, reflective prayer called the *examen* in the illustrated *Sleeping with Bread: Holding What Gives You Life* (Mahwah, NJ: Paulist Press, 1995). On pp. 6–7, the Linns offer a series of questions to ask at the close of each day, including "When did I feel most alive today?"

In *A Pocket Guide to Jesuit Education* (Boston College pamphlet, 2004), Joseph Appleyard, SJ, advises young adults to reflect on their lives and their learning, looking for patterns in their experiences in order to understand their significance. Parker J. Palmer encourages those who are discerning their callings to participate in a "circle of trust," a gathering of companions on a path "too deeply hidden to be traveled without company," in *A Hidden Wholeness: The Journey Toward an Undivided Life* (San Francisco: Jossey-Bass/Wiley, 2004), 26.

Timothy M. Gallagher, OMV, writes that "the life of discernment calls for a person willing to act" in *The Discernment of Spirits: An Ignatian Guide for Everyday Living* (New York: Crossroad Publishing, 2005), 25. The story of Father Pedro Arrupe is told in chapter 7 of Ronald Modras, *Ignatian Humanism: A Dynamic Spirituality for the 21st Century* (Chicago: Loyola Press, 2004). The quotation from Father Arrupe is from James Martin, SJ, *My Life with the Saints* (Chicago: Loyola Press, 2006), 119. "Jesus, 'God-with-Us,' poured his life energy. . ." is from Margaret Silf, *Companions of Christ*, p. 52. A true calling will lead us to give ourselves away, according to Michael Himes in *Doing the Truth in Love*, p. 55.

The quotation from Rainer Maria Rilke's *Letters to a Young Poet*, trans. M. D. Herter Norton (New York: W. W. Norton, 1934) is from pp. 33–34.

LIVING AS COMMUNITY

Technically, monasticism is one of several traditional ways of structuring (or "ordering") a committed Christian life. Monastics have tended to live in stable, communal households; other "orders" have emerged among mendicants, missionaries, hermits, and those devoted to apostolic service. The "new monasticism" described in this chapter understands monasticism in a more popular, less technical, sense, honoring the legacy of a range of movements in Christian history. "We have all known the long loneliness . . ." is from Dorothy Day's autobiography, *The Long Loneliness* (New York: Harper & Row, 1952), 317–18.

The summary of Pachomius's life is based on Thomas Merton's account in *Cassian and the Fathers: Invitation into the Monastic Tradition* (Kalamazoo, MI: Cistercian Publications, 2005), 40. See Jonathan Wilson-Hartgrove, *New Monasticism: What It Has to Say to Today's Church* (Grand Rapids, MI: Brazos Press, 2008). Each of these twelve marks is considered in an essay by a member of a new monastic community in *School(s) for Conversion: 12*

Marks of a New Monasticism, ed. Rutba House (Eugene, OR: Wipf & Stock Publishers, 2005).

University of Virginia theologian Charles Marsh describes CCDA in *The Beloved Community: How Faith Shapes Social Justice, from the Civil Rights Movement to Today* (New York: Basic Books, 2005), 206. Diana Butler Bass writes about becoming an intentional churchgoer in *Strength for the Journey: A Pilgrimage of Faith in Community* (San Francisco: Jossey-Bass, 2002). Jean Vanier reflects upon his life in the L'Arche community in *Living Gently in a Violent World: The Prophetic Witness of Weakness* (Downers Grove, IL: InterVarsity Press, 2008), by Stanley Hauerwas and Jean Vanier, quotation from p. 31.

The quotation from *The City of God*, in *Writings of Saint Augustine*, vol. 8, 21:25, p. 396 is Gerald Walsh and Daniel Honan's translation in *The Fathers of the Church: A New Translation* (Washington, DC: Catholic University of America Press, 1954). For more on Alexander Schmemann's Eucharistic theology, see *For the Life of the World* (Crestwood, NY: St. Vladimir's Seminary Press, 1973), quotation from p. 43.

FRIENDSHIP AND INTIMACY

Ralph Waldo Emerson's essay "Friendship" is an important influence on this chapter, and I recommend reading it in its entirety in *The Essential Writings of Ralph Waldo Emerson*, ed. Brooks Atkinson (New York: Modern Library, 2000), 201–14. The quotations are from pp. 202, 203, 205, 209, 210, and 211. Stephen Mitchell's *Gilgamesh: A New English Version* (New York: Free Press, 2006) is a wonderful modern rendering of the epic, with an excellent introduction.

The quotation from Cicero about the importance of friendship to Epicurus can be found in Pierre Hadot, *What Is Ancient Philosophy?* trans. Michael Chase (Cambridge, MA: Harvard University Press, 2002), 125, and the quotation from Aristotle's *Nicomachean Ethics* can be found in Richard McKeon, ed., *The Basic Works of Aristotle* (New York: Random House, 1941), 1058. The passage from Auden's poem "For Friends Only" is in W. H. Auden, *Collected Poems*, ed. Edward Mendelson (New York: Vintage Books, 1991), 707, and the passage from Virginia Woolf is from *The Diary of Virginia Woolf*, ed. Anne Olivier Bell, vol. 3, 1925–1930 (New York: Harcourt Brace Jovanovich, 1980), 316.

Paul J. Wadell's *Becoming Friends: Worship, Justice, and the Practice of Christian Friendship* (Grand Rapids, MI: Brazos Press, 2002) is a beautiful meditation by a contemporary Christian ethicist who has spent years pondering friendship as a vital Christian practice; quotation from p. 63. Aelred of Rievaulx's *Spiritual Friendship,* trans. Mary Eugenia Laker (Kalamazoo, MI: Cistercian Publications, 1977), is an important medieval treatise on friendship and Christian life; quotations from pp. 46, 66, 96, and 131. The comment on generosity by Saint Ambrose can be found in Aelred's *Spiritual Friendship*, p. 108. Simone Weil's "Forms of the Implicit Love of God" in *Waiting for God*, trans. Emma Craufurd (New York: G. P. Putnam's Sons, 1951), identifies friendship (along with love of neighbor, love of the order of the world, and love of religious practices) as one of those forms; quotation from p. 208. Quotation from *The Confessions of St. Augustine* is from a translation by Rex Warner (New York: New American Library, 1963), 74.

For further insight into the jewel of Wisdom Literature, see Dianne Bergant's *Song of Songs: The Love Poetry of Scripture* (Hyde Park, NY: New City Press, 1998). "The Song of Songs, which is Solomon's," the opening words of this Hebrew scripture, are the source of its most common titles: The Song of Songs (New American Bible, New Jerusalem Bible) and Song of Solomon (New Revised Standard and New International Versions). The Wisdom of Solomon is placed with Psalms and other Wisdom Literature in Bibles authorized by the Roman Catholic Church; Bibles published for Protestant readers omit it or place it in a section called The Apocrypha.

The writings of four contemporary writers helped me think about friendship and intimacy. I quote from p. 26 of Karin Gottshall's poem "The Bog Body" in *Crocus: Poems* (New York: Fordham University Press, 2007); from pp. 20 and 123 of the poet Mark Doty's memoir of the death of his partner, Wally Roberts, from HIV/AIDS, *Heaven's Coast: A Memoir* (London: Jonathan Cape, 1996); and from pp. 92, 94, and 97 of poet Wendell Berry's essay "Poetry and Marriage: The Use of Old Forms," in *Standing By Words* (Washington, DC: Shoemaker & Hoard, 2005). Finally, I quote from Jane Smiley's novella "The Age of Grief" in *The Age of Grief: A Novella and Stories* (New York: Alfred A. Knopf, 1987), 213.

SINGING OUR LIVES

"The Sound of Music" is from Richard Rodgers and Oscar Hammerstein's musical *The Sound of Music*, used with permission. I recommend the insightful and conversational book about this practice by the father-daughter team of Don Saliers (a theologian) and Emily Saliers (one of the Indigo Girls), *A Song to Sing, A Life to Live: Reflections on Music as a Spiritual Practice* (San Francisco: Jossey-Bass, 2004). I quote from the writings of two of my mentors: Gabe Huck, *How Can I Keep from Singing? Thoughts about Liturgy for Musicians* (Chicago: Liturgy Training Publications, 1989), 44, and Marty Haugen, *To Serve as Jesus Did: A Ministerial Model for Worship Teams and Leaders* (Chicago: GIA Publications, Inc., 2005), 54. Wisdom about singing our lives also comes from many traditions. The quotation from Thich Nhat Hanh, a Vietnamese expatriate, is in *Anger: Wisdom for Cooling the Flames* (New York: Riverhead Books, 2001), 17.

Two ecumenical, international communities, Taizé and Iona, have given many simple, prayerful songs to the wider church. "Take, O Take Me As I Am" (© 1995 Iona Community, GIA Publications, Inc., North American agent) was written by John L. Bell. Bell, a pastor of the Church of Scotland, is a member of the Iona Community, which is dedicated to seeking justice, making peace, nurturing Christian community, and renewing worship (www.iona.org.uk). The Taizé community in France welcomes thousands of young people from around the world each week. Brother Roger founded this community in 1940 to bring Protestants and Roman Catholics together in a place of hospitality, prayer, song, and simplicity (www.taize.fr).

Rory Cooney wrote "The Trumpet in the Morning" (© 1998, GIA Publications, Inc.). I wrote "Will the Circle Be Unbroken?" (© 2002, GIA Publications, Inc.).

CARE FOR CREATION

I thank my students Katie Pritchard, Anna Leslie, and Kendra Kallevig for their ongoing work to care for creation, and for permission to use their stories in this chapter. I also thank Asher for permission to use his Bar Mitzvah story.

The first Creation story (Gen. 1:1–2:3) was written for use in public worship. The second (Gen. 2:4b-25) is part of a larger narrative that includes Genesis 3, the story of the disobedience of the human creatures. For a profound exposition and meditation on the biblical theme of the goodness of creation, see Daniel Erlander's whimsically illustrated *Manna and Mercy: A Brief History of God's Unfolding Promise to Mend the Entire*

Universe (Mercer Island, WA: Order of Saints Martin and Teresa, 1992). Theodore Hiebert offers an excellent overview of Genesis 1–2, including the theme of *adamah* as fertile soil, in "Rethinking Traditional Approaches to Nature in the Bible" in Dieter T. Hessel, ed. *Theology for Earth Community: A Field Guide* (Maryknoll, NY: Orbis Books, 1996), 23–30. Gene McAfee examines biblical views of domination in "Ecology and Biblical Studies" in the same collection, 31–44.

Lynn White Jr. charged Christianity with being the most anthropocentric of all world religions in "The Historical Roots of Our Ecologic Crisis," *Science* 155, no. 3767 (March 10, 1967):1203–07.

God and creation are forever bound together because God is always moving toward creation in power and in love, according to Walter Brueggemann in his very readable commentary, *Genesis: A Bible Commentary for Teaching and Preaching* (Atlanta: John Knox Press, 1982), 22–23. Augustine describes God as "ineffably and invisibly great and ineffably and invisibly beautiful" in *The City of God against the Pagans*, trans. David S. Wiesen (Cambridge, MA: Harvard University Press, 1968), 11.4, p. 437. Augustine reflects on Psalm 26 in *St. Augustine on the Psalms*, trans. Scholastica Hebgin and Felicitas Corrigan (New York: Newman Press, 1960), 1:272. The John Muir quotation is from his *My First Summer in the Sierra* (Boston: Houghton Mifflin Company, 1911), 211.

The description of Hildegard is from Anne H. King-Lenzmeier, *Hildegard of Bingen: An Integrated Vision* (Collegeville, MN: Liturgical Press, 2000), xi. For Hildegard's own words see *Hildegard of Bingen: Mystical Writings*, ed. Fiona Bowie and Oliver Davies, trans. Robert Carver (New York: Crossroad, 1999): *The Book of Divine Works*, Vision 1.2.8, 91–92.

For a good biography and analysis of Saint Francis, see Marie Dennis, Joseph Nangle, Cynthia Moe-Lobeda, and Stuart Taylor, *St. Francis and the Foolishness of God* (Maryknoll, NY: Orbis Books, 1993). Pope John Paul II proclaimed Francis of Assisi the patron saint of ecology.

MAKING A GOOD LIVING

I have discussed the social powers that influence our economic behavior in detail in Douglas A. Hicks, "Inequality, Globalization, and Leadership: 'Keeping Up with the Joneses' across National Boundaries," *The Annual of the Society of Christian Ethics* 21 (2001):63–80. James S. Duesenberry describes the phenomenon of "keeping up with the Joneses" in *Income,*

Saving, and the Theory of Consumer Behavior (Cambridge, MA: Harvard University Press, 1962 [1949]), quotation from p. 27. The most accessible introduction to the capabilities approach, as connected to economic and human development, is Amartya Kumar Sen, *Development as Freedom* (New York: Alfred A. Knopf, 1999). See also Douglas A. Hicks, "Gender, Discrimination, and Capability: Insights from Amartya Sen," *Journal of Religious Ethics* 30, no. 1 (Spring 2002):137–54. For good data and background on global economics, including measures of well-being and poverty, the annual Human Development Reports published by the United Nations Development Programme (UNDP) are a reliable source (see http://hdr.undp.org/en and also www.endpoverty2015.org).

For more about communal cooperation and investing ourselves for the common good, see Robert H. Frank's book *Luxury Fever: Money and Happiness in an Era of Excess* (Princeton, NJ: Princeton University Press, 1999). Bono is quoted in Michka Assayas, *Bono in Conversation with Michka Assayas* (New York: Riverhead Books, 2006), 91. One analysis of Bono's theological perspective is *One Step Closer: Why U2 Matters to Those Seeking God* by Christian Batalden Scharen (Grand Rapids, MI: Brazos Press, 2006). I thank Elizabeth Victor for sharing her reflections on how to make a difference.

HONORING THE BODY

The hymn "He'll Understand, He'll Say, 'Well Done,'" written by Lucie E. Campbell, is included in *The Hymnal of the Christian Methodist Episcopal Church* (Memphis, TN: CME Publishing House, 1987), no. 428. Robert Lowry's hymn "Nothing but the Blood" is printed in several hymnals, including *The Hymnal of the Christian Methodist Episcopal Church*. It is in the public domain. "For All the Saints," written in 1864 by William W. How, is in the public domain.

Adina Levine reported on Harvard Corporation's divestment of its holdings in PetroChina in "Major Steps Against Sudanese Genocide a Response to Student Activism," *Harvard Law Record* (April 7, 2005).

I am indebted to Stephanie Paulsell for her wise work on the practice of honoring the body. Kay Northcutt's story of bathing her dying mother is in Paulsell's *Honoring the Body: Meditations on a Christian Practice* (San Francisco: Jossey-Bass, 2002), 38. On pp. 133–34 of the same book, Paulsell addresses the body's rhythm of exertion and rest. She writes about

Sunday-go-to-meeting clothes in "Honoring the Body," *Practicing Our Faith: A Way of Life for a Searching People,* ed. Dorothy C. Bass (San Francisco: Jossey-Bass, 1997; second, revised edition 2010), 21, and about viewing "the world through the lens of Jesus' wounded but resurrected body" on p. 27.

Maya Angelou is quoted from her foreword to the anthology of stories and photographs of African American women in their Sunday hats by photographer Michael Cunningham and journalist Craig Marberry, *Crowns: Portraits of Black Women in Church Hats* (New York: Doubleday, 2000), 2.

KNOWING AND LOVING OUR NEIGHBORS OF OTHER FAITHS

"Ahmad" was not the actual name of my new friend, but otherwise this story is true. *In sha'a Allah* is an Arabic phrase which roughly translates, "God willing." Pious Muslims will use this phrase whenever they talk about the future. It is by no means indicative of a fatalist theology, as some Christian polemicists would have it, but rather is an expression of profound humility in the face of divine providence (that is, "Whatever I say about the future, I must recognize that this will only come to pass if it is God's will").

For an example of Jesus' relationship with tax collectors, see Luke 19:1-10; with Samaritans, see John 4:4-42; with pagans, see Matthew 8:5-13; Luke 7:2-10.

According to most available sources, Stendahl first publicly articulated the idea of "holy envy" in a press conference in Stockholm in 1985 after he had retired from the Harvard Divinity School and become Lutheran bishop of that city. He called the press conference to speak out against the religious bigotry of those who wanted to block construction of a Church of Jesus Christ of the Latter Day Saints temple in the Swedish capital. Leaving room for holy envy was the third of three basic "rules" Stendahl recommended for meaningful interreligious dialogue. In Yehezkel Landau's "An Interview with Krister Stendahl," *Harvard Divinity Bulletin* 35, no. 1 (Winter 2007), Stendahl described these rules as follows: "let the other define herself ('Don't think you know the other without listening'); compare equal to equal (not my positive qualities to the negative ones of the other); and find beauty in the other so as to develop 'holy envy.'"

Lee H. Yearley writes about "spiritual regret" in "New Religious Virtues and the Study of Religion" (Fifteenth Annual University Lecture in Religion, Arizona State University, February 10, 1994), 5, quoted in Judith

A. Berling, *Understanding Other Religious Worlds: A Guide for Interreligious Education* (Maryknoll, NY: Orbis Books, 2004), 56.

Jeremy, Rosa, and Bao: Although this scenario is *per se* fictitious and its characters composite, the events, reactions, perspectives, and feelings that they represent are based on the experience of real people in the context of real dialogue. The fourfold typology of interreligious dialogue was first articulated in "The Attitude of the Church toward Followers of Other Religions" (Vatican Secretariat for Non-Christians, May 10, 1984), secs. 28–35. It was further developed in "Dialogue and Proclamation: Reflections and Orientations on Inter-religious Dialogue and the Proclamation of the Gospel of Jesus Christ" (Pontifical Council for Inter-religious Dialogue: May 19, 1991), sec. 42. The original order in which these two documents treat the four dimensions of dialogue and the original nomenclature of the 1991 document is as follows: the dialogue of life, the dialogue of action, the dialogue of theological exchange, and the dialogue of religious experience. "To live in an open and neighbourly spirit . . ." comes from "Dialogue and Proclamation," sec. 42.

George Weigel, noted U.S. American Catholic commentator, in response to a question about violent episodes in the history of the Roman Catholic Church: "As for the Crusades, while there were deplorable events during those years, it should be remembered that the Crusades began in large part as a defense against Islamic depredations against Christian pilgrims to lands that Islam had conquered by the sword." See "The Vatican and Islam: Pope Benedict XVI Prepares to Visit Turkey" (October 4, 2006), The Pew Forum on Religion and Public Life, Transcript Series at http://www.pewforum.org/events/index.php?EventID=128 (accessed August 12, 2008).

Killing for Christ "is no sin . . ." is from *Patrologiae cursus completus*, Series latina, accurante J.P. Migne, Parisiis (1844–1905), 182, 924 in J. Hoeberichts, *Francis and Islam* (Quincy, IL: Franciscan Press, 1997), 16. An English translation of Bernard's treatise, "*Liber ad Milites Templi de Laude Novae Militiae*," is available as "In Praise of the New Knighthood" (trans. Conrad Greenia) in *Treatises III: The Works of Bernard of Clairvaux* vol. 7, Cistercian Fathers Series 19 (Kalamazoo, MI: Cistercian Publications, 1977), 127–67. For a translation by David Carbon, go to http://faculty.smu.edu/bwheeler/chivalry/bernard.html (accessed August 12, 2008).

See Hoeberichts, *Francis and Islam*, 96–98, and Kathleen A. Warren, *Daring to Cross the Threshold: Francis of Assisi Encounters Sultan Malek al-Kamil* (Rochester, MN: Sisters of St. Francis, 2003), 34–38. For a contemporary "Jericho road" story, read Jonathan Wilson-Hartgrove's account of his experience in *To Baghdad and Beyond: How I Got Born Again in Babylon* (Eugene, OR: Cascade Books, 2005).

For a beautiful discernment of the difference between proselytism and evangelization, see Benedict XVI's first encyclical letter, *Deus Caritas Est*, sec. 31c: "Those who practice charity in the Church's name will never seek to impose the Church's faith upon others. They realize that a pure and generous love is the best witness to the God in whom we believe and by whom we are driven to love. A Christian knows when it is time to speak of God and when it is better to say nothing and to let love alone speak. He knows that God is love (cf. *1 Jn.* 4:8) and that God's presence is felt at the very time when the only thing we do is to love." http://www.vatican.va/holy_father/benedict_xvi/encyclicals/documents/hf_ben-xvi_enc_20051225_deus-caritas-est_en.html (accessed September 16, 2008).

"Dialogue is thus the norm and necessary manner of every form of Christian mission . . ." is from "The Attitude of the Church toward Followers of Other Religions" (Vatican Secretariat for Non-Christians: May 10, 1984), sec. 29. The "Merciful," "Compassionate," and "Sustainer of the Universe" are epithets for God (i.e., *al-Rahman*, *al-rahim*, *rabb al-`alamin*) in the opening chapter of the Qur'an (*surat al-fatiha*), which is also a prayer recited by observant Muslims a minimum of seventeen times each day.

PEACEMAKING AND NONVIOLENCE

The Vow of Nonviolence used in this chapter was adapted from the Pax Christi Vow by the community living at Holden Village in 1998–1999. Read the current Pax Christi Vow at: http://www.paxchristiusa.org/news_events_more.asp?id=55.

Albert Camus defined hope as "reconsider[ing] everything from the ground up" in his *Neither Victims nor Executioners*, trans. Dwight Macdonald (Chicago: World Without War Publications, 1972), 48–49. I quote John Dear from *Jesus the Rebel: Bearer of God's Peace and Justice* (Franklin, WI: Sheed and Ward, 2000), xv.

The documentary *The Danish Solution: The Rescue of the Jews in Denmark* was written, directed, and produced by Karen Cantor and Camilla

Kjaerulff and released in Denmark in May 2005 by Singing Wolf Documentaries, Inc. The paraphrase is based on "History of the Rescue," at http://www.thedanishsolution.org. For further discussion of the prophets' use of imagination, see Walter Brueggemann, *The Prophetic Imagination*, 2nd ed. (Minneapolis, MN: Augsburg Fortress, 2001).

Thomas Merton's prayer is in his *Thoughts in Solitude* (New York: Farrar, Straus & Giroux, 1999), 79. This translation of Matthew 5:39 is from the Scholars Version of the New Testament, which Walter Wink quotes in his *Jesus and Nonviolence: A Third Way* (Minneapolis, MN: Augsburg Fortress, 2003), 11. Carolyn Sharp writes about Jeremiah's defiance in "Voiced in Paradox: Prophecy and the Contemporary Church," *Reflections* 93, no. 1 (Winter 2006):12. Read the story of the king, the prophet, and the scribe in Jeremiah 36. "Getting in the way," the motto of the Chicago-based Christian Peacemaker Teams, and the question "What would happen if. . ." are quoted from the Web site http://www.cpt.org/. To learn about Nonviolent Peaceforce, which is based in Belgium, go to http://www.nonviolentpeaceforce.org/. Walter Wink considers the power of nonviolent action in *Jesus and Nonviolence*; see p. 46.

Martin Luther King Jr.'s phrase "the conscience of this nation" appears in *A Testament of Hope: The Essential Writings and Speeches of Martin Luther King, Jr.*, ed. James M. Washington (New York: HarperCollins, 1990), 286. In *Catholics, Conscientious Objection, and Peacemaking* (Liguori, MO: Liguori Publications, 1985), 4–5, Jim Forest quotes the document "The Church in the Modern World," from *The Documents of Vatican II*, Abbott-Gallagher edition (New York: America Press, 1966). Dietrich Bonhoeffer referenced Matthew 19:17 in this quotation from *Ethics*, Dietrich Bonhoeffer *Works*, vol. 6 (Minneapolis, MN: Fortress Press, 2005), 275. See also p. 282.

Roland Bainton wrote about the practice of nonviolence in the early church in "The Churches and War: Historic Attitudes toward Christian Participation," *Social Action* 11, no. 1 (January 15, 1945):12. Writings from the first three centuries of the church, including those of Tertullian and Origen, are gathered in ten volumes edited by Alexander Roberts and James Donaldson, *The Ante-Nicene Fathers: Translations of the Writings of the Fathers Down to A.D. 325* (Grand Rapids, MI: Eerdmans, 1989–90). Tertullian linked military service to serving false gods in *On Idolatry*, XIX (ANF, vol. 3). Origen argued that the king could not demand that Christians go to battle in *Against Celsus,* LXXIII (ANF, Vol. 4).

For an account of nonviolent strategies that have proven effective in real, historical situations around the world, see Peter Ackerman and Jack DuVall, *A Force More Powerful: A Century of Non-Violent Conflict,* which is available as a PBS documentary and as a book (New York: Palgrave, 2001). Knut Willem Ruyter traces the change in the early church's attitude to war in "Pacifism and Military Service in the Early Church," *Cross Currents* 32 no.1 (Spring 1982):54–60. The United States Conference of Catholic Bishops' pastoral letter on war and peace, *The Challenge of Peace: God's Promise and Our Response* (Washington, DC: United States Conference of Catholic Bishops Publishing, 1983), is available from the USCCB at 800-235-8722, order number 863-0.

For further information about conscientious objection, see Robert A. Seeley, *Choosing Peace: A Handbook on War, Peace, and Your Conscience* (Philadelphia: Central Committee for Conscientious Objectors, 1994), 33. If you are in the military and searching your own conscience, see Alexander Doty, *Helping Out: A Guide to Military Discharges and G.I. Rights,* 5th ed. (Philadelphia: CCCO, 1997). The interview questions for COs are found at http://www.army.mil/usapa/epubs/pdf/r600_43.pdf and http://www.objector.org/files/35625089.pdf (pp. 12–14). For the most current information, or to receive confidential counseling, visit the Central Committee for Conscientious Objectors at www.objector.org, or call the GI Rights Hotline at 1-800-FYI-95GI.

DOING JUSTICE

Portions of this chapter have appeared previously in *Sojourners* (January-February, 1998); *Fellowship* (March/April 2000), published by the Fellowship of Reconciliation; and *Voices & Visions,* a publication of the Southeast Conference of the UCC (May 2004).

For more on the worldwide distribution of wealth, see the "United Nations Development Program Report," 1998. Phillip Johansson addresses this disparity in "United for a Fair Economy Reports on a Decade of Disparity," Dec. 17, 1999. At www.socialfunds.com you can order "Investing in Socially Responsible Funds," a free primer on investing in companies that strive to care for creation, do justice, and make peace. Find the most recent information on poverty in the United States at the Health and Human

Resource Web site: www.aspe.hhs.gov/poverty/. For more about how children are affected by injustice, go to www.childrensdefense.org. For regularly updated facts on global hunger, check at www.churchworldservice.org for the "Food Crisis Fact Sheet" download.

Walter Brueggemann spoke about anxiety and the common good at the Columbia Theological Seminary, Summer Scholars Conference, July 2007. The quotation from Robert Alberti is from "Fight Terrorism with Relentless Doses of Hope and Compassion," published in the Minneapolis *Star Tribune*, September 29, 2001. The observation that there is a "perpetrator in each of us" and "humanity" in the most evil perpetrator comes from my interview with Charles Villa-Vicencio. For an insider's look at the Greensboro process, see Lisa Magarell and Joya Wesley, *Learning from Greensboro: Truth and Reconciliation in the United States,* with a foreword by Bongani Finca (Philadelphia: University of Pennsylvania Press, 2008). Kate Foran's essay is used with her permission. Vincent Harding's reflections are recounted in *Cloud of Witnesses,* Jim Wallis and Joyce Hollyday, eds. (Maryknoll, NY: Orbis Books, 1991), xvi.

LIVING IN THE PRESENCE OF GOD

I am grateful to those whose stories enrich this chapter: my godson, Matthew Des Voigne; Erik Spurrell and his mother, Laura; my daughters, Mary Emily and Magdalena; and "Rachel."

"God's Grandeur" is from *Gerard Manley Hopkins,* ed. Catherine Phillips (New York: Oxford University Press, 1986), 128.

Walk the way of Jesus in John: love one another (John 13:34-35); serve (13:1-20); abide (15:1-17); forgive (20:23); and peace be with you (20:19-23). Read these water stories: Creation (Gen. 1:1–2:3); Flood (Gen. 7:1–9:17); the Crossing (Exod. 14:10-31); Jesus' baptism (Matt. 3:13-17); the woman at the well (John 4:5-42); the man born blind (John 9:1-41).

"Create in Me a Clean Heart," a canticle based on Psalm 51, is in the public domain.

I allude to Denise Levertov's poem "The Avowal," in which the speaker longs to float in Spirit's embrace as hawks rest in air and swimmers in water (*The Stream and the Sapphire* [New York: New Directions, 1997], 6). Levertov's "The Tide" is from the same volume, pp. 25–26. She considers mystery, faith, and imagination in her 1984 essay "A Poet's View" in *New and Selected Essays* (New York: New Directions, 1992), 239–46. Martin

Luther calls scripture a mine and a manger in his "Preface to the Old Testament" in *Word and Sacrament I, Luther's Works,* vol. 35 (Philadelphia: Muhlenberg Press, 1960), 236.

From the beginning, Christian worship practices have been diverse, but many scholars agree that a basic shape—gathering, hearing the Word, praying for the needy, sharing the meal, and being sent to serve the world—has remained since the earliest church. See *Baptism, Eucharist, and Ministry,* Faith and Order Paper No. 111 (Geneva: World Council of Churches, 1982), E27. On Easter evening, the crucified and risen Christ, appearing as a stranger, opened scripture to two disciples on the road and was "made known" to them in the "breaking of the bread" (Luke 24:13-35).

For more on the biblical basis of worship, see Geoffrey Wainwright's "Christian Worship: Scriptural Basis and Theological Frame," in *The Oxford History of Christian Worship,* ed. Geoffrey Wainwright and Karen B. Westerfield Tucker (New York: Oxford University Press, 2006), 1–31. Maxwell E. Johnson explores Christian worship in the first three centuries in "The Apostolic Tradition" in the same volume, 32–75, including excerpts from Justin Martyr's *First Apology* (c. 150), written to the Roman emperor. See Don E. Saliers, *Worship and Spirituality,* 2nd ed. (Akron, OH: OSL Publications, 1996), 1. Augustine (391–430), bishop of Hippo in North Africa, preached on the eucharistic mystery that "we become what we receive" in his Sermon 272.

ON OUR WAY
Martin Luther wrote about the Christian life in his "Defense and Explanation of All the Articles"; see *Career of the Reformer II, Luther's Works,* vol. 32 (Philadelphia: Muhlenberg Press, 1958), 24.

Acknowledgments

The writing of this book was sponsored by the Valparaiso Project on the Education and Formation of People in Faith, a project of Lilly Endowment Inc., a private family foundation in Indianapolis. We are especially grateful to Craig Dykstra, senior vice president, religion, whose thinking and writing about Christian practices that form a whole life lived in the real world in response to God's grace have deeply influenced this book.

The authors are grateful to those who responded to early drafts of this book: Alexx Campbell, Jack DePaolo, Timothy Frazier, Katherine Lytch, John Schwehn, Martha Schwehn, Clinton Trench, and Magdalena Briehl Wells—all of whom had contributed as teens to *Way to Live: Christian Practices for Teens* (Upper Room, 2002)—and also Joel Bergeland and Jason Duba. Others read a later draft and engaged the authors in lively discussion: Alvin Black, Karnell Black, Hannah Cartwright, Daniel Cobbler, John Dahlstrand, Katherine English, Eldon Santiago, LaSheena Simmons, and Lydia Wylie-Kellerman. At the invitation of the authors, Pam Chao, Kate Foran, Allison Frost, Nathan Mustain, Robert Rich, Frank So, and Elizabeth Victor wrote personal essays about how they practice their faith. Much of what is good and true about *On Our Way* comes from the challenging questions, creative insights, and faithful testimony of these readers and writers.

During the writing process the authors gathered twice as a community; Central Lutheran Church (Minneapolis) and Fourth Presbyterian Church (Chicago) graciously received us. In Minneapolis, Mary Preus and Tom Witt, our treasured friends, led us in spirited song and prayer. In Chicago, Enuma Okoro, author of the online study guide for this book, served as a small-group facilitator. At both meetings and all along the way our colleague Don Richter was a trusted companion and worthy conversation partner.

Robin Pippin and Jeannie Crawford-Lee, our editors at Upper Room Books, were generous partners and patient guides as this book took shape. The work for this book was coordinated from the office of the Valparaiso Project on the Education and Formation of People in Faith. This project makes its home at Valparaiso University; the editors are grateful to the university for its support. We also thank Doretta Kurzinski, the Valparaiso Project Coordinator, who tended to the many details associated with author meetings, reader responses, manuscript preparation, and much more.

An online study guide for *On Our Way* and other resources on Christian practices are available at www.practicingourfaith.org, the Web site of the Valparaiso Project.

More resources on Christian practices and a free study guide
for use with **On Our Way** are available at

www.practicingourfaith.org